The Politics of
Self-sufficiency

Michael Allaby and Peter Bunyard

The Politics of Self-sufficiency

Oxford New York Toronto Melbourne
OXFORD UNIVERSITY PRESS
1980

Oxford University Press, Walton Street, Oxford OX2 6DP

London Glasgow New York Toronto
Delhi Bombay Calcutta Madras Karachi
Kuala Lumpur Singapore Hong Kong Tokyo
Nairobi Dar es Salaam Cape Town
Melbourne Wellington
and associate companies in
Beirut Berlin Ibadan Mexico City

British Library Cataloguing in Publication Data

Allaby, Michael
The politics of self-sufficiency.
1. Self-service (Economics)
I. Title II. Bunyard, Peter
640 HD9980.5 80–40112

ISBN 0–19–217695–1
ISBN 0–19–286005–4 Pbk

Set, printed and bound in Great Britain by
Cox and Wyman Ltd, Reading

Preface

In the summer of 1978, we were invited by the Department of Extramural Studies of the University of Exeter to prepare a series of four evening lectures on the subject of 'self-sufficiency' and to deliver them during the autumn. This book is a by-product of the lectures.

We agreed immediately that rather than divide the lectures between us, with Peter delivering two and Michael delivering two, both of us would attend all four. The University accepted this arrangement. Our idea was, that instead of each lecture consisting of one man talking at an audience, it would consist of two men holding a conversation in which members of the audience would be encouraged to join. We felt the less formal approach would prove more interesting for the audience, and more interesting for us as well. Having agreed that, we went on to agree that the lectures should deal only with the theoretical aspects of self-sufficiency. There are many excellent textbooks, handbooks, and evening classes devoted to the more practical aspects and, in any case, these are difficult to describe in a classroom. Erudite discussions about the number of goats that can be accommodated in the garden shed are less convincing or conclusive in the absence of both goats and shed.

As our planning began, it became rather obvious that no one had defined our subject for us. We could not interpret 'self-sufficient' literally because if we did we arrived at the ridiculous notion that each individual should be an isolate, wholly independent of other humans and so deprived of all human concourse. Not only is the idea patently absurd, it bears no relation to the concern about building strong, supportive communities upon which those who practise or advocate self-sufficiency place such great emphasis. If the term cannot be understood literally, though, just what does it mean? More and more of our time came to be spent struggling to construct a definition. In a sense, that is the subject and part of the purpose of this book. We were led to consider the nature of man, the extent to which his technology is a new phenomenon or a mere continuation of the applied creativity that has set him apart from other species since first he appeared. We were led finally to speculate about the kind of society that may be implied by self-sufficiency on a large scale, based on many autonomous, and probably small, communities.

We had to consider, too, the related concerns of environmentalists. The environmental and self-sufficiency movements are distinct but they share so many views that the self-provider may be regarded, in some senses at least, as a kind of extreme environmentalist.

The lectures proved popular and it seemed to us that our approach had distinct advantages. Not least of these was the ease with which we could show that there are no simple answers to the questions raised by self-providers and environmentalists, and that on many issues, views diverge widely. Discussions were often animated.

The book is not based upon the lectures, but the idea for it was derived from them. So, too, was the technique by which we have written it. We could have collaborated to develop a consensus view but we felt that this would force both of us to compromise and that it would present the erroneous impression that only one viewpoint is admissible. So we laid down a set of very simple rules. Having agreed the general content of each chapter, one of us would write the main text. The other would append a comment or criticism that also formed the introduction to the following chapter, which he continued to write. It so happened that Mike wrote the first word and also had the last word, but we should not pretend that life is necessarily fair!

The subjects with which we deal are those we consider fundamental to the position of the self-provider and the environmentalist. They are not those that are debated most commonly and the newcomer to the environmentalist argument may feel certain omissions are strange. We do not discuss the 'population explosion', for example, or environmental pollution, the world food situation, or the conservation of nature. We do discuss energy and the depletion of resources, but only because in our view these are fundamental and because the implications of our discussion of them are political. Our main concern is with differing views of the nature of man and the kinds of political arrangement they imply.

We are dealing, then, with some of the philosophical and political aspects of self-sufficiency and environmentalism. We believe it is desirable, and perhaps necessary, for supporters of the two movements to consider the ramifications of the changes and reforms they propose, to decide on the kind of society it is that they seek to create, and that they discover and then declare their political complexion. Until they do they will not construct the broad political philosophy upon which they may build their programmes. The movements are becoming political, engaging in protest demonstrations and also contesting elections. During 1978 and 1979 parliamentary elections in several European countries, including Britain, have included environmentalist candidates and in 1979, in the USA, the Citizens' Party was formed to contest the 1980 Presidential Election, using a campaign platform that covered the full range of issues rather than only those concerned directly with the environment.

The subject is new and, while we can supply some of the questions, we do not pretend to supply answers that represent anything more than our personal opinions. Often we disagree and sometimes our criticisms of one another are severe. We neither regret this nor apologize for it. It has not strained our friendship and argument is necessary and healthy. We hope that our argument may expand by infecting others.

Both of us have been involved in both movements for some years. Mike began to work full time within the environmental movement in January 1964, when he joined the staff of the Soil Association. At that time the Association was the only voluntary organization concerned with the welfare and health of man as well as of the natural environment. For a time it stood at the forefront of the emerging environmental movement. Peter was, and is, a scientist and science writer and although his special concern is the fate of those primitive peoples whose cultures are threatened by modern development he is presently engaged on a study of the economic viability of nuclear power. We met while working for *The Ecologist*, Teddy Goldsmith's magazine that appeared first in 1970. Later we both moved to Cornwall with the magazine. Mike began to work in *The Ecologist* office, but Peter had bought a small farm and much of his time was devoted to farming. Today Peter still farms. Mike bases his claim to selfsufficiency on the fact that he lives entirely on the proceeds of his writing and he and his family eat with reasonable regularity. Both authors have continued to study and to write about matters that interest self-providers and environmentalists.

We would like to thank John Hurst. He manages the Cornish outpost of the Exeter Extra-mural Department from a small office in Truro and it was he who suggested, and then arranged, the lectures. Without them there would have been no lectures and no book. If our book contributes to the development of a coherent political argument in favour of self-sufficiency and environmentalism, John was the catalyst that made possible the first reaction.

Michael Allaby
Peter Bunyard

Wadebridge and Withiel,
Cornwall, October 1979

Contents

1 What is man?

There is nothing really new in the search for 'self-sufficiency'. The pioneers who first colonized the New World, Australasia, and parts of Africa were self-sufficient because they had to be and, in this context, the term suggests a kind of rugged independence associated with mastering a new and rather hostile environment. For modern seekers of self-sufficiency, however, the term means something rather different. It has lost its pioneering connotation since the idea of 'mastering' the natural environment has become unfashionable. Indeed, one of the sets of concepts motivating such people today describes a relationship between modern man and the natural environment that is unsatisfactory and can be improved by accommodation to the environment, not by further attempts at mastery.

In this, those who seek to become self-sufficient share an outlook with many environmentalists and, although the two movements are separate, from this point of view they may be considered together. If a person is an environmentalist it does not follow that he or she practises or advocates self-sufficiency, but a person seeking self-sufficiency is likely to be an environmentalist, at least by temperament if not by virtue of active membership of an organization.

Self-sufficiency is seen as an alternative way of life or 'lifestyle'. What does this mean?

Each of us lives according to a daily routine that changes little from one month to the next or from one year to the next. We need a framework within which to function, a series of events each day that provides us with a way of ordering the information we must receive from our environment and of performing with optimum efficiency those humdrum tasks that are necessary to secure a regular supply of those materials that are essential to us.

Now it may seem that there are people who avoid this humdrum daily round, people whose lives are 'glamorous' and constantly interesting. There is a sense in which this is true, but in the more important sense it is not. Most of the 'glamour' is the invention of publicists, and whether a person be a film star, fashion model, an airline pilot, or a monarch, each day is dominated by work that must be completed and routine tasks that must be performed. The lives of such people may be interesting or, to be more crude, the source of envy of others, if they lead to the accumulation of personal wealth or provide other, non-material satisfactions, or simply because they appear novel. Once the novelty wears off, and the satisfactory rewards come to be accepted as normal, the daily routine reappears.

What is more, our lives change but little over quite long periods of time. This observation may seem odd, since it is widely accepted that we are living in times of rapid and turbulent change. So we are. After all, in our own century we have seen powered flight develop from the first successful attempt by the Wright brothers to probes of neighbouring planets and the conveyance of human beings to the Moon. We have seen two world wars and the development of weaponry from the machine-gun to the laser-gun, from the explosive shell to the hydrogen bomb. The vast majority of all the scientists who have ever lived are alive today, and their findings are reported in a literature whose output increases exponentially. Yet how much of this change actually impinges on our daily lives? Men have landed on the Moon, but we have not experienced their landing except as images on our television screens. The victims of a war are killed or injured by whatever weapons are used, but their injuries do not change. So far as the individual is concerned the effect of being hit by a cannon ball is very similar to that of being hit by a nuclear weapon. Change is perceived only by looking back, by compressing time. It is quite true that a century is but a moment in historical terms, and so small an interval as to be beyond measurement on the scales that are used to measure biological evolution or geological processes. On a human scale, though, it is a very long time indeed. I have no doubt that in the twenty-first century people will live very differently from the way they lived in the eighteenth century so that historians will be able to refer to this short, three-hundred-year period as one of great change, but for individuals change occurs rather slowly. The way I live is somewhat different from the way my parents and grandparents lived, but not unrecognizably so. I believe that if they were to return from the grave they would be able to adjust to life in the modern world perfectly well and continue to live in a way that was sufficiently familiar to them to feel comfortable.

Our lifestyle, then, the way we live from day to day, is the product of a continuing but very gradual process of development and it demonstrates great stability. If we seek to alter it, in most cases we achieve no more than quite minor revisions, the substitution of one kind of routine for another, but within the same broad context. This is what happens when we change jobs. When, at particular points in our lives, really important changes occur, usually connected with physical changes as we grow to maturity, we use ceremonies to mark them and to ease ourselves through them. All human societies have such 'rites of passage' to mark births, the onset of puberty, marriage, death (or more correctly bereavement), as well as events connected with significant changes in status conferred on adults, as, for example, when a student graduates.

This being so, we need to be clear about what we mean when we talk of changing the way we live. No matter how radical a change may appear, the appearance is likely to be superficial. In essence we will be living as we have always lived and unless our way of life supplies us with those biological essentials, such as food and shelter, and psychological essentials, such as emotional relationships with other humans, that were supplied by our former lifestyle, we will revert to our former way of life, or abandon those aspects of our new way of life that distress us, or we will fail to survive. Thus a 'change of lifestyle' appears to be synonymous with a 'change in means of livelihood'.

Most of us change our means of livelihood at some time during our lives, and perhaps many times, but clearly this is not the kind of change people mean when they talk of 'alternative' lifestyles, of which the self-sufficient lifestyle is one. These terms imply more than just a change of occupation or place of residence. They suggest, and since they are not used synonymously with 'change of occupation' we may assume they are meant to suggest, a change in the system of values by which we order our lives. If this is so, it may be that the significance of the change lies not in the change of occupation or residence, which may be no more than a kind of rite of passage, but in its moral quality. It is somewhat similar, then, to a religious conversion, marked by a ritual but leading to such deep commitment as to require the convert so to adapt his or her way of life as to permit time for devotion, reflection, or necessary observances.

A person who moves from one house to another house does so, presumably, because the new house is more pleasing or more convenient than the old house. The acceptance of the new implies the rejection of the old, at least in some respects. Similarly, a person who changes jobs voluntarily may be presumed to find the new job preferable to the old, so that again the acceptance of the new implies a rejection of the old. These instances are commonplace and of no importance. When a person undergoes a religious or moral conversion, however, the acceptance of a new system of values also implies a rejection of the old values, and this is important. What are the values that are accepted and what are those that are rejected? Is the change rational, in the literal sense, and if it is irrational is it at least comprehensible to others?

What is rejected by those who seek a radical change in lifestyles must be all or part of the system of values that governs the majority of people in the society away from which they wish to move. We will have something to say later about these values, but let us concentrate for the moment on the values that are accepted.

People seldom describe clearly their motives for seeking changes in the way they live, but a frequent explanation is that they are seeking a more 'natural' way to live. They imply, then, that formerly they were living in a less natural way and in future they will live in a more natural way. Of course, one does not need to make so profound a change to feel concern at many aspects of modern life – no matter in which historical period you locate the word 'modern' – and colloquially we often hear people complain of the 'unnatural' way most of us live. The words 'natural' and 'unnatural' occur so frequently in this context that any assessment of the possibility or desirability of such changes must begin with a consideration of the nature of man. What is a natural way of life for us? If we can discover a way of life that can be said to be truly natural, then such a way of life is likely to supply us with all that we need physically and psychologically, and it would make good sense to seek to attain it.

First, though, we must consider the word 'natural'. Throughout history many writers have sought to support their views by claiming them to be more 'natural' than those of their adversaries. Today, to most people, 'nature' refers to conditions brought about by physical and biological laws, so that 'natural' behaviour is behaviour consistent with such laws. It is, however, difficult to devise a lifestyle based on such laws, which require us to do such things as eat, drink, reproduce, preserve our internal homeostasis, and fall to the ground when we overbalance. The laws have little to say about how we achieve these aims and so they offer no moral guidance. There is another sense, though, in which 'nature' becomes a more theological concept. It was used in this sense by St Thomas Aquinas, who wrote: 'Every law framed by man bears the character of a law exactly to that extent to which it is derived from the law of nature. But if in any point it is in conflict with the law of nature, it at once ceases to be a law; it is a mere perversion of law.' To Aquinas, and to many subsequent writers, 'natural law' is precisely synonymous with 'God's law', so that it cannot be divorced from its moral context. This, incidentally, should dispose of the view that the Christian church is necessarily ecologically insensitive.

To many nineteenth-century writers, 'human nature' was taken to mean man's 'animal nature', that dark side of ourselves that we must seek to master if we are to achieve moral advancement. When we talk of people 'behaving like animals' it is this conflict between spirit and flesh we have in mind, and again the concept is theological.

In the writings of Marx, 'nature' means something quite different. On the one hand, it means the whole of reality and, on the other, it also means that extra-human reality, independent of man, that is capable of being mediated by man. 'Nature', in other words, comes to mean the same as 'raw material' and, according to Marx, 'natural history' becomes human history extended backward in time.

It is evident, then, that provided we are careful in our use of the word 'nature', the concept of mastering or exploiting nature has respectable antecedents and can be defended, but so can the concept of obeying nature and of framing human laws to reflect natural laws. In neither case, though, does the concept of nature correspond to the concept that would be accepted by a modern scientist. In one way or another it is theological or metaphysical.

What, then, is 'natural man'? There is a view that holds that the natural way of life for man is that of the hunter and gatherer and that all other ways of life are, therefore, more or less unnatural. If this is so, then our search for a natural life should be directed back into the distant past.

The view is advanced seriously and must not be dismissed on the ground that it is impossible for us to return to such a way of life. The truth of a proposition is not affected by any personal inconveniences that may arise from its implications. If the proposition 'by nature man is a hunter and gatherer' be true, then we must be prepared to live with its consequences. Nor is it relevant to dismiss the view on the ground that it is held by a small minority of people. That does not affect its truth, either. In any case, it seems probable that the view influences many people, at least indirectly. The search for self-sufficiency often directs itself towards the cultivation of the land to produce food, and often by methods that a modern agriculturist would consider obsolete. The defence of this is that the provision of food must be an early step in any progress towards self-sufficiency, but the defence is not convincing. Why is the person who grows food more self-sufficient than the independent person, employed in some other way, who buys food? The move to the land is often associated with a search into the past and sometimes it includes an interest in ancient, pre-Christian religions (actual, or more often invented) that are supposed to enhance respect for non-human species, and it is by no means impossible that it is founded on the belief that man has, and should return to, an ecological niche.

The view is expounded in its most complete form by Edward Goldsmith, who states: 'It is significant that for nearly 99 per cent of man's tenancy of this planet he has earned his living by hunting and gathering and his activities have been limited to the fulfilment of his normal ecological functions in his particular environment without in any way upsetting its balance . . . when we generalize about man, we must mean "man the hunter" '. From this it follows that any departure from this mode of life 'must mean at least a measure of biological and social disruption'.

The argument proceeds, then, from the first premiss that man evolved into and as part of certain ecosystems, which Goldsmith asserts were natural climax ecosystems. Within these ecosystems man occupied a particular niche for which he was well adapted. Climax ecosystems are characterized by great stability, so that while individuals are born and die, and nutrients are recycled constantly, the system as a whole endures over long periods of time. The systems which man has substituted for the natural ecosystems into which he evolved are less stable and so less satisfactory, and modern societies are highly unstable. Since climax ecosystems are usually stable, in Goldsmith's opinion stability becomes a desirable characteristic to be sought in any surrogate system devised by man. Our present ills can be attributed to the inherent instability of our (and by implication all) societies. His earlier ideas were expanded in a later work, *The Stable Society,* which begins: 'Our society is increasingly unstable. It is subject to increasing discontinuities which, if unchecked, must lead to its eventual collapse'. The solution, then, is to seek greater stability, and to do this we must study and if possible emulate those early societies which existed within climax ecosystems, where man lived as a hunter and gatherer.

The reason for the inherent instability emerges when human societies are viewed as systems. The interacting components within a stable system tend to preserve that stability. If certain components behave in ways that are incompatible with the stability of the system, if they pursue objectives whose inevitable consequence is to alter the system profoundly, then it is likely that the stability of the system will be threatened. Whether or not it collapses depends on the extent of the disturbance, and if Goldsmith's argument seems obscure or implausible we might remember that much of the discussion over environmental pollution in recent years has turned about this very point. At what stage do we decide that a particular form of pollution ceases to be an annoyance and becomes a threat? Obviously, at the point where it begins to endanger the health or life of organisms, and especially of humans. In other words, pollution becomes a threat when it disrupts the natural system to such an extent that the environment becomes more hostile to man himself.

If we regard human societies as systems, subject to the laws that govern general systems, then perhaps we can diagnose the cause of a particular malaise and prescribe a treatment in terms of modifying the behaviour of certain components. This is precisely what Goldsmith does, drawing many of his analogies from primitive societies.

So we have three premisses. The first, as we have seen, is that man evolved to fill a niche within climax ecosystems and that he has departed from that niche. The second premiss is that this departure initiated a process that has led, by a more or less direct route, to our present position as members of a society that is on the verge of collapse. The third premiss is that it is valid to regard society as a system subject to the laws of general systems. Let us examine these in turn.

It cannot be denied that man inhabited this planet in his present physiological form for, in human terms, a very long time before the discovery or invention of agriculture. In pre-agricultural, or palaeolithic times our ancestors lived, usually in seminomadic groups, by gathering plants and augmenting this mainly vegetarian diet with more or less hunting and fishing. Either this hunting and gathering way of life was the natural life for man, so that his subsequent departure from it was aberrant, or hunting and gathering represents no more than a phase in man's history, from which his departure was implied from the beginning.

The first objection to the hunter and gatherer premiss is supplied by common sense. If this were the natural life for man it must have supplied all of his needs. If it did, then why did he abandon it? From all accounts of hunting and gathering societies, life is not especially austere or irksome, in that even under conditions that are far from ideal, such as those of the Kalahari Desert or the Australian Outback, groups of people find little difficulty in obtaining ample food and shelter. Such aberrant behaviour demands an explanation, but the theory has none to advance. Some people suggest that there was a major environmental change, perhaps of the climate, that compelled man to invent agriculture. In the regions where agriculture originated, however, there is no evidence for such an environmental change at the appropriate time. The alternative view, that hunting and gathering represent no more than a phase in human development from which man was bound to depart sooner or later, avoids the difficulty. It provides an adequate explanation of why man changed his way of life by locating the reason for the change within the human psyche which, if you like, had always desired change and so impelled men to seek opportunities for change.

If man is naturally a hunter and gatherer, certain consequences seem to follow. It may be that he is, in ecological terms, a climax species. This would allow him to occupy a definable niche in particular ecosystems, as Goldsmith holds he did. If, on the other hand, he is an ecological opportunist, habitually invading ecosystems and establishing himself there either by adapting to fill a vacant niche or by displacing some other species in prior occupation, then we have no reason to suppose this behaviour has changed. Man remains an opportunist, he has never occupied a niche of his own and perhaps history can be explained as his search for ecological security. Once again the hunting and gathering theory fails.

Climax species are well adapted to the niches they occupy, so that they tend to be more or less specialized, the higher the trophic level on which they reside the greater their degree of specialization. The true carnivores, for example, are likely to be equipped with armament to enable them to overpower their prey, and their dentition and alimentary system may be those best suited for a diet of raw flesh. The cats, for example, have strong jaws with a wide gape, teeth designed for piercing and shearing but not for grinding or chewing, excellent binocular vision in most species able to make use of dim light, claws that are retractable for their own protection (except in the cheetah whose digits lack sheaths into which the claws may be withdrawn), and a comparatively short gut into which are secreted strong digestive juices. Clearly, cats are highly specialized for hunting. There are herbivores that are no less specialized. The ruminants, for example, have teeth designed for grinding fibrous plant material and a complex digestive system by means of which nutrients can be extracted from cells contained within walls of cellulose. Mammals cannot digest cellulose, but the ruminants employ bacteria, which can do so, to perform this service for them. Many species carry specialization to its limit. The koala will eat only the leaves of certain eucalyptus trees and is likely to die from starvation rather than eat leaves from the wrong eucalyptus. The giant panda, which is a member of the racoon family, eats only certain bamboo shoots. Many snakes will eat only live animals that they catch for themselves.

the processes of hunting and feeding being inextricably linked.

Man lacks the special armament that would enable him to hunt efficiently without weapons. He runs neither fast nor for very long distances, compared with the speeds and endurances of his competitors among the hunters or his quarries among the prey species. His teeth are capable of piercing and shearing and of grinding and chewing, but he performs all these tasks rather inefficiently. His gut is neither so short as that of a typical carnivore nor so long as that of a typical herbivore. His vegetarian diet is restricted in range and does not include very cellulosic material, but within its range it is very diverse. Man, then, is not very specialized.

Extreme specialization is not invariably an attribute of climax species. There are many orders whose members have close physiological similarities, yet are adapted to quite different diets. Among the Rodentia, for example, all of which have jaws and teeth adapted for gnawing, there are species that subsist on every conceivable kind of vegetation, and many that will eat flesh, especially of young birds, and carrion. Some rodents are climax species, others are opportunists.

There is another indicator that can be used to determine whether a species is or is not truly a climax species. A climax species lives as an integral part of its ecosystem. If it is removed from that system and its place is not taken by some equivalent species, the system may undergo fundamental change. The removal of predator species, for example, may cause a proliferation of those species on which they used to prey. This in turn may lead to over-utilization of the plant resources. The population of herbivores may deteriorate as it comes to include first the old and sick individuals that would have been killed by predators, then weaker individuals that are suffering from malnutrition or ailments linked to malnutrition. The floristic composition of the system is likely to change.

If we suppose that early man lived in much the same way as present-day primitive people, which is a reasonable supposition but a supposition all the same, it appears that the removal of such peoples from their environments causes no environmental change of any consequence, but their invasion of a new system can, on occasion, cause much disturbance. These effects can be attributed to the fact that the diet of man is very broadly based and to the inefficiency of his hunting under certain conditions.

The diet of early man was so diverse that the actual amount of material from any one species that was consumed was so small as to have little influence on the population of that species. According to

Bilsborough the diet of the early hominids probably consisted of nuts, berries, leaves, fruits, grasses, seeds, roots and tubers, augmented by insects, grubs, other invertebrates, fledgelings, reptiles, and small mammals. Later hominids engaged in organized hunting of larger mammals and also ate carrion from large mammals that died naturally or that had been killed by more powerful predators.

The adverse environmental effects of early man derived from his difficulties in hunting large herbivores, so that hunting tribes sometimes stampeded entire herds, driving them over precipices then climbing down and taking as much meat as they needed and could carry. The wastage was extremely large and the effect on populations of prey species was often severe.

Such dietary versatility and hunting inefficiency are not characteristic of climax species, but it is interesting to note that there have been climax species that occupied side branches of the human evolutionary tree. *Australopithecus robustus*, for example, was a highly specialized herbivore who became extinct more than two million years ago. He lived at the same time as other descendants from the early *Australopithecus* population, whose evolution had taken them on a diverging route, were taking to gathering and scavenging for food (*A.africanus*). It was these species that evolved into the more advanced hominids whose remains have been found in the Olduvai and Lake Rudolph region of East Africa. This is the line that led to *Homo erectus* and so to modern man.

It would seem to follow from this that we should consider a man to be an ecological opportunist. If so, we must ask whether man has an ecological niche into which he fits in any real sense?

It seems likely that the increasing seasonality of climates during the Miocene epoch (which began about twenty-seven million years ago) favoured certain of the Dryopithecines that were able to subsist on a more varied diet than that of their competitors. Around twenty million years ago the Dryopithecine stock diverged, one line leading to the great apes, possibly with a separate line leading to the orangutan, while the other line led via the later Dryopithecines to *Ramapithecus*, who lived in a landscape of mosaic woodlands with streams, open areas and grassland, and who probably lived on a wide range of plant foods, possibly with a small amount of meat. During the Pliocene (which began about ten million years ago) increasing aridity led to a contraction of the forests and an increase in the area of grassland. This would have favoured the descendants of *Ramapithecus*, which were better able to live on the ground and which, by this time, had a more upright posture and bipedal locomotion, while increasing competition among arboreal species. This increased competition would have ensured that once a species took to living on the ground its former niche would be filled so that it could not return to its arboreal habitat. By the late Pliocene and early Pleistocene (which began about two million years ago) at least some hominid communities were subsisting on an omnivorous diet.

If this story is more or less correct (and there is a gap in the fossil record between about five and ten million years ago so it is not possible to be absolutely certain) it implies that the major environmental change that is supposed to have led to the development of agriculture occurred much further in the past, long before modern man appeared as a distinct species. The abandonment of the arboreal niche and adaptation to life on the ground had been accomplished by man's ancestors so that man was an opportunist from the start, and descended from opportunists. He never had an ecological niche of his own but lived by invading ecosystems and making the best of whatever he found in them. Thus, life as a hunter and gatherer was neither more nor less 'natural' than any other way of life.

The fact that man has spent more than 90 per cent of his history living in this way is irrelevant, not to say tautological, just as it is tautological to say that a six-year-old child has spent 83 per cent of its life as an infant under five years of age. The one is simply another way of stating the other and it leads to no conclusion.

What is more, man's success as an opportunist has been phenomenal. Probably he has been successful from the start, but there can be no doubt that it is in fairly recent, historical times that he has reaped the greatest benefits. Those who maintain that his departure from a hunting and gathering way of life represented a decline from an ecological norm must introduce some novel criteria against which to measure performance, since the most obvious criteria contradict them. Numerically, human population has increased greatly. Man has expanded geographically to colonize habitats under widely different conditions of climate, topography, and vegetation. Although the natural span of a human life has not been prolonged, far more people live through that span than at any time in the past. Since this can be explained only as a result of better nutrition, better living conditions and better medical care, it suggests that people enjoy greater physical comfort than at any previous time, and a general reduction in mortality implies an overall reduction in the incidence of disease, so that people are healthier. Good health does not necessarily guarantee happiness, but chronic ill health most certainly causes more or less misery, as anyone who has suffered from it will agree. While the victim of a prolonged illness may be cheerful in adversity the fact that we must admit that his or her circumstances are adverse suggests rather strongly that under happier circumstances the person would be happier. It would seem, then, that a population that is healthy is likelier to be happier than one that is unhealthy, all other things being equal. In this respect I think it reasonable to suppose that people today are happier than people were in former times. To suggest that all this amounts to failure rather than success sounds like perversity!

Man's lack of specialization also suggests that his evolution has not yet ended. He has existed as a distinct species for only a short time so that gross evolutionary changes in modern man have not been observed, but are not to be expected. Minor changes are more difficult to detect and the close observation needed to do this has been possible only within the last few centuries. Even so, it is possible that such changes have occurred. For several thousand years, for example, humans have consumed caffeine in its various forms, and they appear to have evolved mechanisms to overcome the deleterious effects of this substance. Caffeine is known to cause breaks in chromosomes, but human cells in which such caffeine-induced breaks occur are also prevented from dividing, so that affected cells cannot multiply aberrantly.

If human evolution continues as it might be expected to continue for any other species, it is possible that eventually man may become a climax species, fitting precisely into an ecological niche from which escape is impossible. At that point his evolution will reach its end because the future of the sp cies will be determined by the condition of the environment and man will be unable to adapt to major changes. It seems unlikely that he will continue to evolve in an entirely random fashion, however, since his highly complex cultural development has led him to a point at which he is capable of manufacturing environments for himself, so reducing the probability of major changes that are beyond his control and his adaptive capacity, and also to a point at which he is capable, at least potentially, of manipulating his own genetic coding so that in future he may be able to evolve much more rapidly, in directions determined by himself. This raises difficult ethical and political problems, of course, but his cultural development does make his early extinction rather unlikely.

This would seem to dispose of the first premiss. Man did not evolve simply to live as a hunter and gatherer and so he has not departed from an ecological niche. The hunter and gatherer lives no more naturally than do you or I and the concept of 'natural man' is meaningless. All men are natural, so we may as well drop the word 'natural' and just talk of men – provided, of course, that we are using 'natural' in its stricter scientific sense and not in its more theological sense.

Is modern society on the verge of collapse? This is a matter we shall consider in more detail later. For the moment there is one general point that should be made, and the issue should be placed in its proper historical context.

We cannot know whether our society is close to collapse for the simple reason that to do so requires us to have knowledge of future events. Since we lack such knowledge any statement that society will, or must collapse is misleading. Furthermore, we must define 'collapse' to provide ourselves with parameters against which we can measure events, and perhaps we may derive such parameters from the history of previous societies which we believe collapsed. Actually it becomes extremely difficult to devise such parameters, but let us assume it is possible. We may then go on to assert that events in our own society appear to form trends which, if continued, may imply collapse according to the definition of collapse we have devised. If our definition is based on past experience, 'collapse' will not imply human extinction or, indeed, any serious long term halt to the development of what (with another definition) we may call 'civilization'. Thus, the collapse of a particular society may be inconvenient for members of that society at the time but it may have little long-term significance for humanity as an historical whole. As we saw earlier, human extinction seems unlikely in the foreseeable future.

The idea that modern society faces imminent collapse became fashionable in the early 1970s, but it is not new. The collapse is supposed to result from the multiplicative effects of population growth (or human success), the depletion of essential materials and land, and the pollution of the environment by toxic substances. These fears are not new, either.

The threat of overpopulation in the modern world is derived from, and adds nothing to, the fears expressed by Malthus in the late eighteenth century, and these were not original, even then. The originator of the theory of population was the French mathematician and philosopher, the Marquis de Condorcet (1743–94) and Malthus came to hear of it through his father, who was a disciple of Condorcet. Condorcet, though, saw no gloomy future for man, for he advocated birth control, so evading the evil effects, and believed that man had proceeded through nine epochs in his rapid progress from barbarism to civilization and that he stood on the brink of the tenth epoch which would see mankind perfected, physically, intellectually, socially, and politically. Malthus, then, was making a political point when he chose a gloomy interpretation.

The depletion of resources has caused concern repeatedly throughout history. It was this concern, with particular reference to agricultural land, that inspired Malthus, and the risk to those resources that are owned communally was expounded in the famous essay by Garrett Hardin, 'The Tragedy of the Commons', based on the work of a nineteenth-century mathematician, William Forster Lloyd.

The pollution of the environment recurs as a theme in the writing of many nineteenth-century authors, including Carlyle and, of course, William Morris. Carlyle and Morris may be taken as representing reforming movements, but of very different kinds, and theirs was a political, economic and, to some extent, philosophical argument.

Malthus argued, and believed he had proved, that human populations are limited only by starvation and that they multiply to the limit of subsistence. The only way in which the poor may improve their situation is to restrict the growth in their numbers voluntarily, so that the labour market comes to favour the labourer. He disagreed with Condorcet in holding that this was impossible since (ignoring the possibilities of contraception) it would require a voluntary abstinence from sexual intercourse of which the labouring classes were incapable. The only alternative was to administer a sharply educative therapy by abstaining from all social reforms so that the starvation predicted by the theory might be experienced in fact. The premiss on which the argument is based is, that while populations increase geometrically, the resources required to sustain them increase only arithmetically.

The Malthusian argument was supported by the English economist, David Ricardo, who maintained that there are distinct limits to the portion of national wealth that can be distributed as wages. Both Malthus and Ricardo favoured the repeal of the Old Poor Law, but opposed the enactment of any substitute legislation. They represented a group called Radical, and the Radicals were reacting against the Utilitarian movement that (late in the life of its principal founder, Jeremy Bentham) became associated with liberal policies. In commerce these were based on the laissez-faire, laissez-passer view derived from the eighteenth-century Physiocrats, the French school which held that the only true source of wealth is the land, since it is only by natural biological processes that goods are produced from nothing, manufacturing industry merely altering the form of materials and adding nothing substantial to them. Since natural laws govern all living organisms, including man, human laws should conform to them and the purpose of governments should be to do no more than educate people regarding natural laws and remove obstacles to their observance. The similarity of this view to that of Aquinas is obvious but, being products of the Enlightenment, the Physiocrats held that man is inherently good and perfectible. This was an atheistic, optimistic view. As the doctrine came to be interpreted, laissez-faire did not mean total inactivity on the part of government, which would have satisfied the Radicals. It meant that combatants must be given every opportunity to remain active in the fight for survival and to achieve this aim ambitious programmes of liberalizing reforms were needed. So the Utilitarians, seeking the greatest happiness of the greatest number, were social reformers seeking ways to remove obstacles to 'natural law' that would permit laissez-faire to operate as it was meant to operate, to the common good of all.

There was a strong element of romanticism in the Radical movement which can be traced back to Rousseau and which we shall examine again in a moment. This romanticism is very evident in the writing of Carlyle and it also appears strongly in the views of William Cobbett. Industry was inherently unpleasant, if not actually wicked, and England would do well to try to return to the days when the country was ruled by a strong landed aristocracy led by a good monarch.

This combination of Malthusian–Ricardian Radicalism and romanticism for a better past led Carlyle and Cobbett to favour what today we would call despotic government. Government should be in the hands of those fitted by birth and education to govern. The worst evil that may befall a society arises from democracy, which can lead only to anarchy. The view is reactionary in the literal sense of seeking to recreate the past and some of it is inherent in certain modern environmental romanticism, whose implications we shall consider presently.

Morris, too, rejected manufacturing industry, but the romantic past he sought to recreate was that of the skilled artisan, and the world in which he believed this might be accomplished was the Marxist Utopia. He favoured reforms of conditions for working people and so, although he started from much the same position as Carlyle, and although the implications of his political views involved the rejection of democratic government in favour of dictatorship, his proletarian dictatorship was very different from the absolute monarchy by heredity advocated by Carlyle. In more formal terms the two views are expressed by Locke and Hobbes and are the origin of contemporary political differences between left and right. The similarities between the left-wing views of Morris and those of some modern environmentalists are also striking.

Having placed modern environmental concerns into some kind of historical context does not dispose of them, of course. By showing that the concern is not new I have not shown that it is unfounded, or that even if it was unfounded formerly it is therefore unfounded now. All I have sought to do at this stage is to suggest that predictions of imminent collapse made in the past have proved wrong. Before we can take this discussion any further we need to consider the third of our premisses, which justifies the view that modern society is inherently unstable.

Is it valid to regard societies as systems subject to the laws of general systems? The technique of mathematical modelling has been tried and proven over a long time. It is useful in two ways. It helps us to understand complex situations or phenomena by translating them into aggregates of their components, each of which is relatively simple, and it forces us to be precise since we are required to attach numerical values to each factor in the model. The technique can be applied to systems because any discrete group of continuous events behaves according to rules that can be induced from the relationships among the events within the group. Where rules exist that can be used to predict future behaviour, the construction of a model requires nothing more than the attachment of numerical values to components of the system so that the model may be expressed mathematically. The validity of the model will depend on the accuracy of the mathematical construction.

The concept of an 'ecosystem' derives much from the theory of general systems, being just such a discrete group of events as the theory explains. The relationships among species within an ecosystem can be known by observation and the flow of energy and materials through the system can be known by measurement. Having studied the real system to obtain sufficient information for the construction of the model, the model itself can be used to estimate the effects that might ensue from changes to the system or to any part of it, and these can be related to other similar systems. In most cases the results will conform to what common sense would suggest (although there may be exceptions) but they are more useful since, being quantified, they are more precise.

The view of the system must be mechanistic. Such models can be made only if the relationships they describe vary only within known limits. When the theory is applied to human societies two results of philosophical importance follow. Since the model must be mechanistic it can make no allowance for free will, so that in the debate between determinism and free will it must fall on the side of determinism. It must also be materialistic, resolving the other ancient debate between mind and matter in favour of matter. This abolishes the dualism that has troubled philosophers for centuries, but it does not solve the problem, it simply ignores it. Modern physics, for example, has effectively abolished matter, so that the argument might be better resolved in favour of mind. Goldsmith has no doubts, casually listing free will and the mind among his list of 'Our Fatal Illusions' along with consciousness and vitalism. In such models of society, Goldsmith also includes religion in its purely mechanistic form, as no more than a cultural phenomenon designed to regulate behaviour. It is this, of course, but theism cannot be dismissed so lightly and in such a mechanistic interpretation there is no way account can be taken of those who believe that one or another religion expresses an absolute truth. Religious belief cannot be affirmed or disproved by reasoned argument and so any departure from a strict agnosticism implies a belief. This is acceptable, of course, but not when it masquerades as fact.

This is but one instance of the inherent weakness of the approach. A further weakness appears when attempts are made to attach numerical values to relationships among humans within societies. This becomes arbitrary and liable to distortion arising, for example, from the outlook of the modeller as this has been conditioned by his or her experience of life as a member of a particular class or society. As the system that is being modelled grows larger, so the model becomes more metaphysical, in that it is based much more on intellectual calculation and estimate than it is on actual measurement. It leads to rigidity, which can be demonstrated by the fact that it is possible to show that modern industrial cities are so dependent on complex networks of communications as to be highly vulnerable to small disruptions, any of which may deprive citizens of essential supplies and so lead to chaos. In fact, cities can withstand very large disruptions with, apparently, no lasting ill effects. They continue to function, albeit in a modified form, while being bombed or invaded, and cities that have been virtually demolished recover remarkably quickly. Humans, it seems, are much more resilient than the models allow.

In fact, there is no way that models of very large systems can be verified with any certainty. Since the purpose of modelling is to reduce the system to dimensions that render it comprehensible, the model must be distorted since the size and complexity of the original are characteristic of it. If we try to overcome the difficulty by constructing a model whose size and complexity is similar to that of the original we have a model that is no easier to understand than the original, so we have defeated our own purpose. If we construct a model that we can understand we can verify it only by comparison with the original, but it was our lack of understanding of the original that led us to make the model in the first place, so we cannot tell whether or not the model is accurate.

Such metaphysical models are made, however, and in some cases their purpose has been to warn us of the error of our ways. Although they are couched in scientific language, such models are intended not to predict the future but to bring about changes in human behaviour that will bring us closer to 'natural' or 'God's' laws.

The modeller of large systems of this kind is compelled to devise entire worlds in which predictions are fulfilled or dangers avoided. This problem is very ancient. Throughout history, those who sought to develop a total view of society found themselves having to invent entire societies in which their theories might be demonstrated. The word 'Utopia' is taken from the society invented by Sir Thomas More, but the first Utopia may have been Plato's Republic. Such Utopias have their uses, but they have disadvantages, too, the most glaring being the lengths to which their creators must go to avoid internal inconsistencies. At times they are compelled by the force of their own argument to conclusions that, as human beings, they would find utterly repellant if they had to live in the society that incorporated them. We will consider one such Utopia in a moment, but first let us examine a modern Utopia that is derived from a holistic view of the world.

The argument begins by stating that the real world is a unified whole, if you like a complex of natural systems operating outside human control and of which man is a part. Human behaviour and human societies are similarly formed and governed in accordance with natural laws. The attempt to violate those laws, to escape beyond the bounds imposed by them, has led us to a crisis that threatens the very survival of our society. This may be described as 'nature's revenge'. Nature must win at last, restoring us to the reality that existed before man subjected nature to rational planning and technology. As we have 'denatured' the natural world, so we have accumulated riches and in doing so we have acquired an ethic that equates wealth with virtue. If we are to escape the crisis that threatens us we must develop a new ethic. We must return to nature, as it were, to our own origins. We must forget ideas of seeking happiness as a goal, although happiness may well result from the application of the higher principles we must adopt. We should cultivate honour, morality, duty and heroism, and poverty should be regarded as a noble state to be emulated. Since it has been rational philosophies and the science derived from them led us to the crisis, by seeking to impose on nature patterns devised by the human intellect, we cannot hope to resolve our problems by rational means. Indeed, we must abandon rationalism and our perception of reality must be intuitive. We will find this reality in the basic things of life, in the tilling of the soil and the comprehension of the organic whole of which we are part.

There are clear similarities between this line of reasoning and that advanced by some environmentalists, but the example is not taken from environmentalist literature. The argument continues by showing how this intuitive awareness of our cultural roots will lead us to identify with heroic figures from the past who can provide us with examples of the ways in which adversity may be overcome. We will find ourselves becoming more and more united, as one people. Cultivating an ascetic way of life, strengthened by our unity of purpose, we will rise to meet any challenge. In this we will be led by a charismatic figure who will be our new lawgiver. Since we have abandoned rationalism, the leader will not need to account to us for his decisions. These will be true and valid because he has made them. The leader may choose to explain some or all of his decisions, but he is under no obligation to do so and since he rules by intuition rather than by reason he cannot be expected to provide arguments in support of his actions except where these follow logically from previous actions that were intuitive. His authority is absolute and cannot be challenged.

This scenario is taken from an essay written in 1934 by Herbert Marcuse, outlining the theoretical arguments underlying German National Socialism. As we know, the development of this theory required the invention of a remote, heroic, history that was unashamedly romantic and in its efforts to remain coherent (so far as it did) its creators were compelled to ignore or suppress facts relating to the real natural world.

The aim of the Nazis was to create a Utopia, the Reich that would endure for a thousand years. Like many authoritarian Utopias, the new state bore many similarities to Plato's Republic. In the Republic, there were to be only three classes, the guardians who possessed all political power, the soldiers, and the workers. Life was to be austere, since both poverty and riches lead to a decline in the quality of workmanship of all kinds, statecraft being no exception. 'Does the potter, after he becomes rich, seem still to mind his art? By no means, said he. But will he not become more idle and careless than formerly? Much more so. Will he not then become a more unskilful potter? Much more so, said he. And surely, if he is unable through poverty to furnish himself with tools, or anything else requisite to his art, his workmanship will be more imperfectly executed, and his sons, or those whom he instructs, will be inferior artists? Yes. Through both these, now, poverty and riches, the workmanship in the arts is rendered less perfect, and the artists themselves become less expert.' The guardians were to rule because they were qualified to do so by birth and education, just as the potter is qualified by birth and education to pursue his craft. Everyone was to mind his or her own business, although some social mobility was allowed. This was to be justified to the people by means of a deliberate lie, children being brought up to believe that some individuals have souls containing gold, some silver and others iron, so that it is natural and proper for power to be distributed in the way it is distributed. Not only was personal property to be limited strictly, but private possessive emotions were to be reduced by the abolition of the family. There was to be some selective breeding to improve the human stock but by and large the sexes would mingle rather promiscuously and children would be brought up in institutions. This led to the problem of incest, since no father – and after a few years no mother – could know the identity of their own offspring and siblings could not recognize one another. This difficulty is overcome, after a fashion, by an elaborate arrangement of age grouping so that for every person certain age groups are taboo. Children born to parents outside the prescribed age limits for parenthood are to be killed at birth. Strict censorship would ensure that young people were exposed only to the most edifying of literature, music, and art. It was this that led Plato to his main unacceptable conclusion, for although personally he loved literature and drama, he found there was no way he could permit it to exist once interpersonal conflict and 'unworthy' emotions and individuals were purged from it, so it had to be forbidden in its entirety.

The guardians were to be appointed by the legislator, or lawgiver. It was mainly Nietzche who introduced the idea of the class of heroes led by a superhero, so perhaps we can allow a Nietzchean promotion to make the legislator into the charismatic leader. In this case the guardians may be likened to party members in any modern totalitarian state.

The purpose of the state is to provide sustenance for its people at a bare subsistence level, to wage war against neighbouring states of more or less equal size, and to prevent change. In fact, the state would resemble its own original model, Sparta, whose soldiers defeated Athens not many years before the Republic was written and by whose political system Plato was much impressed.

If we consider this concept of the state in a modern context, the goals of resistance to change and to moderate aggression from outside are important. If we are persuaded that we live in times of rapid and frightening change, what is more human than to imagine a state in which change is forbidden? Goldsmith expresses this feeling by describing the goal of societies in the language of systems theory.

What is the goal? The answer is stability. This is not defined as a fixed point in space-time but as a course or trajectory along which discontinuities, i.e. disequilibria and their corrections, are reduced to a minimum, and which thereby ensures survival taken in its widest sense. Human societies until recently satisfied this requirement.

If the final sentence of this passage is taken literally, as apparently it is meant to be taken, it seems to imply that the series of events which we call 'history' cannot have occurred, unless the word 'recently' is being used in a special sense. Like other modellers of total societies, Goldsmith has a clear idea of what is the best kind of society. He calls it a traditional society and in it there is nothing that approximates to our idea of government. 'There are rarely kings, or even chiefs, no presidents or courts of law, no prisons or police force. The closest approximation to a political institution is the council of elders which occasionally gathers to discuss important issues. Such a society has often been referred to as a "gerontocracy", or a government by the old men – a term that can be applied to most stable societies. It might be more apt, however, to speak of a "necrocracy", or government by the dead, since . . . the role of the elders is simply to interpret the traditions and customary laws of the tribe, which embody the experience and practices of previous generations. A society of this sort usually displays a high degree of order.'

Once the Republic, or any other totalitarian state, has achieved its millenial goal, it might well resemble this description of the ideal stable society but, as with all Utopias, we are left with a considerable problem in getting from here to there. Just as Plato found himself committed to a ban on all art, which personally he could not have tolerated in practice, so Goldsmith may have committed himself to means of achieving his defined end that he himself would find appalling.

Such societies have existed in some places and at some periods, but very obvious and grave objections to this description of them suggest that they are unusual and far less durable than they seem. During periods of stability, states will be stable by definition. During periods of change, however, according to this description of them they are reduced to employing internal devices to prevent the occurrence of events whose cause lies outside their boundaries and so beyond their control. In other words, the only conditions under which such a state can exist are those under which it exists anyway, and any attempt to create it at other times must fail, unless it is proposed to establish some kind of global dictatorship that can be subject to no external influences.

It is difficult to see how the state could be established, and life within it might not be pleasant. We are accustomed to the view that the freedom of individuals and of groups within societies derives from laws that are framed clearly and unequivocally and that are administered impartially. In the absence of such laws and such administration, the most likely outcome is that society would become dominated by its more vociferous, aggressive members – bullies. It is possible to base law on tradition, up to a point, and in a way this is how case law is accumulated and used, but the tradition must begin somewhere. With case law it begins with a written law that is interpreted by courts of law, but we are to be denied courts of law and written laws, so if such a state is to be created then 'traditions' must be created simply by declaring them to exist, just as Plato invented a lie to justify the distribution of power within classes. How is the law to be applied? Presumably it is public opinion that will determine the guilt of offenders and administer punishment. It would seem there is to be no trial, no opportunity for an accused person to advance a defence, and no appeal, for there are no courts of law, nor higher authorities to whom such appeals may be addressed, unless the plight of an individual is a sufficiently 'important issue' to warrant a meeting of the council of elders. In fact, this is likely to degenerate into the most arbitrary of mob rule, dominated by bullies, in which there is no effective way to protect the weaker or more timid citizens.

Of course, there are many other ideal states in which communities of varying sizes may achieve stability through self-reliance, but these may be closed to us if we insist that the ideal state once existed in a romanticized past.

The idea that 'natural' man lived more peaceably than modern man derives from two sources. The first is the rejection by many environmentalists, based on modern anthropological evidence, of the idea of Hobbes that the 'natural' state of man is one in which individuals are engaged perpetually in a war of all against all. This view has been much misunderstood. What Hobbes actually argued was that: '. . . during the time men live without a common power to keep them all in awe, they are in that condition which is called war; and such a war, as is of every man, against every man. For WAR, consisteth not in battle only, or the act of fighting: but in a tract of time, wherein the will to contend by battle is sufficiently known: and therefore the notion of *time*, is to be considered in the nature of war; as it is in the nature of weather. For as the nature of foul weather, lieth not in a shower or two of rain; but in an inclination thereto of many days together: so the nature of war, consisteth not in actual fighting; but in the known disposition thereto, during all the time there is no assurance to the contrary. All other time is PEACE.

'Whatsoever therefore is consequent to a time of war, where every man is enemy to every man; the same is consequent to the time, wherein men live without other security, than what their own strength, and their own invention shall furnish them withal. In such condition, there is no place for industry; because the fruit thereof is uncertain: and consequently no culture of the earth; no navigation, nor use of the commodities that may be imported by sea; no commodious building; no instruments of moving, and removing, such things as require much force; no knowledge of the face of the earth; no account of time; no arts; no letters; no society; and which is worst of all, continual fear, and danger of violent death; and the life of man, solitary, poor, nasty, brutish and short.'

Hobbes was advancing a theory of (authoritarian) government and argued the need for such government from the supposed consequences of its absence. He did not assert that men actually lived under such conditions, the situation he described being anterior to any society. Certainly he cannot have believed this to be the condition under which any known tribal society lived for, as he describes it, there is no way individuals could achieve that minimum level of co-operation that is needed to hold together a society of any kind. All known societies do have 'a common power to keep them in awe'. Hobbes used the word 'natural' to describe a hypothetical original state, not one in which men live in harmony with their environment or one another.

It may be that we owe to Hobbes the concept of human societies as systems. In his view, the individuals that comprise a society may be likened to the component organs of a body. Each has its special function and if it is to work efficiently it must be contained within a stable environment from which unusual events are excluded. Since it is difficult to think of organs as individuals capable of independent existence, a modern version of this view might substitute cells, since each living cell is, in fact, a self-contained unit. The analogy cannot be carried very far, however, for two reasons. The first is that individual human beings are possessed of consciousness and the capacity for self-determination in a way that individual cells are not, so that the regulatory mechanisms which are satisfactory within a complex living organism (at least when considered mechanistically) cannot be applied to human societies without considerable repression of individual aspirations. The second reason relates to the scales of the two systems. A human society may consist of thousands or, perhaps, a few million individuals, whereas a complex living organism such as a mammal consists of countless billions of cells. It is much easier to maintain homeostasis within a very large system than within a small one, and an organism consisting of as few cells as there are individuals in a human society would have to sacrifice some, and perhaps much, of its homeostatic equilibrium. The evolutionary success of very simple organisms is achieved by the population of those organisms as a whole, and the existence of each individual is precarious and short.

It was the misunderstanding of Hobbes' view of 'natural man' that led to an over-zealous espousal of Rousseau's concept of the 'noble savage', in which Rousseau really did believe. Advancing an alternative theory of government that owed much to his knowledge of Spartan politics and his own Calvinist upbringing, Rousseau nevertheless admired the 'savages', principally of North America, who could be overthrown by European military might. In 1750 he won a literary prize, awarded by the Academy of Dijon, for an essay in which he contended that the arts and sciences have conferred no benefits on mankind. He held that all science is ignoble, that ethics originate in human pride, that all education and publishing are to be deplored, and that freedom and happiness are to be found in the state of innocence in which he imagined his 'savages' to be living. Later he expanded this view to hold that man is naturally good and is made bad by institutions. Of course, his 'noble savage' is as much a literary fiction as is the war-like barbarian attributed, wrongly, to Hobbes. Yet he is a more attractive fellow, provided that we do not consider to closely the implications of his way of life. He appealed strongly to those who found the intellectual climate of the 1700s and early 1800s in Europe disturbing, and Rousseau became very influential as his ideas developed into the romantic, antirationalist movement based on a love of the Earth and of toil and rejection of science, industry and with them, intellectual inquiry and education. As we have seen, this path led fairly directly via Nietzsche to Hitler.

Let us return now to our three premises. We have seen that there is no valid ground for believing that the life of a hunter and gatherer is natural for man in the sense that it is the way of life we were designed by evolution to pursue. Indeed, the term 'natural man' is meaningless. Ecologically, man is an opportunist, with no true niche, and he makes what use he can of the materials and conditions he finds in the environments he invades. It seems that his evolutionary story has not yet ended, and his history may perhaps be seen as a progression towards some evolutionary goal. We may speculate that this may provide him with the niche he has never had, in some natural or man-made ecosystem, but that the price he pays for the apparent security offered by this niche may be his complete adaptation in an evolutionary cul-de-sac. Such speculation is of no practical importance, except to remind us that our future may be at least as interesting as our past.

We have not disposed of the idea that modern society is on the verge of collapse, but we have placed it in its historical context and we can see how it has developed and what some of its implications are. The undoubtedly phenomenal success of our species means that any event or set of events that is to cause serious disruption must now be on a truly colossal scale. Out numbers, distribution, and diversity of activities make us very resilient.

Whether or not it will be possible one day to construct mathematical models of human societies, today such models are largely metaphysical, the degree of abstraction increasing as the size of the society, or system, being modelled. If we are to regard human societies as systems governed by laws analogous to physical laws we must ride roughshod over at least three of the major philosophical controversies that have exercised thinking men for many centuries: theism; determinism and free will; mind and matter. We cannot resolve these matters, we must simply ignore them, and in opting for materialism in the mind and matter debate we are taking a view that may contradict the view of many of the environmentalists for whose benefit the model is being made. In making such large models we find ourselves compelled to invent total societies, or Utopias, and those Utopias that derive from Plato's Republic and are influenced by

Rousseau's romanticism usually develop into a form of irrational totalitarianism more or less similar to National Socialism.

'Self-sufficiency', then, cannot be conceived of as some kind of return to a simpler way of life based on the idea that the ideal way for us to live is by hunting and gathering, for that path leads nowhere. This is not to say that there are no lessons to be learned from our own history, even from our remote history. Nor is it to say that because one idea of 'self-sufficiency' is based on a misconception, all such ideas are similarly mistaken. It does mean that there are dangers in constructing large scale abstract models of ideal societies, and that these dangers are increased when such models are derived from a romanticized view of the past. The future lies ahead of us, not behind us.

*

The search for self-sufficiency is, I believe, as much spiritual and ideological as it is one of trying to reap the basic necessities of life out of the bare minimum of our surroundings. In fact, I doubt whether the bare minimum would ever be enough, and even though agronomists and the like may calculate the land area necessary to sustain a man, it would be a *reductio ad absurdum* to imagine that self-sufficiency means being restricted to such limits. Many of the early North American colonists, in particular the Plymouth Brethren and other puritanical sects, went pioneering through strong religious motivation, and being self-reliant – God helps those who help themselves – was part and parcel of their creed. Despite hardship and initial privation in the bitter New England winter, it was the success of their efforts that paved the way for the industrial development of America. One reason why contemporary primitive man may have remained primitive is that he never had anything like the Puritan ethic of working hard, and being rewarded for his pains.

The nineteenth-century Zionists who left their Shtetls behind them and embarked with revolutionary zeal for the desolate wasteland that Palestine had become after centuries of ravaging and neglect, were also in pursuit of some self-sufficient ideal. They were repudiating the image of their fathers, of the landless, persecuted Jew, and were seeking freedom through physical work on the land. That freedom took the form of the anarchist proposition that each man should give according to his abilities and receive according to his needs. It was thus an important part of the early Zionist's creed that he could obtain independence and freedom only if he avoided either exploiting or being exploited – and hence he must do all manual work himself. Indeed, we hear pathetic stories of haggard, malaria-wracked Zionists digging roads until they dropped. That ideal, perhaps not surprisingly, has long since become tarnished with time and there are not many kibbutzim today which do not employ non-kibbutz labour, whether Arab, Oriental Jew, or volunteer, to do the more menial tasks.

Being spiritual, ideological, or a combination of both suggests something irrational, and this very irrationality makes a hard and fast definition of self-sufficiency problematical. Take our own small-holding in Cornwall, which has been cited in self-sufficiency magazines and alternative directories. We have had many visitors, some for a few days, others for weeks, months or even years. At various times the notion of self-sufficiency raises its head and we have discussions, sometimes even rancorous, over what is or is not a legitimate activity on the farm and in the house. John Seymour tells me of similar occurrences at Fachongle Isaf, his farm in South Wales, where at one time it was considered absolutely against the principles of self-sufficiency to do any activity which could be turned to profit and bring in hard cash. Very often self-sufficiency is associated with vegetarianism and with trying to buy in as little as possible from outside, at least with money. Bartering, on the other hand, has been granted some self-sufficient virtue because it takes place outside the cash economy. But how to procure nails and do you allow machines if you cannot make them on the spot? What about fuel? In the end, sheer necessity and survival dictate a more sensible course than cutting yourself off from those around your self-sufficient circle.

Unquestionably there is a large element of faddism in self-sufficiency and clearly the rules we make for ourselves, our self-generated taboos, are not based on fundamental truths but are rationalizations which tie us implacably to a particular way of life and provide us with an identity. The convictions we take with us when embarking on the road to self-sufficiency in fact are very necessary if we are to sustain enthusiasm for what can become back-breaking toil on the land. We surely do not live by bread alone.

One thing one can say for self-sufficiency: those who have thought about it and even acted on it are taking themselves and what they do seriously, and they certainly do not take for granted that man has progressed to a better state because of industrial development; nor are they prepared to let themselves be swept along by trends just because they can gain more immediate security that way. In considering man and his place on earth it is inevitable that they should look to more primitive societies, whether agrarian or even hunter-gatherer, because there they may find a timeless activity, where development, at least in an economic sense, is simply not part of the vocabulary.

Like Mike Allaby, I find it easy to find fault with the three premisses posed by Goldsmith in *The Stable Society*. Mike is surely right in claiming that man is an opportunist by nature, rather than a climax species; that hunting and gathering may not be the only long-term path available to him, and that trying to tabulate what is good for him by systems analysis is fraught with danger. Yet I feel a great sympathy for many of Goldsmith's views. One problem I have in particular is accepting that the trend towards industrialism necessarily signifies progress, or is a moral solution to the dilemma of human survival. Undoubtely my own abrupt rejection of urban life and my attempt at 'self-sufficiency' were generated by a disillusionment with the ethic of growth and progress, and I believe my reaction was by no means isolated. Moreover, at the time I moved to the country there was a great deal of publicity given to the plight of Amerindians in South America, in particular in Brazil, and it struck me that the confrontation between the two extremes, stone-age hunter-gatherer-gardener man and twentieth-century consumer man was the final stage of a drama which had been going on since Cain and Abel, and I felt an irrepressible sadness for the ultimate demise of the primitive. I also felt a curious loneliness as a human being, since with the primitive gone we with our industrial ethic would have burned our bridges, we had nothing to turn back to, and we had no certainty that the way ahead was anything more than a cul-de-sac, or even abyss.

Could my feelings be no more than sheer nostalgia, especially in the face of the responsibility of modern man implied in the following?

'The compassionate human being, the compassionate scientist and technologist must somehow provide for the coming billions. It seems to me much more likely that our efforts to limit population will be more successful in a world that has avoided the Malthusian dilemma with its raw human misery than in a world strangulated by this dilemma.'

That statement is by Alvin Weinberg, once director of the United States nuclear research establishment at Oak Ridge. But is that really what scientists are working for ... 'to provide for the coming billions'? Isn't Weinberg's emotive statement as false as claiming that every good-hearted farmer has the drought-starved Sahelian in mind? Yet such ideas have become current currency and it is by persuading us that industrial progress is the only way to solve our problems – at least our material ones – that governments can justify terrible acts, even of genocide, against those who stand in the way of the growth ethic. Obviously Weinberg sees the scientist and his industrial colleagues in an heroic role, battling under enlightened government against the vicissitudes of nature, and thereby creating a better world for man to live in. In his eyes the scientist and technologist together are the toolmakers of social democracy and by fashioning new tools they inspire new visions and new potentials for change and presumably betterment.

Let us look at our stone-age Amerindians again. Just what do they get from the deal of development? Do they in one fell swoop get the fruits of a magnificent civilization, which they really would not have been without had they known of it earlier? Surely not. The Indian encounters western civilization's raw ragged fringes where frontier-style opportunism reigns supreme and life is geared to making the quick buck, and even though he may discern the horror of the new way of life with which he is surrounded, he is either unable to resist its power and persuasive force and goes along with it, or hangs on to his 'obsolete' way of life and goes under. How can his own traditional way of life – in Goldsmith's terms, so admirably suited to the timeless rhythm of the equatorial rainforest – stand up to modern man's swift and ruthless conquest of the jungle? How puny and inefficient a stone axe, how absurd such a tool, when man has invented giant earth-moving equipment that literally pushes the forest away from in front of it.

The Indian's instincts tell him, and I am tempted to agree, that the awesome power of those machines is not a liberating and creative force which will free him from the bondage of forest, river, and swamp, but one which will surely destroy him as it surely destroys his aeon-enduring environment. What a psychological dilemma for the Indian, and it is hardly surprising that some have sought refuge deeper in the jungle, hoping they will escape the sharp edge of western civilization as it penetrates the forest for the treasures of land, minerals and of Amazon-derived hydroelectric power. Other Indians, drawn like moths to the light, become little more than drunken vagrants in the new frontier towns, while others still give up the will to survive and overnight an entire tribe stops breeding. Extinction of the stone-age Indian is, therefore, inevitable.

Does it really matter? Isn't it better for the sake of all men and future prosperity that the stone age – a relic of our neolithic past – should yield to progress and the techniques of modern man? Isn't the price that the primitive is now paying no more than the price many organisms have had to pay in the evolutionary process? Philosophically we are caught in a dilemma, as many have realized. On the one hand, the Earth, as moulded by the forces of nature, has the capacity to sustain man without excessive interference: the hunter-gatherer, or even the simple stone-age gardener, like the Amerindian or New Guinea tribesmen, have proved it. On the other hand, the Earth is beautiful only as seen through man's eyes and man's changing of it to suit his purpose has been both to his and to the environment's advantage. Most of us stand somewhere between two such extreme views. We look at nature in its raw, virgin state and are lost in wonder at its power and richness: in that context the savage is a romantic figure in his ability to survive the physical hardships of a life within the confines of a natural environment. Yet at the same time we are products of our own culture and glory in its achievements – those amazing feats of engineering, the exquisiteness of art, and the deeds of men. We cannot really expect to have it both ways, to shed those aspects of the industrial, technological world we do not like, and just keep what we like, when both good and bad are part of the same process. And who decides into which category a particular technology or industrial pursuit falls? As for the savage, we have taken our population far beyond the natural capacity of the Earth to sustain us if we return to that kind of existence: hence Weinberg's powerful words on the role of the scientist.

Mike has certainly posed some fundamental questions. Are we truly part of a progressive improvement of our state on Earth – a sort of historical evolutionary process? Is our future to have food for the asking, to live in comfort, to be able to travel easily? Is our life to be one of inordinate leisure so that we can indulge our minds in all sorts of flights of fancy? Or are such dreams pie in the sky, and if achieved at all, only at the expense of other human beings and of the environment itself?

Our modern industrial state is far from ideal. We have polluted and degraded the Earth: far from freeing man from labour we have reduced much of the population to a life little short of drudgery. Ironically, through embarking on those two prime processes which should have freed us – agriculture and industry – we have somehow managed to enslave ourselves. To judge by the spare time of the Kalahari hunter-gatherer Bushman, Rousseau was surely right to call the savage 'noble'.

Mike has also taken a philosophical line to show that any attempts to return to a more primitive, austere life are likely to coincide with totalitarian beliefs – a rigidity in outlook regarding deviants. I cannot agree with him that those who turn to self-sufficiency are naturally inclined towards the obscenities of Nazism or even of Stalin's purges. On the contrary it is the industrial state, under whatever political guise, which has the potential within it to become totalitarian as it seeks to unite its workers in the common cause of creating affluence. Marcuse has certainly delineated the dangers in *One-dimensional Man.*

Those who seek self-sufficiency, on the other hand, are reacting to conditions they find in industrial society but their solution is to put themselves at a distance from the system rather than remain with those they believe to be trapped in it. It is thus a wholly different re-action to the same pathological situation as brings about totalitarian-ism, and the question then becomes whether such a counter-reaction is productive.

Historically the late nineteenth-century and early twentieth-cen-tury drive back to nature, which affected artists, artisans, and workers alike, was a reaction to the growing industrialism of the age with its emphasis on bourgeois values. Nazism was by no means an intrinsic part of Germany's nature movement – Der Wandervogel – and it was Hitler's sick genius to implant in it his own fantasy of the pure race reclaiming its rightful place in the world. Indeed the German Expressionist painters who created the Die Brücke move-ment derived the title from Nietzche's 'Also Sprach Zarathustra' not because they saw in it the springboard of Germany's fascism but because of its symbol of brotherhood and hope in a world besotted with materialism. Artists such as Kirschner were appalled by World War I and wholly unconvinced by the upwelling of nationalism, and their expressionism was a strong criticism of the degeneracy inherent in industrial society whether in the factory or the fashionable streets of Berlin. In politics the Brücke artists inclined to socialism and it is hardly surprising that the Nazis hated their art and destroyed what they could. It is too simplistic to imagine that the human drive back to nature, the modern self-sufficient movement included, must ter-minate in totalitarianism because of the occurrence in human history of such a fearful aberration as Hitler's Germany.

I would agree that Teddy Goldsmith's notions that man has a sort of preordained role to play in his environment, and woe betide him if he deviates, is a very deterministic thesis. Indeed, its very inflexibility as a posit of man and his nature rules out freedom of choice and other tenaciously held tenets of libertarianism. But there are serious discrepancies in *The Stable Society*, a disunity in the thesis, which makes it impossible to pin Goldsmith down as serving the cause of Fascism. For instance, he is a champion of decentralization and harmonious diversity and is a hater of uniformity. And far from being a racist, he advocates the survival of all kinds of men, including tribes and races.

A debate about self-sufficiency could well encompass such practicalities as how to grow vegetables and whether to keep goats or ban them from the face of the Earth, given their propensity for debarking one's favourite fruit trees. But far more important to the debate are questions about political structure, man's future, freedom, and environmental degradation; the sort of technosphere versus the environment arguments; and whether the seekers of self-sufficiency achieve their ultimate aims or not, one thing can be said for them: that they are looking for a new kind of freedom. It is surely true that the future lies ahead of us, but continual change for its own sake, or rather because of capitalistic or even socialistic drives towards innovation in order to capture markets and political allegiances may not necessarily be the only path.

2 The technological solution and the myth of progress

Ever since Darwin and his theory of evolution, it has become fashionable to look back over human history as the unfolding of a forward process of development and progress. The step from primordial hunter-gatherer to man the cultivator and builder of cities, and now to modern technological man, seems but a logical sequence of events up a long ladder to that mist-enshrouded pinnacle of man's complete dominion over nature.

The well-known ingredients of evolution are those of natural selection operating on a large and changing gene pool with the best adapted, in a mechanistic way, becoming the most successful in the arduous game of survival. But another, too often overlooked, facet of evolution is 'organic selection' whereby the organism actually selects the conditions under which it will later evolve. In *The Living Stream* a compilation of the 1963 Gifford Lectures, Professor Sir Alistair Hardy draws attention to the importance of organic selection and provides evidence for it, with examples taken from the insect and bird worlds. The incredible variety of species of finch on the Galàpagos, presumably from one original species, becomes understandable if the progeny and descendants of the original pair radiated somewhat purposefully into a myriad of different niches. The evolution of their special characteristics then followed, tempered by natural selection. As Charles Elton said in 1930, in *Animal Ecology and Evolution*, '... there is selection of the environment by the animal as opposed to the natural selection of the animal by the environment'.

How does this volte-face of orthodox evolutionary theory affect the evolution of man? It may be that man's special characteristics, his upright stance, stereoscopic vision, opposing forefinger and thumb, extended childhood, were anticipated by his behaviour in selecting his environment. In the same way, his omnivorousness might have been a behavioural tendency before it became reflected in his jaw structure and teeth. Certainly omnivorousness has played a significant part in man's adaptations to a wide range of habitats and different foods. Later it may have acted as an incentive behind the domestication of plants and animals.

If, in fact, early man's behaviour was so important in directing the evolution of his prime characteristics then, with hindsight, it would appear that the potential for his supremacy over the rest of nature was inherent from the beginning of his development. All history has done, therefore, is to reveal that potential.

However, the urges behind organic selection need not be conscious acts of reason – they are certainly not so in the case of Darwin's finches – and in prehominid and early man they may well have been subconscious. But with man, as his brain and his manipulative powers developed, cultural evolution would play an increasingly strong role, amplifying both the effect of organic and natural selection in determining his overall evolution. Indeed, like the ever-expanding annual growth rings around a tree's core it would become possible for mankind to superimpose a dynamically changing culture on the experience of his predecessors.

But has the rapid change that man has brought to bear, however unwittingly, on his evolution, necessarily been for the best? Can we talk of progress in man's physical and cultural evolution as being inevitably a process of betterment? The paradox is that as we come to the finale of the drama of human development, as indeed we come to control more and more of nature, so we begin to see more clearly the dangers of that process. Nevertheless we seem destined to continue on that path, urbanization thus continues apace, the arms race seems unstoppable despite checks here and there and, however much we talk of the evils of the consumer society, we appear inextricably caught up in it. As for the environment itself, we tend to replace the delightful diversity of nature with our own single-minded, uniform and drab monoculture. And any natural component we see fit to eradicate, like the wolf that roamed the now felled forests of Europe, is driven out of existence. So we continue: one suggestion at the United Nations World Food Conference in 1974, taken seriously by all delegates, was for a scheme to spray 1600-kilometre stretches of the African savannah with DDT from B52 bombers to eradicate the tsetse fly. Paradoxically, too, our ability to adapt to a wide range of habitats, from the arctic to the tropics, is the same innovative ability behind the manufacture of the modern standardized urban environment, well epitomized by the ubiquitous Hilton Hotel which springs up in the wake of Coca-Cola, the car, and the first airstrip.

But the misgivings people may have about human activities and their effect on the environment, are generally put aside, for they hope that progress will sort out those problems, too, particularly once the scientists and technicians get to work on them. Indeed, belief in progress towards some ultimate material goal is inherent in much of our political philosophy of the time, whether it be marxist or capitalist.

'We have pursued the idea of a future perfection dependent upon constant economic progress realized by the application of science and technology without any regard for the frightful cost in actual human perfection,' says Robert Waller in *Be Human or Die*. 'Man has sacrificed personality to progress and reason to the rationale of progress. Reason has been confused with that which advances progress. Whereas reason is that which advances the fulfilment of personality.'

The priests of the fundamentalist creed of progress are primarily scientists and technologists, and, just as the priests of ancient Babylon went out in the fields and ploughed to propitiate the Mother Goddess so that the Earth would be made fertile, today's scientists use their skill in the laboratory to demonstrate the reality of progress. As for doubters and unbelievers, they are swept away under a torrent of facts and figures to be shattered on the rocks of knowledge below. Benefit is the magic word to justify a course of action and establishment scientists resort to this emotionally charged formula in making what they claim to be logical progressive statements. Thus, Lord Ashby talked of the 'benefits' of genetic engineering when he chaired a committee set up by the government to investigate the potential hazards of this relatively new technology. And medical scientists who have taken all pretence of 'natural childbirth' from woman by inducing birth and curbing labour pains through epidural anaesthesia, they too claim 'benefits' both to hospital staff and to their patients, even though evidence is accruing that newborn and possibly the mother herself may be damaged by such techniques. Indeed, a problem with birth induction is that a higher percentage of births have to be carried out with forceps with the risk of a higher than normal incidence of brain damage in the newborn. The pagan priests of ancient civilization must also have promised benefits, but whereas they used myth and legend, science, claim its proponents, is at least based on a rational system of knowledge.

'Some idealists argue that the way to improve the quality of life is to renounce technology and all its works,' says Sir John Hill, chairman of the United Kingdom Atomic Energy Authority (UKAEA). 'But realists must accept, I suggest, that improvements in the quality of life depend on, and must be sustained by increases in economic output.' Again the scientist resorts to his magic formulae, in this instance, 'quality of life' and 'economic growth'; moreover, in Sir John's eyes, realism and sense lead to progress: idealism takes man back into the woods and darkness.

Beyond improving the efficiency of energy use, world economic output can be increased only significantly by increasing energy production and consumption, an idea which has been cogently expressed by P. J. Searby, a colleague of Sir John's. 'Energy provides the power to progress,' he says, 'with a sufficiency of energy properly applied a people can rise from subsistence level to the highest standard of living.' Both Searby and Sir John Hill have a big stake in the successful future of nuclear power, and in their minds the only way sufficient energy can be made available to raise the standards of living of the world's masses is by building thousands of nuclear power stations. Indeed, nuclear power addicts such as they, see this remarkable form of energy as the logical heir to fossil fuels, coal and oil, a concept which fits in nicely with the modern idea of a handful of workers controlling a gigantic automated power plant which generates no unsightly piles of waste, but keeps all its effluent contained in manageable bundles finally to be deposited out of sight and mind in subterranean caverns. Those who believe in progress in the modern sense of increased industrialism, see nuclear power as part of that chain of progress; and it is heresy to place obstacles in its path. But when we consider that the future of civilization hangs on a discovery which might not have been, progress becomes either a haphazard affair or one of magical intervention on behalf of some deity who favours our attempts at controlling nature. Could progress have progressed if nuclear power had not been discovered?

The irony is that the civilian use of nuclear power did not come about because of scientists heroically seeking a way to sustain industrial society on its course; and the story is well known how Lord Rutherford who first split the atom gave little credence to the idea that his discovery would lead to a controlled source of energy for our use. Indeed the real impetus to nuclear power came from the need to atone for the horrors of the Nagasaki and Hiroshima bombs. What a beginning for a source of power now enthusiastically hailed as the new flame of progress. As the nuclear physicist, Alvin Weinberg remarks: 'There are very compelling personal reasons why atomic scientists sound optimistic when writing about their impact on world affairs. Each of us must justify to himself his preoccupation with instruments of nuclear destruction (and even we nuclear people are only slightly less beset with such guilt than are our weaponeering colleagues).'

When we scrutinize the progress that has resulted from technology and more recently from scientific enlightenment, we begin to see unpleasant anomalies of which the atomic bomb is but the most blatant. That is not to discredit the intentions of the world's inventors and innovators, but second-hand those intentions tend to become distorted. Indeed all advances, all aspects of progress appear to have negative components, rather like Newton's 'opposite and equal reaction' and the greater the hurry to progress, the greater the counterpoint. More cars mean more traffic jams, more motorways cutting their way through countryside and cities alike, and the more nuclear power plants we build, the more we shall have to be on our guard from accidents, from sabotage, and thefts of nuclear material. And who feels easy about the ever-swelling inventory of deadly atomic waste that must be kept from living organisms for thousands of years hence? Is progress worth that kind of price?

'Let us not delude ourselves that the consequences of Progress have been beneficial to.all,' says the philosopher-historian, Henryk Skolimowski. 'The pursuit of progress has been an elitist enterprise *par excellence*. Not only did we exploit the people and parts of the world that are outside the magic ring of progress, but within the ring itself we have been admirably efficient, which is another way of saying: admirably ruthless. The metaphysics of progress is based on an exploitive and parasitic form of philosophy. Progress has been a cover-up for Western man's follies in manipulating the external world.'

We live in an age consumed by a passion to solve problems and to innovate, forgetting in our eagerness to finance new problem-solving research projects, that many of the problems are entirely of our own making. We spend fortunes for example attempting to find cures for cancer, heart disease, intestinal disorders, and kidney disease when the proper remedy for these degenerative diseases may be a different life-style and different eating habits. And has modern childbirth, with all its machines for monitoring the foetal environment, and its drugs to control the date and time of delivery, solved problems or just posed some more thorny ones? In looking back into the past and trying to determine reasons why civilization developed on the lines it did, we tend to apply contemporary criteria that particular actions of the past must be in response to particular problems. Just as future historians might be justified in thinking that nuclear power was conjured up – in the nick of time – in response to dwindling supplies of easily obtained energy, so Arnold Toynbee, with his 'challenge and response theory' and other believers of environmental determinism might be exonerated from thinking that agriculture was devised under pressure to supply man with urgently needed food. For is that not how we behave today, holding World Food Conferences, to conjure up ways of increasing food production to feed the needy?

A number of parallels can be drawn between the origin of agriculture and of atomic power. With hindsight both technological achievements appear to have emerged when needed, yet in reality neither agriculture nor nuclear power were used to generate surpluses until some time had elapsed after their introduction; their use in extricating man from a crisis is therefore questionable. It has now become clear, that nuclear power could never have got off the ground without an enormous investment in fossil fuels to mine the uranium, extract it from its rocky substrate, enrich it, to build the atomic plants and to reprocess the radioactive waste, and finally to keep the waste safe in stainless steel cooling tanks. Even after more than twenty years' operation the total net yield of energy from nuclear plants including those used for research has barely covered the energy investment. Of course, a net gain in energy was not initially the main criterion behind the construction of plants: their main purpose was to provide plutonium for atomic war heads.

If neolithic man were short of food he would hardly take time to begin experiments in domestication; the risks would be far too great; and it seems much more likely that the first cultivators set about their task in an unhurried manner, even out of fanciful curiosity. As Carl Sauer tells us in *Agriculture and Origins*: 'People living in the shadow of famine do not have the means or time to undertake the slow and leisurely steps out of which a better and different food supply is to develop in a somewhat distant future ... The improvement of plants by selection for better utility to man was accomplished only by a people who lived at the comfortable margin above the level of want. The needy and miserable societies are not inventive, for they lack the leisure for reflection, experimentation, and discussion.'

The desperation and hopelessness seen on the emaciated faces of the starving people of the Sahel, Ethiopia, and Bangladesh certainly add weight to Sauer's words.

It is indeed a curious position that man has placed himself in, for through his achievements, such as the technology of agriculture, he has undoubtedly opened the way for many more people to survive than would be otherwise possible. Yet by the same token more people are put at risk when the technology fails, and the price for what has been considered progress can be heavy. It is also important to realize that dependency on a technology comes only after the use of that technology is widespread and has become fundamental to society's well-being. Fifty years ago the majority of mankind could manage perfectly well without the motorcar. Today the car and its needs have come to dominate western society, and there is a serious crisis in the offing with the diminishing reserves of petroleum.

Nevertheless many people today find it hard to accept that necessity is not necessarily the mother of invention, that man is capable of remarkable innovations for the hell of it rather than in response to environmental challenges. That great historian of the neolithic age, Gordon V Childe, was certain that agriculture was conceived in response to spreading drought. He envisaged a sudden climate change at the end of the last ice age, which deflected the rain-bearing winds away from the Near East, and caused man and beast alike to huddle into the remaining oases. This proximity and the desperate urge to establish a sound food supply gave man the idea, suggests Childe, of domestication and of crop cultivation to feed both himself and the animals which he had corralled for fattening. The same conditions would be repeated in many different oases, and each one could be a likely site for the origin of agriculture. According to this challenge-response theory it is even possible that agriculture had a multiple origin.

The oasis theory of the origin of agriculture has a convenient logic about it. But the theory in its original form has had to be discarded because of a lack of evidence of major climatic change in the Near East some 10 000 years ago. Not that the idea of environmental determinism has died. Lewis Binford, for example, agrees with Childe that the most likely motivation behind the domestication of plants and animals must be a dwindling supply of food and sees the task of historian and scientist to unravel the reasons why. He suggests that because of a rising sea-level at the end of the Pleistocene through the melting of the ice, man was able to settle down for the first time in substantial numbers next to the sea and rivers where he was able to exploit highly seasonal but rewarding sources of food such as migratory fish and fowl. This new sedentary life with abundant food would attract more and more people from the arid surrounding areas, thereby overloading the carrying capacity of the land and creating what Binford calls 'tension zones' where there would be insufficient food to feed everyone.

The tension zones are the key to Binford's theory, for in these the incentive would be sufficient, he suggests, to try any means to increase food production, and plant and animal domestication would soon prove themselves to be the best solution.

All this seems excellent pragmatic reasoning, and all it needs is corroborating evidence. Some evidence has been forthcoming. In 1966 Harlan and Zohary discovered natural stands of wild wheat in

Turkey which were almost as dense as cultivated wheat fields, and the two researchers could not help asking themselves why anyone should want to cultivate wheat when it was so plentiful in the wild. There is nothing like experiment in the field and with a flint-bladed sickle Harlan harvested enough wild wheat in one hour to produce a kilogram (2 pounds) of clean grain, which on analysis proved to be almost twice as rich in protein as modern domestic wheat. 'Farming,' he remarked astutely, 'may have originated in areas adjacent to rather than in the regions of greatest abundance of wild cereals.'

One supporter of the Binford hypothesis, Kent Flannery, thinks that people out on the fringes of abundant food supply would not only have discovered the advantages of cultivation, they would also have set about diversifying their food base, selecting all manner of animals and plants which under better circumstances they would discard or simply overlook. In certain parts of the Near East, he says, in the Zagros mountains, for example, abundant remains of snails, mussels, and crabs have been discovered, these invertebrates being an unusual ingredient of human food. According to Flannery '. . . the broad spectrum revolution was real, nutritionally sound, and it constituted a move which counteracted disequilibria in population in the less favourable hunting areas of the Near East'.

Flannery's own research into the diet of neolithic man in the Near East indicates that initially at least cultivation provided no more than a supplement to hunting and gathering. His investigations in an early dry farming village on the Khuzistan steppes of south-western Iran indicate that in the period from 7500 to 6500 BC most of the total weight of meat and plant foods came from wild resources. Among the carbonized seeds discovered at Ali Kosh, only 3 per cent were cultivated cereals although, because of their relatively bigger size, they constituted nearly one-third of the total weight of plant food.

Certainly cereal cultivation increases considerably the carrying capacity of the land even when only a supplement to hunting and gathering. Flannery points out that in northern Khuzistan dry farming of wheat produces on average 410 kilograms per hectare (370 pounds per acre). This quantity is equivalent to the usable meat from sixteen sheep, or the weight of 400 million small legume seeds. 'Cultivation,' says Flannery, 'was a decision to replace the native, high-protein wild legume cover with a lower protein grass which would grow more densely and was probably less work to harvest, in spite of crop failure.'

But can we be certain that the origin of agriculture was linked so closely with human needs? Robert Braidwood dissents from this functionalist view; indeed it was he who set out to find evidence for Childe's theory of a challenging climate change in the Near East during neolithic times and become convinced that '. . . no evidence exists for such changes in the natural environment . . . as might be of sufficient impact to have predetermined the shift to food production.'

Braidwood suggests that the origin of agriculture in the Near East was a one-time phenomenon, devised not because of the stark realities of necessity but because neolithic man had acquired enough knowledge and awareness of his local environment to begin experimentation with plants and animals. Agriculture then spread outwards from its point of origin gradually transforming the mode of life of people in Europe, Asia, and Africa. In some areas where the ice was still retracting and climatic conditions were still harsh, cultivation may possibly have been embraced as a useful supplement to hunting and gathering, just as Flannery found in Khuzistan.

The view that agriculture had a unique origin spreading like ripples in a pond from a nuclear zone has certainly been challenged. Lewis Binford for one, finds Braidwood's thesis based on hazy, unscientific and, therefore, untestable concepts. 'Vitalism,' he argues in *New Perspectives in Archeology*, 'whether expressed in terms of inherent forces orienting the direction of organic evolution or in its more anthropocentric form of emergent human properties which direct cultural evolution, is unacceptable as an explanation. Trends which are observed in cultural evolution require explanation; they are certainly not explained by postulating emergent human traits which are said to account for trends.'

Binford is certainly unfair to upbraid Braidwood of 'vitalism', for the latter never implied that some kind of supernatural spark or divine inspiration lay behind the first act of plant and animal domestication, any more than he might suggest the same for the innovations and techniques that Stradivarius applied to his violin making. Nevertheless, the two theories – the oasis theory and the nuclear zone theory – are different in a fundamental respect: the former implies a multiple origin of agriculture, each oasis or tension zone stimulating some kind of survival-oriented responses, while the latter stresses the originality of the discovery of agriculture in terms of cultural evolution. The historian has a difficult task distinguishing between the two theories. Imagine a historian some 9000 years hence asking himself about the origins of nuclear power. Assuming by then that nuclear power stations were as widespread as agriculture is today, the historian could possibly jump to a similar conclusion as Childe, Binford, and other environmental determinists, that in response to dwindling energy supplies and political expediency many different industrial countries developed nuclear power themselves, each one by itself learning how to split the atom. We know differently of course, and are able to discriminate between the rapid spread of knowledge from Neils Bohr's and Rutherford's laboratories and the subsequent development of different reactor systems in different countries by different teams of physicists and engineers.

It is conceivable that agriculture had a unique origin, just as the Semitic alphabet emerged from Palestine and, mainly through the migrations of the Phoenicians along the Mediterranean, became the common property of many different peoples, or jazz or flamenco or any other cultural trait becomes absorbed and integrated into the cultures of people outside its origin. Some rather interesting evidence does seem, if anything, to support the nuclear zone theory. L L Cavalli-Sforza and his anthropologist colleague, Albert Ammerman, at the University of Stanford, have computerized the carbon-14 datings of the oldest remains of domesticated plants in the Near East and Europe and they find what seem to be two nuclear zones with evidence of domestication before 7000 BC, one on the Jordan Valley, and the other east of the Black Sea. By following carbon datings the two scientists find that plant domestication appears to have spread in a north-westerly direction across Europe at a rather regular one kilometre (two thirds mile) per year, reaching Britain and Scandinavia around 4000 to 3500 BC.

How did the new technique spread? Was it by word of mouth, or did people migrate carrying the message with them? Kingsley Davis in *Scientific American* (September 1974) believes that, far from being induced to a sedentary life through agriculture, neolithic farmers were ever-migrating. 'Technological improvements in production, weaponry, and transport kept appearing and that created inequality and hence migratory potential between one territory and another. Pastoralists or shifting cultivators could evict hunters and gatherers because hunters and gatherers required more land per man and therefore could mobilize less manpower at any one spot.'

The historian would surely agree with Kingsley Davis. History is peppered with examples of one people's conquest of another, of destruction, annihilation, assimilation and, rising out of this turmoil, of new cultures, and it would be hardly surprising that Near Eastern farmers should look for new lands to try out their cultivation techniques. Moreover, with the new techniques to hand a colonizing people could take over virgin land and make it productive without first having to come as closely to grips with the environment as would the hunter–gatherer.

Thus, agriculture has led to colonization, just as western technology has in recent times. And Cavalli-Sforza has come up with substantiating evidence for such a migration. By mapping out an evolutionary tree for ten population groups as diverse as Europeans and Australian Aborigines, from a common beginning some 40 000 years ago (the date given to the oldest known fossil of *Homo sapiens*) he has discovered that Caucasians appear to be a genetic mix between Africans and Orientals. He explains his finding on the grounds that Caucasians are initially derived from Near-Eastern farmers who intermixed with indigenous contemporary Europeans.

Agriculture, when properly established, enhances enormously the carrying capacity of the land by harnessing natural biological productivity to one end – that of feeding human beings. Through agriculture one family can survive adequately off less than 0·5 hectares (an acre) of land. Two-and-a-half square kilometres (one square mile) and more is usually the figure given for the amount of land necessary to provide a hunter–gatherer with sufficient food. This substantial difference between the carrying capacity of agricultural as distinct from hunting and gathering land has led many to the conclusion that hunter–gatherers are permanently on the brink of starvation and that population pressure within any one group of such men and women must be acute.

But Malthus was by no means absolutely right. Contemporary studies of hunter–gatherers, the Kalahari Bushmen, for example, or even of stone-age horticulturalists such as the Tsembaga, indicate that those peoples are rarely, if at all, short of food and, moreover, they seem to be able to keep their populations well within the carrying capacity of the land. Richard B Lee spent some time with the Kung Bushmen and, from examples of food brought into the camp, was able to show that Bushmen not only had an adequate and very varied diet, but a high percentage of it was protein, mostly from vegetable sources. Moreover, Lee made his observations during the second year of a severe drought which seriously dislocated the pastoral and farming economies of the Bantu. Then again, Robert Carneiro, from his rigorous studies of the Kuikuru Indians, found they always had food to spare. The Kuikuru are horticulturalists, and Carneiro calculated that if they wanted they could have produced several times the amount of food they did by spending a little more time planting and harvesting. Yet, after producing enough food to meet local demands, that was it, they made no further effort. Equally important they kept their population in check.

While traditional peasant economies remain free of outside market forces, they also appear to generate their own stability. Alexander Chayanov, who was director of the Institute of Agricultural Economy after the Russian Revolution, but was later arrested by Stalin, made the then challenging observation that the peasant was more intent on meeting his family's needs than in making a profit. The peasant therefore tried to find a balance between his subsistence needs and his basic dislike of manual labour. Indeed, by measuring the sown area as representative of a peasant's activity, Chayanov was able to show a strong correlation between it and the number of dependants in the family. More often than not, the Russian peasant had unworked land in his possession; in fact, when his family had grown up and moved away, his own activity would also diminish to suit his own limited needs. Clearly, too, the more hands available to him, the more work a peasant could achieve, and the more land he could cultivate.

People close to the land, whether hunter–gatherers, tribal horticulturalists, or peasant farmers, have an awareness of the carrying capacity of their environment and make it in their interest to keep their populations or families well within the limits. The runaway growth in many peasant populations today is more than the simple arithmetic of births for once swamping deaths because of modern medicine and hygiene introduced from outside. Heinrich von Loesch, an economist specializing in demography, is probably as close as anyone to the right explanation of the surge in numbers of peasant families. He lays the blame on 'imported progress' which '... offered an unexpected chance for social and economic improvement to the peoples of poor countries. Wholly inexperienced in matters of progress they react in a logical way ... by sacrificing personal mobility and consumption to have more children for the better future of their families.' Von Loesch stresses the link between the superego of the peasant and the number of his children, particularly male children, and he derides the current idea that peasants have increased the size of their families because they lack the psychological or physical techniques of restraint.

Parents thus tend to keep their family's numbers down to levels at which they can clothe and feed them. When people, tribes, and populations push up against the limits of their environment, it is either through mismanagement of their resources, or because their conception of the carrying capacity of their land has become distorted through powerful outside interests and influences. As Edward Deevey says in *Scientific American* (1960 vol 203), 'A forest is full of game for an expert mouse hunter and a palaeolithic man who stuck to business should have found enough food on two square kilometres instead of twenty or 200. Social forces were probably more powerful than mere starvation in causing men to huddle in small bands.'

If palaeolithic man were so good at keeping his population within the carrying capacity of the land as far as it could support him through hunting and gathering, why then should he bother with agriculture? Binford is well aware of the current concept that primitive man keeps his population well within bounds especially when he remains part of an isolated group. The tension zone theory of the origin of agriculture is thus a tidy way out of a conceptual dilemma for, in such zones, the relationship between man and his environment would have to alter because of new pressures. But investigators into the origin of agriculture suffer from murky hindsight millennia after the event, and perhaps they should give more credit to Braidwood's concept of cultural evolution, despite its inconclusiveness. Like the artist who is under no obligation to create, perhaps those early Near-Eastern cultivators were giving reign to their own creative fantasies about nature and the environment. John Huizinga dared suggest in his book *Homo Ludens* that all culture was a form of play, and Lewis Mumford extended that idea by examining '. . . the broad streak of irrationality that runs through all human history, counter to man's sensible, functionally rational, animal inheritance . . . Man's proneness to mix his fantasies and projections, his desires and designs, his abstractions and his ideologies, with the commonplaces of daily experience were, we can now see,' he says, 'an important source of his immense creativity. There is no clean dividing line between the irrational and the superrational; and the handling of these ambivalent gifts has always been a major human problem. One of the reasons that the current utilitarian interpretations of technics and science have been so shallow is that they ignore the fact that this aspect of human culture has been open to both transcendental aspirations and demonic compulsions as any other part of man's existence and has never been so open and so vulnerable as today.'

Few modern farmers, let alone ministers of agriculture, appreciate that some of their basic agricultural techniques did not arise from some bright guy searching for a means to improve productivity. Ploughing, for example, was a sacred activity carried out by priests and Mumford has suggested that the first plough was a fertility rite in which a giant symbolic phallus penetrated the vaginal furrow of the earth. Only later, presumably when ordinary people began to see the advantages of planting seeds in ploughed land, did ploughing become secularized and its symbolic meaning pushed back into the subconscious.

We are also used to seeing herds of domesticated cattle standing quietly in the field or farmyard that unless watching the spectacularly aggressive beauty of the bull in the corrida it is hard to imagine how fearful a task domestication must have been. 'Man must have had a strong motivation', says Erich Isaac in *Science* (20 July, 1962), 'since the wild urus was a powerful intractable animal.' In fact, the nineteenth-century geographer, Eduard Hahn, postulated that the motive for capturing and domesticating the urus was for religious purposes, the animal being sacred to the lunar mother goddess over an immense area of the ancient world, presumably because the animal's gigantic curved horns resembled the lunar crescent. The economic uses of the animal as a beast of burden and draught animal would therefore have followed a domestication which was religious in origin.

Human progress begins to lose some of its rational purpose when we begin to unearth the motivations behind the origin of agriculture. Mumford agrees. 'The overwhelmingly material preoccupations of our own age,' he says in *Myth of the Machine*, 'its impatient efforts to turn pinched subsistence economies into affluent industrial societies, tempt us to regard the whole process of domestication as a more or less deliberate effort to increase the supply of food. Only belatedly has it dawned on a few scholars that primitive man did not look at the world in this way; and that what is a primary motive for us played only a secondary role, if any at all, in his life . . .'

By alluding to the irrational and what we would consider primitive as a basic ingredient of our technology, Mumford has in essence cast doubts on the reasonableness of human progress, and on the logicality of the path it has taken since man discovered the potential of fire some hundreds of thousands of years ago; for how can anything logical arise from fantasy? We have made it seem very logical because we have been able to add one building block of human experience upon another until we were able to create the nature-busting edifice of industrial enterprise. But how sturdy are the foundations of this enterprise? Could it not be that by mortifying the living processes of nature to make way for our inorganic substitutes we have started knocking out the very pillars which support us? In this respect it is something of a humiliating process to see the consequences of man's activities on the Earth as a cultivator.

Cultivation began in earnest in the Near East, but there is the possibility, that mankind already had some ideas about the life cycle of plants and the generation of new crop from seeds, tubers, and root cuttings. Women were the gatherers, while the men went out hunting to bring in uncertain but nutritionally important supplies of meat. While gathering it is likely that woman began to tend small areas in the forest where there were particular concentrations of plants that might be used as staple foods, as flavourings, as medicines, or even for their scent and colour. In time the simple tending of plots, keeping them clear of unwanted weeds, might well have led to simple cultivation and the attempt to aggregate as many of the wanted specimens as possible. Contemporary stone-age horticulturalists, the Tsembaga in the highlands of New Guinea, for example, while wholly ignorant of the cultivation techniques developed in the Near East, are able to create remarkably productive gardens with a medley of different plants growing together. The highly varied polyculture of these tropical gardeners seems to mimic in microcosm the tropical forest itself with its incredible variety of different species.

Lewis Mumford claims that cereal cultivation did not take place first in the grasslands or swamps of the Near East, owing to the difficulties in breaking up the heavy grass roots. On the other hand, prehistoric man, like his stone-age counterparts living today, would have been perfectly capable of chopping down trees with his flint axe, and clearing away the debris by slashing and burning, to get down to the easily worked soil beneath.

Whether cereals were first cultivated in forest clearings or whether man had to wait until he had devised the plough cannot be answered, although from evidence of grinding stones and of changes in the teeth of Natufian man in the Near East, the eating of cereals was well underway by the time we have evidence of cultivation; those 'natural stands' of wild wheat apparently did not pass unnoticed. One fundamental change took place when cereal cultivation began to take place on a more lavish scale. Cultivation, previously the province of women, became the labour of men, and it changed from simple handwork to work with tools and beasts of burden. It was these monoculture techniques that spread out of the Near East into Europe, the Near-Eastern farmers presumably taking their knowledge with them in just the same way as modern western technologists export their own ideas when they go overseas to developing countries.

Relative to the food that previously was available to the hunter-gatherers, farming created an enormous food surplus and the human population was able to increase from an estimated eight million in 8000 BC to 300 million at the time of Christ. The great civilizations of this period, the Egyptian, Greek, Persian, Phoenician and Roman, for example, all depended on the great numbers of men that were then supported by the fruits of agriculture. The slaves who built the pyramids were very much the products of successful agriculture as too were the Roman legions who held the Mediterranean and parts of northern Europe under their dominion.

Today agriculture supports a mighty industrial venture and a trade network that covers the entire world. In western Europe and other industrialized regions, where food has been plentiful over the past few decades, few of the millions now living in urban areas give more than a passing thought to the origin of the neatly packaged and processed food stacked along the supermarket shelves. The tendency is to think of food rather like any other industrial product, as a commodity which obeys the economic laws of supply and demand. In this respect some demographers talk 'optimistically' if not glibly of the possibility of feeding a world population that has increased in size by three, four or even ten times its present level.

Such demographic dreams are based on the concept that agriculture is part of the industrial process and that by increasing inputs — fossil fuel energy, artificial fertilizers, and pesticides, for example — farm yields can be expanded enormously. But such dreams overlook the importance of sustaining soil fertility as part of continuing productivity. The lands bordering the Mediterranean, those very regions where agriculture of the kind we have inherited began, show what can happen if care is not take to prevent soil erosion, salinization, or the silting up of rivers. Their present-day barrenness is not a consequence of climatic change, but tells a history of exploitation and mismanagement. Nor has the past necessarily proved a lesson for the present, and desertification in the world has increased by as much as 25 per cent since the turn of the twentieth century.

Soil fertility is a valuable often vulnerable resource that has built up painstakingly slowly since the Silurian period some 350 million years ago when the first primitive plants and animals began to colonize the land which was pushing up through the surrounding waters. That aeons-old soil fertility can be lost in one generation through exploitive farming practices, as occurred with such staggering impact when the American dust bowls were created in the 1920s and '30s. One of the first steps in the destructive process is the wholesale chopping down of trees. As usual those who perpetrate such acts are not the ones to suffer; it is those in subsequent generations that find themselves at the mercy of swollen rivers overburdened with mud and debris which burst their banks leaving ruined crops and villages, as well as drowned men and beasts in their wake. The cutting down of forests in the Himalayan foothills has repercussions hundreds of kilometres away in Bangladesh, and hardly a year goes by without cyclones, flooding, and the grim fight for survival of millions of Bengalis. The deforestation of Lebanon, once renowned for its cedars, has been a direct cause of that country's devastated landscape with its eroded rock and pitifully thin topsoil. And in Mesopotamia, a cradle of Western civilization, erosion took its toll, too, once the forests that covered the Armenian hills to the north were chopped down and the land overgrazed. The Tigris and Euphrates have carried such an enormous quantity of silt down to the Persian Gulf since the time of the Sumerians some 4500 years ago that the mouths of the two rivers are now 209 kilometres (130 miles) further south. Averaged out over the years, the twin rivers must have been building 30 metres (100 feet) of marsh land at the head of the Gulf each year. Inland this burden of silt clogged the irrigation channels which had been assiduously constructed over centuries of civilization, causing the rivers to change their course continuously and carry off even more topsoil. One ancient city after another has been swamped in the silt of this flood erosion, some of the former palaces of Antioch being nearly 9 metres (30 feet) under present ground-level. Some irrigation channels in Iraq have up to 18 metres (60 feet) of silt piled up along their banks, testimony of the desperate age-long struggle to keep the channels clear.

Walter Lowdermilk gives a vivid description of the devastation caused by erosion in Syria. 'Syria holds some of the greatest ruins to be found in the ancient world, such as Baalbek and Jarash. But to a soil conservationist the most striking ruins are found in the graveyard of a 'hundred dead cities'. An area of about a million acres in north Syria, lying between Aleppo, Antioch and Hama exhibits soil erosion at its worst. Here are ruins of villages and market towns resting on the skeleton rock of limestone hills, from which three to six feet of soil have been swept off. Evidence of the depth of soil eroded from these slopes is found in doorsills of stone houses now three to six feet above the bare rock.'

Throughout the Mediterranean, in Spain, Italy, Sicily, Greece, and Turkey, erosion has taken its toll on soil fertility as it has, too, throughout the Americas. The dangers of soil erosion have been known for a long time, hence the incredible terracing begun by the Phoenicians in Lebanon and Palestine and later by the Romans throughout the Mediterranean. Even Plato was dismayed at the changes occurring in his own Grecian landscape. As Critias says in one of Plato's dialogues '. . . what now remains of the once rich land is like the skeleton of a sick man, all the fat and soft earth having wasted away, only the bare framework is left. Formerly, many of the present mountains were arable hills, the present marshes were plains full of rich soil; hills were once covered with forests, and produced boundless pasturage that now produce only food for bees. Moreover the land was enriched by yearly rains, which were not lost, as now, by flowing from the bare land into the sea, the soil was deep, it received the water, storing it up in the retentive loamy soil; the water that soaked into the hills provided abundant springs and flowing streams in all districts. Some of the now abandoned shrines, at spots where former fountains existed, testify that our description of the land is true.'

Agriculture need not be destructive, but history and the evidence of our own eyes, indicates that the destructive forces of erosion unleashed by malpractice in agriculture have far outdone in damage the increases in productivity which have been consequent upon good soil husbandry.

'In *Food, Energy and Society* the Pimentels, from Cornell University, point out that the rate of soil erosion per hectare of agricultural land in the United States is on average 27 tonnes (11 tons per acre). At that rate 80 million hectares (200 million acres) are estimated to have been either totally ruined for crop production or so seriously eroded that they are only marginally suitable for production. 'This relatively high rate of soil erosion has resulted,' say the Pimentels, 'in the loss of at least one-third of topsoil from US cropland in use today.'

Too often exploitation and the profit motive have governed the way man has handled the land under his care; at other times plain ignorance or indifference has led man to brutal acts against his natural heritage. Most historians view the barren landscape of the Middle East and other parts of the Mediterranean as a consequence of political and social upheaval in the early nation states. If man had not battled unceasingly over the land as in Palestine, but lived in peace, then we are assured by these historians, that we would find a prosperous agriculture today and the land still in good heart; for are not the Israelis recapturing some of that forgotten potential? Or alternatively we are told by Toynbee, for example, that the harshness of the Mediterranean landscape was the challenge which drew the resourceful response from the peoples that settled there, as if the harshness and barrenness of the environment had always been there since time immemorial, and that if the land became productive and fertile it was despite nature and its resources.

Vernon Gill Carter and Tom Dale, two American soil conservationists have come up with an entirely new and revolutionary idea. They claim that the lands inherited by the peoples who moved into Africa, Asia, and Europe, and even into the two Americas, were then fertile and that it was the loss of this fertility through deforestation and other malpractices which dealt the main blow to civilizations. Once a particular civilization, the Phoenician for example, had destroyed the agricultural base upon which it depended, then its fate was sealed, even though in its struggle for existence it created colonies elsewhere to provide the mother country with food and other raw materials.

'By the time of Alexander's conquest, there were few resources left in Lebanon,' say Carter and Dale in *Topsoil and Civilization*. 'Most of the forests were gone, and the remaining trees disappeared within a few centuries under the Greek and Roman axes. Most of the topsoil was gone from the hills, lowlands were covered with erosional debris, harbours were silting up with mud from the eroding highlands, and river deltas were marshy pestholes infested with malaria-bearing mosquitoes. Civilization in Lebanon could not rise again, as it had in Mesopotamia and Egypt, because the resources were no longer there to support it. The total life span of progressive civilization in Lebanon was little more than 1500 years (about fifty or sixty generations).'

The rise and fall of civilizations in Egypt over a period of 5000 years are more a function of the Nile's role in bringing each year a new layer of fertility than because of some indomitable spirit of the people living in the Nile valley. The Nile begins some 2400 kilometres (1500 miles) away in the forested highlands of central Africa and each year approximately 1·3 millimetres (0·05 inch) of silt covers Egypt's cracked and baked soil. That thin layer has been the secret of the Nile farmer's success for countless generations. Nevertheless, the American soil conservationists question with some foreboding whether this fertility will continue now that the Aswan Dam is in operation. As they point out, Egypt's population has jumped from a traditional seven million in 1882 to some forty million today and it is expanding even more rapidly. The rationale behind the dam is to furnish water for an expanded irrigation area, and to provide electricity for industry, but by 1971 Lake Nasser, after seven years of filling was less than half full and some pessimists reckon that it will never fill again because of the greatly increased evaporation from its large surface area. Even more significant, Egyptian farmers can no longer depend on their natural coat of fertility brought down by the floodwaters each year, and must instead buy fertilizer at increasingly high costs. The last straw perhaps for Egypt is that the forests at the Nile headwaters are now being cut down and the land overgrazed. Erosion is occurring at an increasing rate and the burden of silt carried downstream by the Nile is bound to clog up the Aswan Dam and in time make it unworkable. Ironically then, industrialization and progress could prove the ultimate ruin of Egypt.

With more than 6000 million people expected to be living in the world by the year 2000, much more is expected of agricultural land than when the great civilizations of Egypt and Mesopotamia were at their peak, although ironically, Mesopotamia can today only feed one quarter of the population it once fed. The modern way to feed the world's inflated population is primarily through monoculture of certain staple crops such as rice, corn and other cereals, maintaining fertility through heavy dressings with artificial fertilizers. Rarely do modern farmers practice soil conservation; the emphasis now is upon cash crops and upon high yields irrespective of how they can be gained or of the affect upon the soil. Consequently, erosion is hardly diminished and the basis of man's civilization is yet again seriously undermined. Typically enough, most people in the cities are ignorant of what is going on in the countryside and even if they did know would not necessarily care. As for agronomists, they are for the most part too caught up in the industrial techniques of agriculture to bother with the subtleties of natural soil fertility. In Tuscany, for example, one hillside after another is stripped of its trees, any terracing is bulldozed away and row upon row of grapevine is planted up and down the denuded hillside. Erosion, already the force behind much of Italy's degradation, has now a free run down the Chianti slopes, and the money pouring into the coffers of the Tuscan landlords will be shortlived. What a shame that modern Tuscans and their agronomic advisors seem incapable of learning the lessons of history. As Gordon Rattray Taylor describes:

The great floods of the Arno, such as that which bathed Florence in mud in 1967, have been experienced ever since the fourteenth century. When the woodlands round Florence were cut down and used as pasture for sheep and goats, these nibbled so close that the grass dried and the ground turned to sterile baked clay. Brooks and wells dried up. By the eighteenth century, the woollen mills of Florence had to import wool and hair from elsewhere. The earliest flood on record was 1333 . . . Since then there has been a flood in Florence every twenty-four years, and a major flood every hundred years.

The United States now feeds a large population in other parts of the world with its corn, wheat, and soyabean. But even that 'benevolent' situation will soon become history if American farmers continue to maltreat the soils as they have in the past. In 1935, Congress was forced to pass its first soil conservation act because of the huge dust storms which were blanketing large areas of the country. Nevertheless, despite a Soil Conservation Service, with a corps of 7700 professional conservationists and 4500 technicians, in 1970 according to Carter, two-thirds of the nation's cropland was eroding at a destructive rate, with soil losses of up to 100 tonnes per hectare (40 tons/acre) per year on millions of hectares of rolling to steep grain belt land. 'What lies ahead?' he asks. 'Fifty million acres are eroding at a highly accelerated rate. In 25 years if it is not stopped those acres will be ruined. In 25 years, 50 million more acres of good land will have been taken over for urban uses; airports, subdivisions, factories, ports and so forth. That is 100 million food acres off the production line. (In 1970 we had about 400 million acres of cropland.) If population increases as predicted by 1999 our food safety margin may have grown thin, even though we have additional land that can be brought into production.'

As Carter and Dale point out, soil conservation techniques are well known, and when applied they can be very successful. By reforesting eroded slopes, terracing, contour ploughing, carrying out a proper crop rotation involving a nitrogen-fixing legume, and by making sure that the organic humus content of the soil is kept high, erosion can be held within acceptable limits and farming continued, theoretically at least, for countless generations longer. The tragedy is that such conservation techniques are practiced all too little, for they demand great care and appreciation of the soil, and more of the farmer's time and more of his money. If the farmer were concerned about the land his children would one day inherit and their children after them, he might try to leave the land in a better state than when he took it over from his own father. But today the emphasis is on cash crops, and a quick turnover. Moreover, because fertility can be artificially maintained through industrial inputs, the devastating effects of erosion on soil fertility can to some extent be ignored. The soil scientist who views the soil as little more than a substratum to hold the plant upright while it absorbs the chemicals and water he pours upon it, betrays the kind of concern of modern man for the very substance of his existence. In time, if erosion continues at its present pace, man may find that he, like the plant, no longer has anywhere to put down his roots and draw sustenance. When this happens, it will mark the end not of an individual civilization, but of man's entire civilization.

Modern man is so bound up with the power of energy that he is by no means daunted by the prospect of an ever-diminishing land surface on which to grow his crops. Britain, which imports more than 50 per cent of its food, makes little more than a token effort to keep its best agricultural land from being encroached upon by industry. Industry's needs in fact come first, for disruption in industry is rapidly felt, through mass unemployment, and a balance of payments problem. Agriculture employs relatively few and there is no tradition for strike action, consequently the government makes little effort to pacify farmers and farm labourers compared with its efforts in industry. Time and again good agricultural land is swamped by industry. Some of the most fertile land in Scotland lies along the Ayrshire coast in the Hunterston–Largs area. That land has now been compulsorily taken over by industry, as a site for manufacturing concrete platforms for North Sea oil production, for a massive 'greenfield' steel works and iron-ore port, and for landing and refining oil as well, all those within a few kilometres' radius of Hunterston A and B nuclear power stations. That encroachment of industry upon good farmland is typical of our attitude towards the foundation of our own existence.

Energy is the panacea for all problems if obtainable in sufficient quantities at a reasonable price. Energy can indeed be used to grow plants, as in an entirely closed environment in which the plant roots are held within a tube and all the necessary minerals are circulated to create the maximum growth conditions. The Libyans have shown interest in such an aeroponic venture. Oil is the fuel to be used, and the sun will serve no other purpose than to provide daylight and a thermostatically controlled quantity of heat. The soil's role will be entirely usurped, its function as firm substratum, as provider of the nutrients, including water, nitrogen and oxygen, as detoxifier, as putrefier, as the core of the cycle of life made irrelevant.

The tragedy is that we are not master, nor have ever been master of our creations, but rather than admit this failing, we push blindly on, rationalizing that this path is forward, progressive. Professor Siegfried Gideon captures well the real spirit of progress. 'The one-way street of logic, has landed us in the slum of materialism', he observes with bitter irony. What we must ask ourselves is whether we are safeguarding our future survival by rushing headlong along the path of progress with its commitment to a boundless energy source in the guise of nuclear power. Or whether this very pursuit of energy will paradoxically seal our fate by destroying the natural processes of existence beyond their capacity for self-repair.

*

'Progress' is a word we use very loosely to describe changes and innovations of which we approve. Our approval of them is based on our judgement of their value and people who disagree with our value judgement may condemn them. The condemnation may hold that the changes and innovations in question do not represent true progress, but since we have come to accept that almost all change and innovation amounts to progress, the condemnation is often reduced to one of the concept of progress itself. The person who condemns such 'progress' thus appears reactionary, and inevitably so because of the linguistic trap that has been laid for opponents of novelty. Perhaps we should reclaim 'progress' for the English language!

'Progress' means movement or development in a particular direction. Since it proceeds in a direction, it must proceed towards a goal, even though the goal may be implicit rather than explicit. It is possible to describe something as 'progress' without having any clear idea of the goal towards which progress proceeds. The word also embraces the possibility of its own negation, so that if progress is possible, regress must also be possible, at least in theory. According to this definition, it is incorrect to describe biological evolution as progress, since evolution is unidirectional. The process may be illustrated by a somewhat fantastic example. Consider a human population that is engaged perpetually, generation after generation, in warfare, so that all able-bodied young men must become soldiers and fight. Battles are fought using guns. Large men are more likely to be hit by bullets than are small men, so that in the early stages of this long war armies enter the fray with more or less equal numbers of large and small men, but since a higher proportion of large men are killed it is predominantly the small men who return home, where they are demobilized, marry, and produce families. The propensity to grow to a particular adult size is determined genetically so, over a number of generations, the children born to small fathers come to outnumber those born to large fathers and, little by little, the genes that produce small people dominate and the entire population consists of short people. If we allow the war to continue for long enough — but to stop before it has eliminated the small people as well — the genes that produce large people are lost from the population. Our

war has imposed a kind of natural selection. Small stature has acquired a survival value and so a population of small people has evolved. These people cannot grow to a large size once the war has ended
because the genetic information needed to produce large people was
lost when the original large people died without issue. The process is
unidirectional and can be 'reversed' only by out-breeding with people
some of whom are large, or by an alteration in the genetic information within the population, by mutation. Even then, the reversal is
only apparent. In reality it represents further evolutionary change
that in this special case appears to recreate a form that existed earlier. Fantastic though the example is, it is interesting to note that
contemporary pygmy peoples, all of whom are small, appear to have
no ancestors who were small among the original populations of
Africa. It seems that their stature is the result of evolutionary adaptation to conditions in the forests where they live. Natural selection
tends to favour individuals within a population that possess some
special structure or ability that is useful and that increases their
success at obtaining food, shelter, or mates. Since such individuals
are more likely to breed than their less-favoured rivals, in time they
will take over the particular environmental niche to the exclusion of
those rivals, who may become extinct. The process is one of increasing specialization. It cannot be reversed because its reversal – in the
literal sense of species reverting to their earlier forms – would require the existence of individuals lacking those structures or abilities
for which their immediate ancestors had been selected and possessing more primitive features that had been eliminated from the
population. If species cannot evolve, as it were, backwards they can
at least evolve sideways, as certain individuals possessing talents that
were irrelevant in one environment discover an ability to exploit
different environments or old environments in new ways. This leads
to the evolution of different species from a common ancestor and it
can be seen in many organisms but most dramatically, perhaps, in
the most numerous of all mammals, the bats. From a common ancestor bat species have evolved to feed on fruit, nectar, insects, and
mammalian blood, with each species highly specialized for its own
way of life. A species cannot evolve in reverse to forms possessed by
its predecessors, and even if we were to allow that evolution is progressive, what is it that progresses? Individual organisms do not progress. I am different from my prehominid ancestors, but I have made
no progress in any real sense. I start from a different position, but
that is not the same thing. Had I once been, say, very sick, or wholly
ignorant of a particular branch of learning, I could legitimately count

as progress my recovery from illness or my acquisition of knowledge. The goals are defined, as health or wisdom or expertise, and at any time I might regress by falling sick again or by forgetting what I had learned. I cannot claim as progress the difference between myself and an Australopithecine.

When we look at the history of human societies it is obvious that they have changed over the millenia, at least superficially, and with the compression of time that comes with long hindsight it is tempting to see these changes as a steady continuum, a chain of events following one another fairly smoothly to bring man from there to here. History was not like that, of course, and although the collapse of civilizations – whatever that may mean – may appear regressive, can we talk of human progress? If we do we imply that history has a goal and that if and when this goal is reached progress will come to an end. It is a millenial view which could be correct, but without a good deal more information about the goal it is of little help. At best our progress towards it must be haphazard and outside human control, for we cannot direct our efforts towards a goal that remains utterly intangible and undefined. If we regard human history as progressive, had medieval Europe progressed further than Roman Europe? Was the cultural peak achieved in Athens in the sixth century BC something from which we have progressed or regressed? By any reasonable standard the philosophers of that period were remarkable and their work has been profoundly influential, but modern philosophers and scientists reject many of their ideas. Does this mean we have progressed beyond them? The Athenian dramatists of that period composed plays that in the view of many students of drama have not been excelled, and in various ways the Greek dramatic style has been imitated by all subsequent European dramatists. Have we regressed from the standards set by Aeschylus, Sophocles, Euripedes, and Aristophanes? If so, it would seem that in relation to ancient Athens we have both progressed and regressed. In fact, the concept of historical progress is muddled and any attempt to apply it leads only to confusion.

Within particular societies, at particular times, it may well be that people generally accepted a defined goal as desirable and sought to achieve it. This might be called progress. Christians might strive to create the Kingdom of God on Earth, and the degree of their success might be used as a measure of their progress. There have been many societies, though, that were governed by extreme conservatism and in which change was to be opposed. The goal of such societies was to remain exactly as they had been for some time. If they succeeded in avoiding change, clearly they had progressed, but can progress require no change or development? On the other hand, it may be that they believed their goal had been achieved in the past, and that their purpose was to remain in their perfected state. If this is the case, how are we to view their more recent absorption into other societies that do not share their views? Have they regressed or was their former belief mistaken so that their interrupted progress has been resumed? If we leave aside the obvious moral question concerning the right of one group of people to impose their own views on another group without permission, the question cannot be answered because it has no meaning. It cannot have a meaning unless we can define the goal towards which they and everyone else is supposed to be progressing.

From the European Enlightenment until quite recently, most members of the powerful European middle classes believed in a definite social and political goal towards which progress might be measured. The progress was to be achieved by the application of reason, the cool, logical analysis of problems that would lead to valid solutions, and the goal was to be a society from which avoidable suffering was banished. The goal was a noble one and the rational thought that was the principal tool in its realization has led us to profound insights into ourselves and the universe in which we live. Yet the concept was flawed by its universalism, which resulted from the confusion of natural law – in the strict sense – and human aspiration, the assumption that irrationality could be made rational.

The European goal was limited. It was a goal derived from the history and intellectual development of particular people and it had no necessary relevance to other peoples whose histories were different. During the years in which this view of 'progress' was developed, scientists were discovering the laws by which natural phenomena are governed. These were, and are, much misunderstood. They are not prescriptive laws promulgated by a lawgiver with penalties for transgressors. The apple that falls upward is not fined or imprisoned. They are descriptive of apparent causal links in observed events. If an apple were to fall upward we should seek for a cause and if we could not find one perhaps we should question our understanding of the 'law' of gravity. The use of the word 'law', in this special sense, derived from the theological concept of God's law, which is prescriptive, allowed people to believe that the laws made by God for the regulation of phenomena were qualitatively similar to those made by men, under divine guidance or inspiration, for the regulation of human affairs. Since the natural laws had a universal application – apples fall downward in all parts of the world – there was no real reason to suppose that human laws were not equally universal in their validity. Thus, peoples whose codes of behaviour were based on different beliefs could legitimately be coerced into accepting codes based on the true law, in the interest of their enlightenment, and this enlightenment could be regarded as progress towards the enlightenment of all people. The missionary movement that had existed since the Middle Ages to bring the truths of Christianity to people who had had no previous access to them, was joined by the new educative movement based on essentially European ideas and values. The effects were never so obvious or immediate that action could be taken to modify the outlook of the religious or educative missionaries. In some cases, and most especially where Europeans encountered peoples whose technology was much inferior, the results were disastrous, but even here the tragedies that befell colonial peoples could be attributed to unscrupulous exploitation by European commercial interests rather than to their moral or cultural corruption by new ideas. This is very evident from Hemming's accounts of the early colonization of Brazil, when the only understanding and sympathetic friends the Indians had among Europeans were often particular, usually Jesuit, priests.

Even so, the goal of the Enlightenment became obscured as Europeans became more and more fascinated by the means for its realization. The scientific discoveries were so impressive, so interesting, and the technologies derived partly from science and partly from a more straightforward application of reason to problems, were so powerful that people became bemused by them. It became possible to relieve much suffering, to provide ordinary people with better food, better housing, and better care than they had ever known – at least within living memory. Living conditions in modern Europe are much better than they were a few generations ago and it is hardly surprising that many people imagine some future time when all suffering will vanish. This sounds like the goal of which the Enlightenment philosophers dreamed, but it is very different, for it is based on personal material gain, as an end in itself. On the day when we can all eat three large, juicy steaks a day, have a car for each day of the week, a robot programmed for every dreary task, and holidays on the Equator or the Moon whenever we wish, on that day all human problems will evaporate in the pink glow of the technological paradise. The philosophers of the eighteenth century had a different goal. They would abolish avoidable suffering – the important word being 'avoidable' – and they would limit the unfair exploitation of men by men, but their paradise was one of spiritual, intellectual, and cultural achievement. They would not have people go hungry, but neither would they have them fall into the materialist trap that leads to the deification of wealth.

Their view developed into Utilitarianism, by which we are still guided in many respects. Again, the attempt was noble, but the technique unworkable. Left by the Enlightenment with no concept of absolute values, the Utilitarians sought to create a moral philosophy on the simple premiss that those things and actions are deserving of moral approval that bring the greatest possible happiness to the largest number of people. Bentham even went so far as to devise a calculus according to which decisions could be made on the basis of a numerical valuation of the outcome of alternatives. The attempt failed for two main reasons. The first arises from the difficulty inherent in defining 'happiness' and allotting a measure of it to everyone. I might be made happy if certain of my enemies were made to suffer. How are we to weigh my happiness against the evident joy they experience in tormenting me? Or what of the minorities who may suffer as a result of measures taken to enhance the happiness of the majority? This is a very real dilemma in all modern democracies, and the Utilitarians can offer us no guidance in resolving it beyond the dismal one of leaving minorities to their fate in the interest of the majority. The other and more serious reason for the failure of Utilitarianism arises from our inability to predict the future. Given several alternative courses of action, how can we know reliably which one will bring the greatest happiness? Dare we actually impose temporary suffering in the cause of the long-term good? If we were motivated by nothing more than Utilitarianism could we have justified our uncomfortable and dangerous opposition to Hitler? On any Benthamite calculation our chance of success would have appeared small and the Utilitarian solution might well have been to capitulate and accept Nazism. Clearly, the philosophy is inadequate.

Perhaps we can begin to see that our ideas of 'progress' are at best local and at worst extremely muddled. The idea of 'human progress', in the general sense, seems to be meaningless, and when we seek to attach a meaning to it we do no more than universalize our own opinion. Judged by this standard there must be many historical events that appear to us irrational. As Peter has pointed out, the discovery of the techniques of crop cultivation cannot have been the result of food shortage. In this case, and in others, the idea that necessity was the mother of invention does not make sense. Agriculture began in other ways and for other reasons. It was not irrational, however, except on our scale of evaluation. When people belonging to other cultures do things for reasons we cannot understand it does not follow that they do them for no reason at all! It is simply that their values differ from ours and that their view of the world is one that sets different goals for them. They may – if they wish – measure their progress towards their goals and talk of 'progress' just as we talk of 'progress', even if they and we appear to be 'progressing' in opposite directions.

That our own, limited and quasiutilitarian goals have become distorted is demonstrated clearly by the examples of the proposal to eradicate the tsetse fly and by all of the arguments used by those seeking to expand the nuclear power industry. It seems that problems are being expressed in terms of the machinery available to deal with them, to the extent that the machines can determine the problems. The discussions become heated, as is inevitable when such basic terms as 'progress' are not defined, so that Sir John Hill can use sweeping and emotional generalizations as an alternative to argument.

'Economic growth' is another phrase that is so vague as to cause much confusion. Strictly speaking, it means an increase in the sum total of economic activities of all kinds during a stated period of time, and as a concept it is so general as to be of only restricted value. To support it without qualification is as misguided as to oppose it, for if we seek nothing more complicated than a growth in economic activity we could achieve this in many ways that would be socially unacceptable. We might encourage and promote prostitution, for example, opening brothels in every town, submitting applications for price increases to the Prices Commission, and creaming off surplus income by taxation. Encouraged by large advertising campaigns and supported by Parliament and the clergy the enterprise might be highly successful, increasing economic activity at, as one might say, every turn. The investment cost would be much lower than that required for starting any kind of manufacturing industry and the risks would be less. What is more, the industry is economical in its use of resources and it is difficult to see why it should require an expansion of nuclear power – although economically this would be a disadvantage. Blanket opposition to economic growth is no less absurd. I would be delighted if the number of theatres increased. I would welcome a renaissance of the film industry. I would welcome more orchestras, more records and, for that matter, more restaurants, and I cannot see how expansion in any of these areas could harm anyone. Their expansion would contribute to economic growth. The confusion arises from our failure to discriminate between one kind of economic activity and another, and, as Peter points out, from our assumption that an increase in economic activity of any kind must necessarily lead to an improvement, or reduction, in our standard of living. As soon as we begin to discriminate, the phrase 'economic growth' becomes superfluous, and we are able to say that we favour more of this kind of activity and less of that, which at least has the merit of making it possible to discuss concrete suggestions.

The importance of the modern environmental movement lies in its challenge to such muddled thinking. Often, although not always, the challenge itself is muddled, but that is not so important, at least in the early stages of the debate. What matters is that the challenge itself forces those who favour 'progress' and 'economic growth' to explain themselves, to state clearly the goals they would establish for society and the means by which they would attain them. When they have done that, the real debate can begin.

3 Human creativity

It is fashionable to believe that technology is essentially modern. This is meant not in the more obvious sense that anything productive of environmental and social change must render previous environments and societies obsolete, or at least 'old fashioned', but in the sense that the very existence of technology is new. We associate it with the twentieth century, and with devices and machines that have been invented recently. With a little more thought we can see that modern technologies are based upon other technologies from an earlier time, so that the history of technology can be traced in an unbroken line to the early eighteenth century and the industrial innovations that prepared the way for the Industrial Revolution.

Some environmentalists and most advocates of 'self-sufficiency' reject a large part of modern technology. Later we will discuss their reasons for doing so, which may or may not be seen to be well founded. For the moment it is enough to recognize that to the environmentalist nuclear power is almost certain to be unacceptable, overseas travel by jet aircraft is likely to raise moral qualms, and microprocessors are viewed with a distinct feeling of unease. The would-be self-provider is compelled to adopt a more extreme view, one that leads to an inevitable compromise with each individual making a personal decision about the level at which the line must be drawn that divides the acceptable from the unacceptable. Since no one can expect the proprietor of a smallholding to design, manufacture, and refine fuel for a private aircraft (although that may be less impossible than it sounds), air travel may be considered unacceptable. Yet mail sent from Britain to other parts of Europe usually travels by air, in civil airliners, and it is doubtful whether this inconvenient fact would deter the smallholder from writing a letter. Some may feel that the use of horses is preferable to the use of farm machines but, in rejecting one piece of technology, they are unable to reject the use of implements drawn by those horses, which themselves are products of an older, but highly sophisticated technology.

The list of possible examples is almost endless, as is the list of levels at which the necessary compromises are struck. Many may appear absurd, as the rejection of one technology in favour of another that differs from it most obviously in being less efficient. Others are easier to justify. None of them, however, succeeds in exchanging modern technologies for no technologies at all. Even the handspinner's spindle, or the knitter's knitting needles, are technological devices, and they were revolutionary in their day. The traditional spinning wheel, by comparison, is a very advanced and fairly recent invention, for all that it is made from wood and often decorated with carvings.

Clearly, then, the rejection of technology as such is impracticable. All of us need it to survive, and when the technologies of today are traced to their origins, these are found to be far more remote in time than they may seem. The microprocessor, for example, enables us to store and retrieve large amounts of information. We need this facility because of the large and increasing volume of information our society generates. It generates this information because of advances made earlier in communications. It is not simply that information can be communicated very rapidly by radio or cable, but that the amount of information generated is increasing. Modern printing has made it possible for more books, journals, magazines, and newspapers to be published than at any previous period in our history. This technology can be traced back directly to the invention of printing by means of movable type. That development occurred in fifteenth-century Europe, but it did not occur in isolation. At that time there was a large and growing market for books. The universities were expanding and the middle classes were largely literate. Paper, introduced to Europe two centuries earlier, was accepted and plentiful. Many technologists throughout the continent were seeking ways to accelerate book production. It was Johannes Gutenberg who is credited with drawing together many strands of what today we would call 'research and development', and inventing the printing press. That is believed to have been in 1440. Even so, it was not the beginning of the process because demand for books could not have been large unless books had existed already which, of course, they did. The oldest printed book in existence, discovered in 1900 and now in the British Museum, dates from AD 868, and is a copy of the Buddhist Diamond Sutra. It was printed from wood blocks, which were invented much earlier, and it is possible that they may have begun as carved seals used to make impressions in soft clay. Such seals are known to have been in use in China in the third century BC. If, then, we trace our present need for improved means of handling large amounts of information back to its origin, it is not difficult to work our way back through more than 2000 years. Nor is it entirely fanciful to claim that the truly modern version of the ancient wooden seal is the printed circuit. Both are designed to communicate complex messages.

The invention of printing derived, in turn, from the invention of writing and it was the invention of a simple phonetic alphabet for all the European, Near-Eastern, and some Asian languages that enabled them to proceed to a printing technology based on movable type many centuries before a similar development could occur in China or Japan, whose ideograms are much more difficult to manage in this form. It may not be too unreasonable, then, to trace the microprocessor back to the invention of writing. Writing, of course, derives from speech, and had we not learned to write it is possible that we would have needed to develop some alternative means for the storing and transmission of information of a kind more complex than could be remembered and recounted orally, and over periods of time that might allow for the omission of one or more complete generations, a task impossible within an oral tradition. The Peruvian Inca civilization, which did not invent writing, had evolved a system for information storage based on the *quipu*, a cord to which other cords of varying lengths and colours were knotted. Unfortunately that line of development was interrupted by the Spanish invasion and the introduction of European writing. It would have been interesting to see whether the *quipu* system continued to develop and if, as is possible, the Inca statisticians managed to adapt it into a binary method of writing.

The choice of the microprocessor as an example of a technology that is still so modern as to be almost futuristic yet that has a long history, was quite random and there is no reason to suppose that any other choice would have led to a substantially different conclusion. To attempt one more, the NASA Space Shuttle, still under development but with a very large potential, is developed from aircraft, whose engines depend on discoveries about the behaviour of heated gases that were first stated formally by the English chemist and physicist, Robert Boyle (1627–91), in a reply to a criticism of an earlier work that had been made by a Jesuit priest called Franciscus Linus, in the early 1660s. It is made from metals that could not have been used without the knowledge of metallurgy that brought an end to the stone age, it uses wheels in the way wheels have been used since the first carts were made in the Tigris-Euphrates Valley around 3500 BC, and if it has military implications these, too, should not surprise us. The first important advance in wheeled transport came when the Hittites invented the spoked wheel and used it on delicately balanced two-wheeled war chariots, some time before 1800 BC. The aircraft largely displaced the ship as a means of passenger transport, and the ship is older even than the wheeled vehicle. Men have dreamed of flying ever since they have dreamed at all, and the exploration of the Universe, to which the Space Shuttle may contribute, began when human beings first looked at the Sun and at the night sky and wondered.

No group of people should understand better than philosophically inclined ecologists the simple fact that nothing exists in isolation, that all phenomena must be seen in the context of the environment in which they occur if they are to be comprehended. While the fact is accepted in respect of biological species and events that affect them, it tends to be disregarded in respect of human inventions. This leads to a lack of appreciation for the historical dimension of the modern situation, allowing the view that 'modern technology' is recent and aberrant since it possesses no true historical roots. Nothing could be further from the truth, and it is impossible to make clear distinctions between 'modern' technologies and those of any other period except chronologically. They are linked indissolubly and, if we are to make choices, they must be between particular technologies that we like or dislike for whatever reason. There is no evidence for an historic hiatus that would separate us from our forebears.

Certain of the most extreme environmentalists are well aware of this difficulty and have attempted to resolve it. In doing so, though, they have succeeded merely in pushing this notional hiatus back to a more remote period.

On 1 June 1974, the Nypro chemical plant at Flixborough, Humberside, was destroyed by an explosion and fire. Twenty-eight people died and many more were evacuated temporarily from the surrounding area. As disasters go, Flixborough was sufficiently serious to be entered in the global records, but even in that year there were more severe catastrophes elsewhere. It is important to see Flixborough in context, just as it is important to see all phenomena in context. Only a little while later, on 17 June, there was a fire in a building in Lahore, Pakistan, in which forty people lost their lives. In Port Chester, New York, there was a cellar fire on the 30 June that poured smoke and fumes into a neighbouring discotheque. The lights failed, dancers panicked, and twenty-four people died. Later in the same year, in September, a riverboat caught fire in southern Nigeria, killing sixty-seven people and injuring more than 180. In all, there were fourteen major disasters caused by fires and explosions during 1974, and several of them were more serious than the one at Flixborough.

Nevertheless, the Flixborough incident prompted an official inquiry in Britain and stimulated a lively controversy. Officially, the cause of the disaster was traced to a failure in a pipe but, in his examination of the case, Edward Goldsmith sought to penetrate more deeply. In his view, failures such as that of the Flixborough pipe are inevitable in complex industrial installations and to regard them as the true, or final cause of the explosion is to treat the matter superficially. 'Even if we design indestructible pipes for our chemical works, this will not prevent future accidents. The only way to do so, and by the same token to prevent life on this planet from being annihilated by inevitable, increasingly numerous and increasingly lethal accidents to such things as nuclear power stations and nuclear waste treatment plants, is not to build them.' In other words, the accident is inherent in the concept of complex technologies and can be avoided only by tracing back to its origin the development of such technologies and from there proceeding afresh in a different direction. Obviously, the implications are extreme and, if we are to be consistent, it is not only industrial complexes that must be dismantled, but large public buildings and riverboats as well, since these seem to be prone to accidents of comparable magnitude. Of course the idea is preposterous, but there is a sense in which Goldsmith is perceptive. If we are not prepared to accept some risk from our technologies, then we have no choice but to abandon them – some would argue with much greater risks attendant upon life without them – but once we seek to dismantle the apparatus of modern society it is difficult to know where to stop. It is not merely for practical reasons that most of us are content to settle for a simple, and often crude, comparison of risks and costs with benefits. The alternative is at best forbidding and at worst, as I would maintain, quite impossible.

As we have seen, each development is based upon earlier developments. At various times Goldsmith and others have proposed that the ideal situation may be one that is historically anterior to the Industrial Revolution, a kind of seventeenth-century solution. Unfortunately, the seventeenth century is no more satisfactory than the twentieth, because it contained within it the individuals and ideas that produced the eighteenth century and all that followed. The process of industrialization was already too far advanced. Nor is any earlier period any better, since each contained that which led to the succeeding period. Thus perplexed, some would hold that the process began with the domestication of crop plants and livestock, with the innovation of farming.

This is plausible, up to a point, for it can be argued that once settled farming permitted populations to increase in size people became dependent on farming for their survival and a point was reached quickly, and passed, beyond which the enterprise could not be abandoned. The remainder of history became no more than a postscript to that fundamental change in human behaviour as each innovation necessitated the next. It follows, therefore, that the idyllic life that men enjoyed before they learned to farm is the life for which we should aim, as best we can. We have considered and criticized in an earlier chapter the cultural primitivism that holds that by nature man is a hunter and gatherer. Here I shall raise a further objection to the concept of the introduction of agriculture as the most important of all innovations. Two innovations preceded it, each of which dwarfs the introduction of agriculture in importance as an event in human history.

Excavations in the caves of Chou-k'ou-tien, near Peking, revealed remains of a near-human creature that was called *Pithecanthropus pekinensis*, Peking Man. Peking Man was not entirely human. He was an ancestor of *Homo sapiens*. His history ran its course and ended before ours began, yet in some senses our history arose because of his. Evidence from the cave showed, beyond any possible doubt, that Peking Man used fire. Not only did he take advantage of any fire that occurred naturally, he tended fire in his cave and, almost certainly, he carried it with him when he went away from home.

It is this use of fire by an ancestor of modern man that provides one of the very few indications that in this species there was something qualitatively different from all other species. Prehumans, including Peking Man, made and used simple tools, but many species make and use tools, although not to the same extent. Other species, such as the prairie dog and, most dramatically, the parasol ant, depend for food on plants they have cultivated. Only man ever learned to overcome his fear of fire and to use it to his advantage and he, or rather his ancestors, achieved this a very long time ago. The remains of Peking Man are about 500 000 years old. Because he could use fire, early man and preman could colonize new regions, at higher latitudes and altitudes, so placing within his grasp new food resources. He could cook food, which broadened the range of his diet. Most important of all, he could use fire to drive game and so increase the amount of meat in his diet. It was these game fires, repeated countless times over thousands of years, that produced the pure and stable stands of grasses that occupy the Russian steppes, the North American prairies, the South American pampas, and the African veld.

For the first few thousands of years no one knew how to make fire. Fire had to be 'caught' from natural fires and then preserved with great care. Natural fires cannot have been uncommon. It has been estimated that each day there are, in the world as a whole, about 10 000 thunderstorms and about 100 000 strokes of lightning, any or all of which may start small fires. Once man began to use fires, the incidence of bush and forest fires must have increased. A party leaving home, or even a temporary camp site, is unlikely to have extinguished its fire. More probably it would have left the fire well banked up against the possibility of its being needed again, and fire would have been carried to start the fire needed the next evening. If the fire were lost the group would have to wait until the next storm or man-made fire, or 'borrow' fire from another party. Sparks must have blown and the landscapes of entire continents were changed. The importance of fire to our remote ancestors is recorded in the myths of its origin, most commonly holding that the fire was given by or stolen from the gods by a folk hero, and in the symbolism we continue to attach to the concept of an 'eternal flame'. We still associate fire with life, in such expressions as 'the spark of life' and 'living fire'.

The accidental clearance of large areas of forests would have encouraged the growth of grasses, so leading to an increase in the numbers of grazing animals, and the same clearance made it possible to commence crop cultivation when the time for that arrived. Without fire, agriculture would have been impossible. With fire, all subsequent developments were made feasible. The nuclear reactor is a direct result.

Such clearance, and the organization of hunting parties to perform difficult tasks, also required a very advanced form of social collaboration, as did the fashioning of tools that became increasingly elaborate. Such collaboration required communication, and it is assumed that human language reached something like its present level of sophistication a million or so years ago, among our hominid ancestors. Again, most animals can communicate with others of their own species but, in man, there is a qualitative difference. In other species, the messages that can be communicated are confined to particular, isolated expressions. They may be numerous, but no mechanism exists either to link two or more such expressions together to form a sentence or to invent a new sentence that will be certainly understood. Human languages all consist of an infinite number of true sentences (that is, sentences constructed according to the rules of syntax and possessed of meaning) only a small fraction of which will ever be used. Yet each of us is capable of uttering a sentence that has never been used before, and provided we observe the rules governing the construction of sentences in the language we are using it is certain that our new sentence will be understood by all humans who are familiar with that particular language. For those unfamiliar with the language, in the vast majority of cases the sentence can be translated. The sentences that cannot be translated are those whose meaning is derived from an experience that is confined to a particular culture, so that the failure may be attributed to the absence of that experience and not to a failure of language itself.

No one knows how human language originated or precisely when but, in the world today, and for as far back into history as we are able to penetrate, there has been no such thing as a 'primitive' language. All languages are complex, elaborate, and capable of expressing all that its users require it to express. All of them share the essential quality of language, that they be composed of an infinite number of sentences. Nor is there anywhere a normal human being who lacks language. Existing languages, and there are about 3000 of them, share certain features in common. They are, for example, composed of 'phones', sounds produced in the throat and head that are joined together to form 'morphemes', or sounds that have meaning. These in turn are joined according to rules peculiar to each language or group of languages to produce further groupings and, eventually, sentences. This sounds obvious, but it is not. Although most languages, and perhaps all of them, are accompanied by gestures made with the hands, movements of other parts of the body, and by facial expressions, these are aids to communication and form no essential part of the language itself. 'Tone of voice' is often important in conveying nuances of meaning, but if it cannot be represented in the written language usually it can be ignored, and all human languages can be written. Further, all languages share similarities of structure and some linguists, most notably Noam Chomsky, argue from this that the faculty of learning and using language must be endowed genetically. It is true and relevant that all languages are constrained in similar ways. All of them refer to objects in the external world and properties possessed by those objects, all of them describe human feelings, and all of them must serve the basic functions of making statements, giving orders and asking questions. While these factors may account for certain shared characteristics of languages, there are more fundamental features that are also shared and that are not explained in this way.

Chomsky reinforces his argument by reference to the way children learn to talk. All normal children learn to talk readily and usually with no formal instruction. They make arbitrary sounds that evoke responses in others so that in time these are modified to form words associated with particular people or objects. The child then, and spontaneously, begins to arrange these words to form simple sentences. Children are not born with a particular propensity to learn any specific language. English, Russian, Eskimo, Tibetan or Yap are learned with equal facility and the child soon becomes a native and fluent speaker of the particular language that is spoken by those around it. Almost from the start, the child is capable of using its vocabulary to construct new sentences, so that with no instruction at all it can acquire mastery of one of the essential characteristics of human languages – their ability to produce an infinite number of sentences. This task, which is so simple to any human child, in fact is very complex and no other animal is capable of it so far as we know. (The complex communications of cetaceans have been studied to some extent, but there is no evidence at present that these animals possess any true language.) This shows, says Chomsky, that children begin life with a highly developed capacity for language that amounts to possession of an essential and universal grammar. If this is so, it must have been acquired genetically. If it is not so, how do we account for the facility with which children learn to speak and the comparative difficulty with which they learn to read and write despite the fact that their necessary muscular and manipulative skills are more than adeqate for the task?

We are drawn to the conclusion that of the two characteristics that distinguish man from all other species, the possession of language and the mastery of fire, one was acquired by man's hominid ancestors before *Homo sapiens* emerged, and the other is still older and may be innate. Yet it is these characteristics that have made it possible for man to develop in the ways he has developed, and it is to them that we must trace the origin of modern, and all other, technologies.

This suggests that not only is man inquisitive and innovative, which are qualities we might expect in any opportunist species, but that he is inherently creative and inventive. This is something rather different. Most primates live in stable social groups, most use simple tools and weapons, all of them care for other members of the group and collaborate in performing many tasks. It is only among men that members of a group plan those tasks in advance and seek to improve on past performances. It is only men who seek to understand the Universe in which they find themselves.

In seeking to trace modern technologies back to remotely distant roots, it may seem that I am resurrecting the concept of 'progress'. It is easy to imagine that the possession of a particular technology, a way of performing a particular task, encouraged people to improve that technology or to adapt it to other purposes, to the solution of other problems. It is possible to infer that by and large, necessity has been the mother of invention, that those early men sitting around their camp fire were discussing earnestly an improved hunting strategy that might save the family from starvation during the coming winter. For all we know, this may have happened, but it is unlikely and there is no evidence for it. Certainly there have been occasions when the need for a particular innovation has stimulated a search for such an innovation. We have considered printing and we may add most modern aids to the navigation of ships and aircraft, which are products of deliberate searches. There are other examples, but over history as a whole they may not be very common. It was not a need for improved transportation that stimulated the race, in the late nineteenth and early twentieth centuries, to invent the first heavier-than-air flying machine. Few people at that time believed the aeroplane had a future as anything more than a toy, and its inventors were motivated mainly by the challenge of their skills and by the prospect of realizing the ancient dream of flying (more or less) like a bird. The boat was invented before the beginning of recorded history and we know little of how it happened. It seems unlikely, though, that it was invented by some genius sitting by the waterside tormenting himself with the need to find a better way to move goods and people over long distances. It is more likely that the boat, too, began as a toy, a thing that provided endless amusement for children and adults alike, and that it existed in this form until the day someone used it to visit friends down the river. The sail, on the other hand, may have been a direct response to the need for a form of motive power that was better and less exhausting than poling or rowing. The role of play in human history is very important and we shall return to it, but first we must dispose once again of the myth of 'progress'.

Even if we allow necessity to be the mother of invention, it does not follow that the history of technology amounts to progress. That it should be thought to be so results, if you like, from a kind of linear thinking. We tend to arrange historical events in a neat, straight line, so that they appear to lead from one to another, and it seems reasonable to project the line, so providing ourselves with a goal of sorts and a substantiation of the claim that we are progressing, as it were, from historical A to futurological B.

It is possible to take a more lateral view. Let us invent an oil tanker. Our problem (the necessity that will give birth to our invention) is that we have a large quantity of oil that must be delivered to those who will burn the oil. The trouble is that our customers live a long way away. If we transport the oil by land the cost will be very high. This is because we cannot find a way to build a land vehicle with a large enough capacity. The larger the vehicle, the more power it needs to move it, so the larger the engine it must carry and consequently the larger its fuel tanks must be, and this increases the weight, which necessitates a still larger engine if the payload is to remain constant. The problem runs in circles and even if we could solve it we would need to build entirely new roads to support the weight of such a vehicle, and it would have to move in rather straight lines. The thing is impracticable, but if we use smaller containers, the unit cost of them is high, and we require a very large fleet of them, as well as two people to crew each vehicle. We could build pipelines, but in the initial stages that, too, is expensive and it lacks flexibility. It would be difficult to change customers. What is more, pipelines are vulnerable to sabotage and accidental breakage, so that their maintenance would be expensive.

Perhaps, though, we could send the oil by sea? As we develop this line of thought we notice that a long time ago some Near-Eastern people invented craft that were capable of travelling across oceans. They were powered by sails, and later European vessels were larger and carried more sails. Then there was someone else who discovered that when heated, a gas expands, and someone else again who used this principle to make engines. So we can use one of these engines in our vessel, which will mean it can be larger and more reliable. By borrowing bits of knowledge from here and devices from there, we construct our oil tanker, complete with its radio links to shore and its radar navigation system. It sounds like progress, but from a human standpoint it is not. The design of ships may have advanced, at least in the sense that our oil tanker is larger and better equipped than its predecessors, but we have not progressed. All we have done is to borrow from the past to find a solution to a particular problem that was worrying us. Our need is our own, and peculiar to our immediate circumstances. Our great-grandchildren may not burn large amounts of oil – indeed, it is almost certain that they will not – and so they may well discard our oil tanker, unless they can find some novel use for it.

We are the latest products of a historical process, but no more. When we think of that history as a 'progress' it is because we find it convenient to view it in a linear fashion. It is no less reasonable to view it laterally, abstracting from it items that interest or are of use to us, as though those items were arranged in a circle around us or, for that matter, heaped together in front of us, in a jumble through which we must rummage for whatever it is that we require. It is true that with each new addition to an old idea, the accumulated experience of our species increases, but the accumulation of experience is an entirely random business. If our oil tanker had sunk at its launching, a dismal failure never to be repeated, so that we abandoned all ideas of sending our oil by sea, would that, too, count as progress? Probably not, but it would certainly become part of our accumulated experience.

This view of history may be unorthodox, but if it can disengage us from the idea that we are progressing from somewhere to somewhere it is helpful. As we shall see later in this book it may be useful in other ways as well.

Let us return to the notion of 'play'. By 'play' I mean all those activities that are not part of and do not contribute to the regular business of daily life. They produce nothing that can be eaten or used for any practical purpose. Some people would call them 'leisure activities', but this can be misleading. Indeed, this view of non-essential activities has led to one of the more serious misconceptions about the life of people who obtain their food by hunting and gathering.

Many studies of such 'primitive' peoples have shown that the number of persons engaged in obtaining food is rather small, and that even they need to devote little time to the task. Other necessary activities, such as the building of shelters, are performed by everyone collaborating. These require little time, either, partly because the labour force is large, but mainly because the shelters themselves are not difficult to make from materials that are immediately to hand. The result is that people lead a life that allows ample time for games, sports (many such peoples become avid footballers when once introduced to the principles of the game), religious rituals that include much singing, dancing, and playing of music, decoration of themselves and their possessions, drinking, and gambling. Since none of these activities contributes directly to the provision of food, shelter, or other material necessities, they tend to be regarded as leisure activities. This encourages direct comparisons with the lives people lead in industrial societies which, very clearly, are dominated by work and allow little time for leisure. If, however, we examine industrial societies to discover the number of people employed in those tasks we regarded as necessary in more 'primitive' societies we find it is rather small. In the early 1970s, for example the working population of Great Britain numbered about twenty-five million men and women. Of these, about 420 000, or 1·68 per cent, were employed in agriculture, forestry, and fishing. A further 1·3 million were employed in the construction industry, which embraces the building of dwellings as well as other buildings. That is about 5·3 per cent of the total. So just under 7 per cent of the total working population is engaged in 'essential' activity. The total population in Great Britain at that time was about fifty-four million people, rather more than twice the working population, so that the proportion of the total population of what we may regard as a typical industrial nation that was employed in the essential tasks of providing food and shelter was about 3·25 per cent. Even if you include the employers of these workers and, generously, double the figure, it still compares very favourably with the similar figure from any hunting and gathering society. If we are to be fair and consistent we must conclude that our society is far more 'leisured' than theirs. We do not feel leisured, of course, which is why we should not regard non-essential activities as 'leisure activities' in pre-industrial societies.

We do not feel leisured, although the vast majority of us contribute nothing to the physical survival of ourselves or of anyone else. If Peter and I ceased to write this book the amount of food produced on the farms of Britain would not change as a result, and neither more nor fewer houses would be built. Yet all of us take our non-essential tasks seriously, and we regard them as work. What is more, the majority of them (with the possible exception of the writing of this book!) do make a positive contribution to the lives of others. We must ask ourselves, therefore, whether such non-essential tasks are really non-essential at all? Do we actually need to perform them, and if we do, should we not ask ourselves whether the non-essential 'leisure' activities of pre-industrial peoples may not be equally necessary to them? If they are, our inventory of tasks necessary to supply us with all that we need must be widened considerably. It may be that musicians, artists, priests, and footballers are as necessary to us as are farmers and builders. It may be that we need large public monuments, such as pyramids and cathedrals. We may even need Concorde! It may be that 'play' must be included in our survival kit.

When the first Europeans reached the shores of what was to become Brazil, early in the sixteenth century, they found the coastal belt populated by large numbers of Amerindian tribes. To the Portuguese, the lives of these peoples seemed to be very simple. The climate was warm, so that clothes were not necessary, and all the Indians were completely naked. The houses in which they lived were apparently rudimentary and made from materials gathered from the surrounding forest. They gathered plants and hunted animals, and ate well. Further inland other tribes were discovered, later, who cultivated crops, sometimes to the extent of fully developed and highly productive farming, but the coastal tribes were hunters and gatherers. Their possessions were very few, beyond the weapons they used in hunting and fighting, and the implements they required to carry and to prepare their food. It was tales of these peoples that returned to Europe, improved in the telling, and inspired the notion of the 'noble savage'. They lived, it seemed, in child-like innocence. Later experience showed that all was not quite as it seemed. The tribes were constantly warring with one another and, invariably, prisoners of war were ceremonially executed and then eaten, usually to insult the victim's tribe and so ensure the continuation of the war, but occasionally as a source of food. The interesting fact, though, is that despite the self-evident simplicity of their lives, despite their lack of material possessions, all of these people were adorned, most of them with great elaboration. They wore plugs of bone in holes made in their lower lips, they were painted and sometimes tattooed, the men of some tribes wore penis sheaths, both men and women removed all of their pubic hair (adding to their child-like appearance), and far from having an unkempt look, all the tribes wore elaborate coiffures. Clearly, personal decoration and adornment were very important to them.

Far from being unique, the Amerindians are typical of all pre-industrial peoples. The first contact with the Biami, a tribe that lives in the forests of New Guinea, many thousands of kilometres from Brazil's east coast, was described by David Attenborough in his television series 'Life on Earth', and his book includes a photograph of two Biami men. Both have elaborate hairstyles, the hair being very short except at the back of the head, where it is made into tight, upright 'spikes' that radiate around the head like a halo. One man wears a large ear-ring. The other wears a band around his upper arm and many thin bands worn loosely around his waist. Other men in the group, described by Attenborough, wore necklaces of animal bones.

It might be argued that body decorations may serve as badges, rather like military uniforms, enabling members of a tribe to identify friends and foes at a distance, but the extent of the decoration and the fact that very often it can be seen only at close quarters, suggests that its importance extends far beyond this. So it does with us, of course, and so it did with those early Portuguese explorers, whose dress conformed to the fashion of the day as surely as does our own. Whatever may be the purpose of such adornment, its ubiquity suggests that human beings need to express themselves in this way.

Inanimate objects are also decorated. Where construction materials lend themselves to it, buildings are often carved or painted. Everyday utensils are decorated in a great variety of ways and, from the very earliest times, decoration and adornment have been accompanied by true art. In many parts of the world, works of art are made using perishable materials so that our knowledge of very ancient artistic achievements is restricted to those, such as cave paintings, that have survived. These are highly accomplished and there is every reason to suppose that all early peoples included skilled artists among their numbers. The skill with which their work was performed varied according to the amount of time that could be devoted to it, and the quality of work is much higher among peoples whose artists were full-time professionals.

It is evident from this that without resorting to any kind of chronological or cultural primitivism we may be confident that all human societies include individuals working in the visual arts and that whenever a society achieves an economic state in which individuals can be spared from the 'necessary' tasks, some of them will become artists and will be admired by other members of their society for their skills.

The performing arts are as old. It is probable that the visual arts, other than those devoted to pure decoration, were of religious origin. It is certain that the performing arts were. The first musical instrument was the human body itself. People clapped their hands, slapped other parts of their bodies, and stamped their feet to mark out a rhythm for dancers performing religious rituals. Later instruments, though, were often ritual objects themselves. They produced 'voices' by which those who played them could communicate with spirits. Again, music, dance, and drama developed independently among all peoples. Sometimes we can trace the course of their development. The drama of western Europe began in ancient Greece where it grew out of rituals performed at Dionysean festivals. According to one version of the legend, the popular *kabuki* theatre of Japan began when local dignitaries hired a prostitute, O Kuni, to perform a seductive dance in a dried river bed in front of the cave in which the sun had hidden himself in a fit of pique, to entice the god into the open and placate him. The more plausible, historical account is no less religious. The original Japanese form of drama, which developed into the *Nō* plays, began as religious ritual. The highly formalized *Nō* plays were performed only at court, and the common people were excluded from them and also forbidden to use human actors to impersonate persons. This led to the development of the *bunraku*, the popular entertainment using life-sized puppets. Eventually human actors came to impersonate the puppets, neatly avoiding the restriction, and so *kabuki* was created. Initially it is said to have employed women dressed as men, men dressed as women, and to have been highly bawdy. It was banned and boys took over the women's roles, which proved even worse and it, too, was banned. Then older men took over the roles and the theatre survived, but it still has about it much that is sacred, most especially the stage on which it is performed, which is a holy place.

The Portuguese missionaries who sought to convert the South American Indians to Christianity were delighted with the enthusiasm shown by the Indians for their rituals. They loved to sing and appreciated the drama of the Christian celebrations with evident delight. The optimism of the missionaries turned to pessimism when they discovered that the Indians appreciated the music and drama, but were not at all impressed by the religious implications of either, since they were secure in their firm knowledge of the workings of gods. They had a religion of their own that suited them and their experience of the Universe, and in common with many religious converts, where they adopted the new religion they did so in addition to their own beliefs, which were not abandoned.

Many European missionaries made the fundamental mistake of assuming that because their lives were simple the people among whom they preached were irreligious, religion being assumed to be the product of a sophisticated and enlightened culture, complicated by the fact that where it is believed that religious truth is derived from the revelation of its founder, people can be aware of such truth only through communication to them of that revelation. While it is true that sophisticated and enlightened cultures produce sophisticated and enlightened religions, it is also true that all cultures produce religions of some kind.

'Religion' is a word that is not easy to define if the definition has to distinguish between 'religion' and 'magic' which is essentially irreligious. If we imagine that the world is controlled by invisible forces that are mechanical and impersonal, then we may also believe that by certain performances we can modify the ways in which those forces operate. This is magic. If, on the other hand, we believe that the forces that control the world are manipulated, actually or potentially, by sentient, conscious beings, then if we seek to modify the operation of those forces we must do so through the mediation of those beings. This is religion. Most peoples, including ourselves, believe in both magic and religion, and it may be that magic preceded the appearance of religion, but the fact is that all known cultures are religious. What is more, in all their stages human religions are much more remarkable for their similarities than for their differences. Like human language, they contain many common elements. The belief that there are conscious supernatural beings that influence natural phenomena seems to be universal. It leads to the observation that this supernatural influence may be evident in nature and also in human behaviour, which gives rise to the concept of the sacred. The spiritual beings themselves are usually represented in some way and the representations form the focal points of rituals directed to communication with the beings represented. There is much room for cross-cultural misunderstanding. People have accused others of worshipping 'nature' when in fact they were worshipping gods whose operations were, to them, manifest in natural phenomena. They denounced as idolators people whose 'idols' were mere representations for use as focuses, as is the crucifix used by Christians. Later, a moral philosophy is usually added, which gives rise to an ethical code, and since the purpose of this code is to guide people in their relationships with one another, such codes are generally similar. Every system of ethics that is meant to strengthen social bonds and to encourage cohesion and collaboration is bound to discourage theft, assault, the oppression of the weak by the strong, and all other forms of behaviour that tends to be disruptive, and hence antisocial.

So far as we know, *Homo sapiens* has undergone no important physiological change since the earliest records we have of the existence of human cultures. There is no evidence that might lead us to suppose there has been any change in his intellectual capacity or manipulative skills. We may assume, therefore, that to all intents and purposes we are biologically indistinguishable from our ancestors. We are no more talented than they in any respect. Similarly, although peoples from different parts of the world may differ superficially, there is no known fundamental difference among them. In fact, the earliest humans were potentially capable of everything that has been accomplished by members of their species at any subsequent time. Indeed, this fact can be demonstrated. Articles that were of importance to peoples living at former times were brought by them to a level of perfection on which we cannot improve. A 'living archaeology' experiment conducted in Denmark, in which families volunteered to live for short periods of time under conditions that obtained in the iron age, found that the iron age felling axe was in some ways superior to the modern article. The head and haft were made in such a way that they were fitted together by sliding the head up the haft from the bottom, rather than by fitting the head from the top as with a modern axe. The haft was tapered slightly, being wider at the top than at the bottom. The result was that the iron-age axe, apart from being perfectly balanced, could not lose its head. The bow and arrow, which has a serious claim to being the most successful weapon of all time, was invented independently in many parts of the world, in a wide variety of sizes. Some bows were so long that the archer lay flat on his back and braced the ends against his feet. Many peoples invented the crossbow, and the Saracens made one small enough to be hidden in its owner's sleeve. The 'English' longbow, invented by the Welsh, allowed a trained archer to fire six aimed shots a minute with an effective range of 180 metres (600 feet) or, in really expert hands, up to twice that range. In Brazil, the Portuguese settlers encountered at least one Indian tribe among whom it was considered very shameful for a warrior to miss his target, so that every arrow produced an injury, to the great distress of the Europeans. The returning boomerang, invented by Australian peoples belonging to a stone age culture, is capable of such remarkable aerobatic feats that it was never used by its inventors as a serious weapon, but only for games and contests. It was not until the last century that European scientists were able to understand its complex aerodynamic properties. Traps used by hunting peoples are as effective as, and often indistinguishable from, traps used by modern trappers and poachers.

The list can be made very long indeed, and its implication is clear. All peoples, of all cultures, throughout the whole of human history and prehistory, have been fascinated by technology and have employed their intellectual and manipulative skills to invent and perfect whatever weapon, tool or toy caught their fancy or fired their imagination.

We began by considering the fashionable rejection of 'modern' technology. We found that although certain technologies are recent, even the most futuristic-sounding of them can be traced to ideas, items, articles from the past, so that everything in the present has antecedents. We found that technology itself, far from being new, is very ancient indeed, and perhaps older than man himself. We may choose to date the beginning of technology – or industry, for that matter – from a particular period, such as the commencement of crop and livestock husbandry, but the choice is entirely arbitrary. The introduction of agriculture was obviously important, but just as modern technologies depend on earlier technologies, so agriculture would have been impossible had men not first learned to use fire, an event that took place before the emergence of *Homo sapiens*. Language was also necessary, and we can say little about the origin of that except that there is some reason to suppose that the capacity for language is endowed genetically.

We reject the somewhat simplistic concept of 'progress', implying as it does a story with a beginning, a middle, and a final goal to provide a satisfactory ending, preferring to picture people at different times and in different places experimenting, playing, borrowing from the ideas of others, and so devising new toys for their amusement and, as often as not, for their practical use. Man is nothing if not a plagiarist!

This idea may help us decide which technologies we prefer to keep and which we feel may be better abandoned, for it is self-evident that there is no way any of us can abandon technology as such. If we are not concerned to return to some former stage in what we regard as progress, but can pick and choose among all the ideas that have accumulated over the years, just as we would hold that people have always done, then the distinction between 'modern' technologies and any other technologies becomes properly blurred. We are free to be entirely practical, making use of what is useful and rejecting what is useless, regardless of whether it is 'modern' or not.

What we must beware of doing is falling into a dogmatic rejection of the concept of technology itself and closing our minds to the possibility of new invention and innovation. There is good reason to suppose that man is inherently creative and that any attempt to suppress this trait amounts to an attempt to deprive him of a need more subtle, but no less real, than his need for food.

Nor must we overlook the need for 'play', for those activities that are not connected with the business of obtaining food or shelter. These, too, are as old as man himself and they are related very closely to our need to understand ourselves, the Universe in which we live, and our position within it, to the need that led to our religion, philosophy, and science. In this connection we observed that such non-essential activities become most highly developed in those cultures that are able to support individuals who devote the whole of their time to them. The full-time professional musician, artist, scientist and priest will serve his or her community better and will develop much higher skills for their benefit, than the amateur can hope to do. We noted, too, that comparisons between industrial and pre-industrial or even pre-agricultural societies that suggest that at some time in the past people had far more 'leisure' than they enjoy today are very misleading. 'Leisure' may be defined as 'free time, time at one's own disposal', so that it depends upon our definition of 'work'. In discussing earlier societies the confusion arises from the assumption that all work has as its object the provision of food, shelter, and such other physical necessities and, therefore, that all time spent on other activities is leisure. We cannot, then, compare the 'work' of a hunter with the 'work' of a musician because already we have consigned the activity of the musician to a category of leisure pursuits. The citizens of industrial societies enjoy far more 'leisure' than do the members of any earlier societies, if by 'leisure' we mean no more than freedom from the tasks of obtaining food and shelter, and apart from the statistics that support this view we may note that the output of works of art of all kinds and the numbers engaged in scientific research or other academic activity has never been higher, absolutely or as a proportion of the population, than it is today.

Our conclusion, then, is the slightly banal one that 'man does not live by bread alone'. It implies that any human community that hopes to endure as a society must contain within itself the capacity to produce sufficient surplus to allow members to specialize in those activities for which they are most suited, and it must recognize that although such people may produce no food, their contribution to the community is no less than that of anyone else. It is an interesting fact that the 'communes' that have endured for centuries rather than for a few years are invariably religious communities in which members are drawn together by the attraction of a life devoted to the study, practice, and observance of their faith, and that within most religious communities individuals are permitted to specialize in the secular work that they do.

*

Over-reaction to the established trend is far more likely than carefully balanced adjustment, and it is hardly surprising that seekers of self-sufficiency behave irrationally in their rejection of the machine. Mike rightly points out the continual process that underlies the development of technology, and the frequent referring back to the ideas of previous ages. Da Vinci himself derived many of his inventions from those already conceived in the Middle Ages, and the notion of manufacturing tanks and submarines is hardly peculiar to the twentieth century. Yet for all the logical process of development and the subsequent illogicality of wanting to reject this or that aspect of technology while being perfectly prepared to accept some antiquated forerunner, the self-sufficient man is trying to discover himself through self-reliance in a world increasingly dominated by machines, made by others for purposes of which he has not necessarily approved. But what to reject: what to permit?

Self-sufficiency seekers have a wide diversity of opinion concerning where to draw the line. To be logical, even though perverse, self-sufficient man should restrict himself to only those tools which he can make himself from materials readily available by gathering. Such people do exist. One man who makes his living in Cornwall from basket-making has prepared and developed a commercial herb garden literally by working the ground with his hands and he spurned the use of conventional garden tools. His father, moreover, was a conventional arable farmer in Norfolk.

Others believe technology should stop just before the internal combustion engine. Perhaps the most famous example is the Amishes in Pennsylvania, a strict puritanical group which uses horses for farm work and for transport. Such people exist in England, too. One old man I once met in Suffolk had never been in a motorized vehicle in his life, nor had he any intention of doing so. He was still then working his 28-hectare (70-acre) farm with a pair of Suffolk Punches, but expected to retire in a couple of years when he relinquished his tenancy. The awful irony was that a decision had been approved to run a four-lane road through the middle of his farm and a few metres away from his house where he had been born and bred.

But is there any particular virtue in restricting oneself to what one can do with one's hands, or in utilizing only renewable resources of power, whether they be beasts of burden, windmills, water wheels, wave machines, or even wood and other combustible, but replenishable materials? The man of reason will immediately claim that petroleum, natural gas, tar sands, coal, and equally uranium are as natural as renewable energy resources, with the one proviso that once consumed they cannot be replaced. Why not, therefore, use them, especially as they liberate man from chores and the humdrum? And there is always the hope that some new energy source – like fusion – will be found for the future.

We are faced with a real dilemma: whether technology has outrun our control of it, or whether we can indeed mould it to benefit all humanity in a complete harmony of interests — social, functional, environmental, and aesthetic?

When did technology start? Undoubtedly it was a dual process. On the one hand man was becoming aware of himself and through language was learning to articulate the flood of ideas that were passing through his mind; on the other hand he was trying to overcome his impotence in the face of natural events; consequently once he started manipulating his environment the rewards were evident and self-reinforcing and they included a more secure food supply through the manufacture of improved animal traps and weapons, shelter through the interweaving of vines and branches, and ultimately the exploitation of fire. The evidence of that distant epoch lies in the ubiquitous chipped flints and the carbonized hearths where he had his fires.

But our modern gluttony for tangible evidence, the need for hard facts, is probably leading us astray from really comprehending the motives of early man, and is even distorting our view of ourselves. Thus, many archaeologists equate tool-making with intelligence and, having found a fractured skull together with some worked flints, they take that as the mark of an intelligent hominid ancestor. But intelligence is perhaps more subtle, its manifestations less tangible than a simple expression of tool-making. While respecting research into man's early origins and his achievements, Lewis Mumford is rather scornful of the excessive emphasis given to the tool-making aspects of *Homo faber*. Many animals use tools and sometimes with equal or better dexterity than early man. Tool-making does not, therefore, necessarily exhibit intelligence. On the other hand, man's capacity to symbolize and reflect is a proper manifestation of intelligence and it places him at the head of the animal kingdom in that regard. 'Minding' and 'symboling' have anticipated language in man, and Mumford is convinced of their over-riding importance in the development of intelligence. He suggests that '. . . at every stage man's inventions and transformations were less for increasing the food supply or controlling nature than for utilizing his own immense organic resources and expressing his latent potentialities in order to fulfil more adequately his super-organic demands and aspirations'.

Our own experience tells us that manual dexterity, however valuable as an asset, does not necessarily imply a particularly developed intelligence (in human terms) and poets, philosophers, mathematicians, and politicians may lack skill when it comes to the use of their hands. Yet if we are looking back into the past we tend to look for material artefacts since anything else would be idle speculation. But building up a picture of early man from a few artefacts gleaned here and there is to exaggerate one small facet of man out of proportion. Indeed, it is a particular problem for the investigator that material artefacts survive the passing of time, while cultural achievements, particularly the oral ones of pre-literate man, remain only as elusive remnants in our own figures of speech and dreams. If we wanted to know something about Shakespeare, and nothing of his writing remained, we would be better off, suggests Mumford, studying the plays of Shaw and Yeats, than scutinizing microscopically a few rotted planks from the Globe Theatre. It may well be that the motives of the modern aspirant to self-sufficiency are more interesting than his possession of a few hectares of land and a straggle of animals.

Nor is it simply in our interpretation of the past that we make mistakes. In today's zeal for studying animal behaviour, comparisons are continually being made between the development of human and chimpanzee babies, with the conclusion that '. . . intelligence in the chimpanzee develops more rapidly than in the human infant during the first eighteen months or so of its life, and that during that period the chimpanzee displays a great ability for solving problems and learning new skills'. In his *Challenge to Survival*, Len Williams points out how fallacious is such a conclusion, for again the emphasis is on manual dexterity and on motor skills in general. Williams has no doubts that the human infant is far more advanced in intelligence compared with the chimpanzee at any rate within the first couple of months after birth, and he refers to the baby's smile, with its expression of '. . . recognition, expectation, communication and the need for another . . .' as something which is uniquely human and unobtainable by the most intelligent chimpanzee. 'Put simply,' he says, 'the actual behaviour (not merely potential) of the human infant at only nine months of age is more advanced than any chimpanzee at the age of thirty.' And for those who accuse Williams of excessive anthropomorphism, it must be said that his monkey colony in Looe, Cornwall, has become famous because of its healthy social structure and the naturalness of the monkeys' behaviour, given that they have to contend with human beings. Williams sees one of the prime differences between the young chimpanzee and human exhibited in each's attitude to play. 'The chimpanzee,' he says, 'is a wonderful animal and born innovator, but the human child is a divine actor.'

However much of a dreamer and actor, man's desire for putting order into his Universe has probably featured from the dawn of his self-awareness. Nature is seemingly disordered, at least to the anthropomorphic mind. Thus, edible plants grow inconveniently out of reach; shelters, whether of twigs and vines or even of hewn stone, dissolve and collapse with time unless continually repaired; and the weather rarely seems to suit man's requirements. In putting order into his Universe by corralling his cattle, tending his gardens, fashioning stones for his dwellings and smelting metals for tool- and weapon-making, man had to make his fantasy and his sense of play become realities, and the means of achieving his purpose was through the development of technics.

By its very nature farming implies some control over the environment and ever since man turned to growing his own crops and raising his own livestock he has had to plan his surroundings to accord with his schemes. That hegemony over nature has given man the illusion of creating order, for it has enabled him to substitute his artefacts for the seeming higgledy-piggledy of the natural. In fact, the chaos and disordering which now takes place as a consequence of man's activities are far greater than would occur through natural processes, and it requires increasing quantities of energy to sustain the artefacts, whether they be transportation systems, household gadgets or crops in the field, and to control the debris and pollutants which accrue in the process. Yet man clings tightly to his illusions and glories in his technology for it is in that man-made world that he feels most secure – he is like the man in the space capsule rejoicing in the wholly-man-made life support systems which enable him to travel in an unliveable environment.

The self-sufficient man is looking for a different kind of security. He wants somehow to return closer to the natural, even though his own journey is something of an illusion since the wholly natural, the wilderness, has long since passed away. What particularly disturbs him is that he is enveloped in a technological, artefact-strewn world not of his own making or choosing, and yet being a member of society he has to comply, he has to use what is there, the monetary system, the motorcar, even the jet for carrying his letters to friends elsewhere in the world. And how proportionately few are those who develop and impose their technologies on everyone else, using the gentle art of advertising to ensure that their products are irresistible. Technological development is, therefore, hardly democratic and the decisions taken to send men to the Moon, to develop supersonic aircraft, to build motorways, to construct urban skyscrapers, are by no means thrashed out by all members of society. It is that lack of democracy, that having to live with another man's technological creations – however superb they may be as manifestations of man's creative energy and intelligence – which offends those who opt out of the technological society. Such drop-outs are not *ipso facto* anti-technology, but they would like to limit themselves to those technologies which they feel immediately in control of, and nuclear power stations or Concordes hardly rank in that category. A prime motive for self-sufficiency is the need to do things for oneself, to put dignity back into work and to escape from the mind-shrinking rigours of the production line process utilized in many of the big manufacturing industries. Not that contemporary society has the monopoly on technological enterprise and control over people. Lewis Mumford has drawn some illuminating parallels between the mega-machine process of the ancient civilizations of the Middle East, in Egypt and Mesopotamia, for example, and that of today. The ancient civilizations also had their technological elite who worked out giant schemes and put them into effect. The result, even though on a gigantic scale like the irrigation schemes of Mesopotamia, or the pyramids of Egypt, was of extreme precision, and Mumford likens the use of thousands of slaves to the use of energy slaves today – petro-leum, coal, and the atom. Again today we have our technological elite, although we call them scientists rather than priests.

In the Middle Ages, too, particularly in Europe, all manner of machines were devised, including metal stamps and forges, which worked off water and wind power. Indeed it was the later develop-ment of those machines which gave a spur to the Industrial Revo-lution of the eighteenth century, for the very limits had been reached, given the engineering ability and knowledge of materials, in the use of renewable energy resources. Indeed, in England at the time of Domesday there were some 5000 water mills recorded and in some rivers there were two mills to every kilometre. In Paris in 1323 there were thirteen floating mills under the Grand Pont.

The self-sufficient man should welcome the use of energy outside his own limited muscle power to help him sustain himself, his family, and those around him. But first and foremost he wants to feel that the energy he is exploiting is not being squandered so that future generations will go in want. Secondly, he wants to have personal control over the purposes to which that energy is put, just as much as everyone else in society should have control. The outcome of that democratic control might well be the end of such a sophisticated source of energy as nuclear power. In fact society needs a revolution

– a complete turn around – according to the tenets of self-sufficiency. The accepted philosophy is that the world needs to consume increasing quantities of energy to alleviate human poverty and suffering, and the model chosen is the westernized one of technological development. But if people can become more self-reliant, more in control of their daily destinies, whatever the individual risk, then, say the aspirants of self-sufficiency, the needs of those in the westernized world where industrial consumption is highest will be markedly reduced. People will be better off on less.

Thus, the self-sufficient person is out to shape his own destiny by getting back to basics, and he can only find his way through rejecting much of the technologies which he feels are inflicted willy-nilly on society. There are bound to be inconsistencies in that rejection. Yet ironically, for man to become self-sufficient again he has to return to being *Homo faber*. It is only in doing for himself and in taking responsibility for his own actions that he can escape from the stranglehold of a society in which the prime movers are faceless, inanimate machines operated too often by mindless men.

4 Living off the land

It is surely one of the great ironies of our time that our farmers should scarcely eat produce from their own farms. Indeed what better symbol of the growing detachment of our civilization from the living process that sustains it than the television advertisement of the farm worker getting back to his breakfast after the morning milking and there on the table in front of him, with all its connotations of farm freshness, stands a packet of a famous brand of cereal. In modern farming the farm worker is increasingly isolated from the soil he is tilling; he sits encased in the cab of his tractor, either with ear-muffs to shut out the noise, or with radio blaring, and what goes on behind the tractor has more to do with the wonders of technology than with the wisdom of countless generations of his predecessors. Meanwhile the farmer has become less concerned with husbanding natural resources than with manipulating purchased inputs in the form of artificial fertilizers, chemical sprays, and animal feedstuffs. The soil, instead of being treated as a living substrate has become a factory floor. No wonder then, that farmers and the men who work for them, see no discrepancy in sitting down to a breakfast of processed food.

The industrialization of agriculture and food production has had profound effects on society. It has eliminated the need for a large workforce on the land, and a single man is now expected to manage on his own the farming of more than 40 hectares (100 acres) where traditionally between five and ten men would have found employment. And because farm equipment is now manufactured by giant companies rather than by local firms and even by the village blacksmith, many others in the countryside have also been made redundant. Overall then, industrialization of agriculture has eroded rural life.

Appalled at the trends, the seeker of self-sufficiency has set out to redress the balance. He wants to grow and eat his own food, he wants to feel the soil under him when out in the fields and he wants to see the countryside peopled once again by families who are deeply involved with its cycles of sowing and reaping.

Self-sufficiency, whether practised by individuals or by communities, has come to represent a struggle for Utopia. But does it have any real place in society? Is it not likely to be an inefficient way of producing food and thus incapable of providing for an expanding population and one which is increasingly against the limits of world food resources?

One problem in evaluating total yields from self-sufficient farms at present is that they operate with a modern industrial system. In addition the movement is in its infancy, making a negligible contribution to total food production, and is largely supported by those new to farming. In Britain, anyone can own land and farm it more or less as he likes as long as he abides by regulations concerning the quality of produce sent to market and that he maintains certain standards in looking after his livestock. There is no obligation to be productive other than for personal economic reasons. But what happens if world food shortages force Britain to reduce drastically its food imports and to strive for far greater overall self-sufficiency; will inefficient producers be allowed, and by what criteria will they be judged? May it not be that farmers will again find themselves facing something akin to the War Agricultural Committee and having chemical fertilizers pressed upon them as happened during World War II?

Given that kind of pressure, the self-sufficiency movement will have to show that it offers a real alternative to the present system, and its supporters will therefore have to demonstrate that they have sufficient ability in working the land to meet the major proportion, if not all, of Britain's food needs.

Petroleum has become the key to much of farming practice. Its products provide fuel for an ever-increasing array of either self-powered or tractor-drawn implements, it forms the basis of most chemicals used on the land, whether they be fertilizers, herbicides, or pesticides, and its use has become essential for the transport of goods.

British farmers, urged on by a large agroindustry, have been second to none in equipping themselves with labour-saving devices and an armoury of chemicals. According to Gerald Leach of the International Institute for Environment and Development, in 1920 the average energy input for each hectare (2·47 acres) of farm land on the basis of fuel consumption alone was approximately 150 megajoules (42 kilowatt-hours) per year. Then only 6 per cent of farms had electricity, their combined consumption being 25 gigawatt-hours. Fifty-five years later the fuel bill amounts to 9000 megajoules/hectare/year (1000 kilowatt-hours/acre/year) – which is a sixty-fold increase, and electricity consumption to more than 100 times its 1920 level. Leach also points out that although modern machines are far more efficient than their 1920 counterparts, yet the increased energy consumption on the farm has reduced farm efficiency when measured in terms of energy input per output. In 1952 the ratio was 0·47 and in 1968 it had fallen to 0·35. That ratio is still falling as farmers utilize more and more machines to replace human labour.

In Britain, less than 3 per cent of the work force are employed on the land and the number is still dwindling as the process of capitalization of farms continues. It is thus estimated that by 1980 the full-time agricultural labour force could decline to 179 000 employees and 132 000 farmers – a drop since 1968 of 45 per cent in employees and 24 per cent in farmers. Not that less land is under cultivation, just that the size of farms has been increasing inversely with the labour required to work it.

Typically the United States has established the basic trend and since 1940, the number of its farms has declined from 6·3 million to 2·8 million and the farm population has fallen from 31·9 million to 9·4 million. 'The result,' says Professor Michael J Perelman of California State University, in *Environment* 'is that there has been a marked increase in average farm size. In 1940 the average farm size was about 167 acres; by 1960 the average size had jumped to 297 acres and in the last ten years another 92 acres has been added, making the farm average close to 400 acres.'

The rationale behind modern farming is that less men can manage much more, and consequently can earn far higher wages and salaries than they would if they remained limited to their family small-holdings. The modern farm worker is thus placed in a similar category to the factory worker.

Former secretary of agriculture in the United States, Clifford Hardin, is unhesitatingly enthusiastic about the trends in farming. 'Using a modern feeding system for broilers, one man can take care of 60 000 to 75 000 chickens. One man in a modern feedlot can now take care of 5000 head of cattle. One man with a mechanized system can operate a dairy enterprise of 50 to 60 milk cows. In short, agriculture does an amazingly efficient job of producing food.'

Like many agricultural experts Hardin has failed to assess just what makes that high productivity of labour possible. Nor has he taken into account the damage done to the environment and to people's health by intensifying agriculture in the way he describes. Coping with the effluent from large feedlots as well as the effluent from the factories that produce pesticides and herbicides has become a major problem in the United States and Barry Castleman relates in the *Ecologist* that several United States pesticide manufacturers have been indicted many times for violating federal anti-pollution laws.

At present the pesticide industry produces a billion pounds of pesticide for use in the United States and another 2 430 000 kilograms (six million pounds) for export. 'The manufacture of pesticides by US firms has generally been carried out in the States,' says Castleman, 'but as more cases of cancer, sterility, and diseases of the central nervous system among chemical workers come to light there is much unease in the industry and widely used products find themselves on the banned list.'

Castleman tells of one pesticide *Kepone*, manufactured in Virginia by Life Science Products Company and sold to banana growers in Latin America, Asia and Africa. 'This pesticide has caused sterility and apparently permanent nervous disorders among seventy-five Life Science employees; has severely polluted the James River and wreaked havoc on the local seafood industry. The Allied Chemical Corporation and Life Science were indicted for over a thousand violations of federal water pollution control laws and criminal charges were filed against Life Science owners. Astronomical fines were imposed and Allied set up an eight million dollar fund to clean up James River. But the damage was virtually irreparable.'

When the first large settlements were formed in neolithic times, they were wholly dependent on those tilling the land for their survival. Agriculture today has become part of a giant manufacturing industry and, by opting for machines and technology rather than for labour and simplicity, farmers have bound themselves to a system which increasingly controls their activities. Without manufacturing industries modern farms would collapse. Professor Howard T. Odum has put it poignantly in *Environment Power and Society*. 'Much of the power flow that supports the agriculture is not spent on the farm but is spent in cities to manufacture chemicals, build tractors, develop varieties, make fertilizers and provide input and output marketing systems which in turn maintain mobs of administrators and clerks who hold the system together. As we stand on the edge of the vast fields of grain with tractors and production as far as the eye can see, we are tempted to think man has mastered nature, but the plain truth is that he is overcoming bottlenecks and providing subsidy from fossil fuel . . .' What a sad joke that a man from an industrial-agricultural region goes to an underdeveloped country to advise on improving agriculture. The only possible advice he is capable of giving from his experience is to tell the under-developed country to tap the nearest industrialized culture and set up another zone of fossil fuel agriculture. As long as that country does not have the industrial fuel input the advice should come the other way.

The citizen in the industrialized country thinks he can look down upon a system of man, animals and subsistence agriculture that provides some living from an acre or two in India when the monsoon rains are favourable. Yet if fossil and nuclear fuels were cut off, we would have to recruit farmers from India and other underdeveloped countries to show the now affluent citizens how to survive on the land while the population was being reduced a hundredfold to make it possible.

Just the fuel consumed in tractors in the United States is equivalent in amount to the energy value of the food crops consumed by Americans. In addition, American farmers use electricity – reckoned to be 2·5 per cent of the total electricity production of the United States – as well as fertilizers, foodstuffs for livestock, and farm buildings constructed of high-energy materials such as concrete and asbestos. Perelman calculates that each American consumes the equivalent of 685 litres (150 gallons) of petrol, or about five times the energy contained in his food, to feed himself. 'Even here,' he says, 'we have not taken into account the energy required to produce the farm equipment, nor the energy used to store and distribute the food. For instance farmers purchase products containing 360 million pounds of rubber, tons of steel in the form of trucks, farm machinery and fences. Farms consume about one-third as much steel as the automotive industry.'

The trend towards greater farm mechanization and dependence on chemical technology is self-reinforcing, for as agroindustries expand their sphere of influence accordingly they have to protect their interests and ensure that their products are competitive. The western world is now so committed to the agroindustrial approach to agriculture that it cannot consider any alternative as likely to provide the necessary food to sustain the population. A typical attitude is that the agroindustrial approach must be expanded further to embrace the entire world if Malthusian food limits are not to be reached early in the next century – given the expansion of population.

Some years ago William H Pawley, then director of the Food and Agricultural Organisation's Policy Advisory Bureau, conjured up a scenario by which a world population ten times bigger than today would have sufficient food to eat well. He envisaged arable farms in the Amazon Basin and a fertile green Sahara made to bloom by the simple expedient of desalinating seawater and pumping it hundreds of kilometres across the desert sands. Taking the Netherlands as his base – they obtain an average 4 tonnes of grain per hectare (1·6 tons per acre) with applications of 360 kilograms (795 pounds) of NPK fertilizer – he believed that total world production of food from the land could be increased some fifty times. To bring about that miracle of production, Pawley calculated that the fertilizer industry would have to expand its output from its present total of sixty million tonnes a year to 4300 million tonnes – a seventy-fold increase. To give him credit he did foresee tricky problems such as soil break-down in the tropics, wholesale unemployment brought about through the massive displacement of peasants from the land, and a consequent reversion to illiteracy.

Such a vision as Pawley's derives its substance from the notion that the global economy will continue to expand until the entire world has reached a high level of industrialization. As we shall discuss later the total energies involved will be many times greater than today and the sources of energy will no longer be cheap petrol-eum, natural gas, and other easily procured hydrocarbons. The ferti-lizer industry alone would be absorbing a considerable proportion of present energy consumption if expanded to meet Pawley's as-sessment of future requirements. Thus, Britain's consumption of nitro-gen manufactured from hydrocarbons has risen more than eight times since 1945 and of phosphorus and potassium fertilizers some thirty-fold: indeed, the present total energy involved in fertilizer pro-duction for British farms amounts to some two million tonnes of oil equivalent. This quantity is approximately 1 per cent of total primary energy consumption in the United Kingdom which may seem fairly insignificant compared with total energy consumed in heating houses and in transport. But on a per capita basis that same United Kingdom fertilizer consumption extrapolated to the present world population would mean that energy equivalent to the entire annual North Sea oil production would have to be diverted to fertilizer production alone: and Pawley was talking of a population ten times greater than that of today.

Nevertheless the use of chemicals and the absolute control of the growing environment of man's crops are beguiling propositions. On a mini-experimental scale and divorced from any considerations of economics, the food-yielding potential of the environment has been put to the test in growing potatoes and certain other crops. Thus, in 1967 M B Alcock set about assessing the theoretical maximum crop that could be grown outdoors assuming the ultimate limits to be the solar input for photosynthesis. On that basis he reckoned that 85 tonnes of ware potatoes could be grown on a hectare of land (34 tons per acre) compared with the average yield in Britain of 31 tonnes per hectare (12·5 tons per acre). Two years later the Agricultural Development and Advisory Service of Yorkshire and Lancashire carried out experiments to test the feasibility of the theory. Initially they sterilized the soil and then planted twice the average number of chitted seed potatoes per hectare. Over a three-year period the ADAS team succeeded in producing average yields of 87 tonnes of marketable potatoes per hectare (35 tons per acre). Following those experiments, other farmers have tried the 'blueprint' technique with some success. A Kent farmer reported a yield of 74 tonnes per hectare (30 tons per acre) after regular aerial spraying against blight; but the main problems for the average farmer have been those of finding a plot with the very special conditions of the pilot experiment and of coping with machinery that was devised for planting potatoes at the conventional rate. Naturally the blueprint techniques required high levels of fertilizer application, irrigation, and constant attention against disease. And what would happen if all potato growers opted for the blueprint technique and there were a potato glut? How would prices be maintained to justify the high input costs?

The idea of solar inputs posing the ultimate limit to yields immediately puts the tropics in a new perspective and, at a meeting in London, Dutch agricultural researchers proposed to the British fertilizer industry that world food production should in future be left to tropical and subtropical countries where, with the requisite application of technology, production could be boosted some forty times higher than its present level. Britain, they said, should abandon any pretence of growing for itself and should concentrate its efforts on the manufacture of industrial goods – a policy which Britain has in fact half-heartedly pursued since the mid-nineteenth century.

If we divorce the blatant absurdity of the Dutch suggestion from the accepted dogma that chemical farming is the only option we have for increasing the world's food supplies, then we are left with the crucial debate on our hands, whether we in Britain will have the resources to continue developing agriculture on its present industrial lines – pursuing the blueprint technique – or whether self-sufficiency farming can provide a real alternative. Since food is the basis of existence, it is not surprising that those of the self-sufficiency movement should take seriously how their food is produced. Undoubtedly faddism distorts the picture, but for the most part those of the self-sufficiency movement want their food untainted with chemicals and fresh. Many of the movement subscribe to vegetarianism, seeing in the production of meat a kind of evil exploitation of animals, but even those who eat meat set out in the main to do so sparingly. For some it is important that they know the animal they are to eat and one man who stayed with us for a year refused all meat unless he helped in the raising and slaughtering of an animal; then he felt both respect for the animal and responsible for his actions. His attitude must surely have parallels in those of prehistoric man when depicting the hunter and hunted. One outcome of the new attitude (or the regaining of ancient attitudes) towards food is that the waste and indulgence presently embodied in the eating habits of industrialized countries can be drastically reduced. If the entire population of Britain were able to emulate those of the self-sufficiency movement in their reverence for the living processes that underlie the provision of food, then the country as a whole would probably come much closer to self-sufficiency in food.

Britain, with fifty-six million people, is a heavily populated country, and if it, with its temperate climate, is able to achieve self-sufficiency in food, then that fact in itself should be enough to silence those Dutch agronomists with their fanciful notions of Britain becoming none other than an industrialized workshop. But self-sufficiency in food cannot be achieved by sparing diet alone; there must be proficiency in the growing of food, and here we come to the matter of techniques.

In all farming and gardening systems the problem of maintaining fertility is a critical one. In a natural ecosystem the basic inputs are energy from the Sun, water from precipitation, and flow of air, as well as soil nutrients, all these inputs passing cyclically through the system, becoming first part of one organism and then another during the processes of life, death, and decay. In theory the system is sustainable for as long as the Sun shines. In farming and gardening the first stage is to replace the diversity of a natural ecosystem with a few or even a single species, the purpose being in effect to channel those nutrients into crops and livestock which otherwise would have gone into the composite biomass of the original system. But there is a snag; whereas the natural system seems somehow self-sustaining, when man grows his crops year after year on the same ground, the land becomes tired and increasingly infertile. There have been outstanding exceptions, such as along the banks of great rivers like the Nile in which a thin layer of nutrient-rich silt is deposited each year.

In fact, by damming the Nile this deposition occurs no more and Egyptian farmers have lost in one stroke the essence of their land's aeons-old fertility.

Thus, unless something is returned to the soil each year, the farmer finds his crops failing and, not surprisingly, the notion of each crop draining the Earth of its nutrients would seem to explain soil infertility. The most common way of replacing lost fertility is through manuring the ground either with animal excreta or with composted vegetable remains, the composite of straw and excrement probably being the best. But there is more to fertility than simply adding lumps of manure, and very early on man discovered the efficacy of leaving land fallow. The fallow idea probably antedates the injunction on the Israelites to leave their land alone every seventh year if they wished to avoid food shortage and famine. In the tropical rain-forests of South America and New Guinea, stone-age tribes who practise a mixture of hunting, gathering, and gardening, abandon their plantations after a couple of years, allowing them to grow back into forest. According to Professor Roy Rappaport of the University of Michigan, the Tsembaga tribe of New Guinea have to weed their plantations assiduously to prevent their crops being smothered. Yet in their weeding they are extremely careful to leave young tree saplings which have reseeded themselves, and to avoid trampling them, even though the rapid growth of these trees soon makes gardening difficult. After two years the gardens have to be abandoned because of the saplings which are called *Duk Mi* meaning 'Mother of Gardens'. Clearly the Tsembaga are fully aware of their importance in restoring fertility to the thin tropical soil.

In Europe from Roman times until the early Middle Ages, farmers operated a two-field system by which one half of the tilled area was left fallow each year, the other half growing the crop. The Romans too, were limited to using oxen as beasts of burden in the fields, because horses at that time did not appear strong enough to pull a heavy implement through the ground. But, as Jean Gimpel points out in *The Mediaeval Machine*, the Middle Ages were a period of great enterprise and innovation, and the groundings of modern agriculture were laid down then. The climate was good, particularly in Europe, with temperatures on average a degree or more higher than now (the evidence comes from glacial movement and the size of the tree growth rings). That better weather accounts not only for the vines grown so easily in England at that time, but also for the cultivation higher up the hills than was possible later, when the good weather again gave way to a mini-ice age. But the really dramatic change was in the development of the three-field system in place of the Roman fallow system, and the substiution of the horse for the ox.

In the Middle Ages a pair of large horses could be expected to haul a wagon loaded with up to 4 tonnes of stone, the wagon itself weighing 2·5 tonnes on top of that. The Romans were explicitly forbidden in the Theodosian Code of AD 438 to harness two horses up to loads of more than half a tonne. The reason for the extraordinary discrepancy between Medieval and Roman horses was not one of a difference in size and breeding, but simply one of breakthrough in technology: the Medieval carters had learnt from the Mongols to use a collar and haims rather than the modified ox-yoke harness used by the Romans, and in 1931 a Frenchman, Lefebre des Noettes, experimenting with a yoke harness, discovered that above loads of half a tonne, the yoke would pull against the horse's neck and semistrangle it. Such strangulation would explain, he suggested, the thrown-back wild look of the horses of the Parthenon.

The three-field system, which first appeared in the eighth century, had the advantage over the two-field system that one-third of the cultivated area was left fallow at any one time rather than one-half. In both instances animals were grazed and kept on the fallow part to help manure it and restore fertility. Another consequence of the three-field system was the greater diversity of crops that could be grown, spring corn as well as winter, for example, thus insuring against total crop failures. The farmers also tilled spring oats, giving their valuable horses a source of feed. Medieval farmers also planted more green crops and vegetables than their ancestors and by all accounts the nutritional standard was remarkably high.

'In 1289,' Jean Gimpel relates, 'on the manor of Ferring belonging to Battle Abbey, the carters expected cheese in the morning and meat or fish to go with their rye bread and beer at noon. And in the years 1300–05, the workmen building the spire of the church at Bonlieu-en-Forez were offered cheese, meat, and a large quantity of wine, as well as rye bread and bean soup.'

Another invention was the heavy wheeled plough with its vertical coulter and long, curved moldboard for turning the slice of ground on to its side. With a powerful team of horses to draw the plough, and working under a good climate, the Medieval farmer was able to extend considerably the land under cultivation. Also to gain manoeuvreability, the ploughman increased the length of his furrow and so altered the shape of the field from its square pattern to one more oblong. Deep ploughing also brought about the invention of the harrow, which lopped off the ridge of each furrow and created a good level tilth. Previously the soil had to be levelled by ploughing at right angles to the original direction.

Through using the new plough, farmers improved considerably their grain yields, getting double or even more the harvests they had previously. In one place, Gosnay, a record harvest of 1335 yielded fifteen measures of wheat for every one sown – a figure not so much lower than average yields obtained in France today.

The prosperity of the Middle Ages is reflected in population figures, and during the 300 years between 1000 and 1300 the population of Europe grew from forty-two million to seventy-three million. In France the population reached twenty million, just half that attained at the beginning of World War II. Gimpel suggests that France's relatively large population in Medieval times explains why France became a leader in the industrial and agricultural revolutions that were then taking place in Europe. A similar, though far greater burst in population took place in Britain some 450 years later with its own industrial and agricultural revolutions.

Records of farming techniques and of yields date back to antiquity and they give us some sort of perspective in looking back over the history of agriculture. From hieroglyphic records, cuneiform scripts, and wall paintings we know a great deal about ancient Egyptian and Mesopotamian agriculture. Nor were Medieval commentators any less thorough in leaving records of farming and, from the various Book of Hours and other manuscripts, we have a wealth of meticulous illustrations of daily activities in the fields. Walter of Henley, for example, tells us how to plough and manure the fields, evaluates the economics of using a horse instead of an ox, and informs us how many sheep were sheared in England. Indeed in 1273, some eight million sheep were sheared, a figure not so much lower than that today, the monasteries such as Fountains Abbey in Yorkshire, being major land and sheep owners.

Farming may have seemed to have marked time between the end of the Middle Ages until the eighteenth century, and the Age of Enlightenment. Yet farmers were still grappling with ways to overcome the fertility problem and to increase the productivity of their land. New crops were then being introduced from other countries, including the potato, turnip and, a little later, the swede. Animal breeding was also being carried on very successfully as was the development of new machines, including Jethro Tull's seed drill and his equally famous one-horse light implements. The new crops, in particular the turnip, stretched the seasons for the farmer, by giving him extra winter feed for his animals. Furthermore they forced him to look for new kinds of crop rotations so that he could squeeze them in. In essence, the land that traditionally had been left fallow became that used for growing the new crops and, in one stroke, four course rotations, such as the famous Norfolk rotation, came into being.

With the need for leaving land fallow gone, the farmer could now experiment with all kinds of rotations in the quest for productivity and, by the mid-nineteenth century, crop rotations had become exceedingly elaborate, some of them involving seven or eight courses. Moreover, successive enclosure acts, in particular, that following the Civil War, led to a shrinking of common land, and to the emergence of a new kind of farmer who was not a traditional landowner, but who had made money out of business and wanted to buy respectability through investment in the land. Competitively aware of new developments, and not being bound by tradition, such farmers would use the latest techniques and implements.

Science was flourishing at that time and, not only had magnetism and electricity been discovered, but also the chemical elements and some of the laws governing their interactions. Consequently, farmers wanted to know more specifically what soil consisted of and how its composition and structure affected fertility. Indeed, given the booming science of physics and chemistry, the actual composition of crops could be ascertained and their mineral requirements determined. The consequences of the new chemical knowledge were as great as any other revolution in agriculture, for now the farmer could be told exactly how much his crops were taking from the soil and could be given precise formulae to replenish the soil after each harvest. Furthermore he could now plant the same crop year after year in the same patch of ground, rationalizing equipment, and for fertility needing to do little more than sprinkling on the right mixture of chemicals. Baron Justus von Liebig, the nineteenth-century German chemist made the farmer's life even easier by showing that fertility could be maintained by adding in the main, three elements, nitrogen, phosphorus, and potassium.

The self-sufficient farmer has on principle to avoid applying chemicals to the land and must therefore be 'organic'. But how in fact should he farm? Curiously this dilemma came to its pitch in the mid-nineteenth century just when the chemical revolution in farming was taking place. Farming by then had reached a kind of perfection, with man, machine and horse working in extraordinary harmony to get the most out of the land and, in his *Book of the Farm* published in 1851, Henry Stephens describes in detail every aspect of nineteenth-century farming, from nurturing calf gut for cheese-making to draining a field with a horse-drawn mole plough. Indeed, he has a lot to tell anyone wishing to learn the foundations of farming.

Stephens himself had a good inkling of the conflict that was emerging between the traditional 'organic' style of farming with its emphasis on crop rotations and the new 'high farming' with its productivity increasingly dependent on the application of manure imported into the farm from elsewhere and the use of imported feedstuffs to feed livestock. He was unequivocally excited by the new discoveries in science, by Faraday's experiments on magnetism, Dalton's and Davy's in chemistry, and the reader is given insight into the chemical compositon of soil, of plants, and of manures. He also disputes the then, as now, accepted notion that Liebig was the first to come up with the concept of 'specific manures'. Instead, Stephens informs us with some pride, that it was an Englishman, Mr Grisenthwaite of Nottingham, who in 1818 published the doctrine of specific manures and of the existence of saline ingredients in plants. Later in his *New Theory of Agriculture* published in 1830 – ten years before Liebig's publication – Grisenthwaite unfolded the logic of his argument, and Stephens quotes: 'In the grain there always exists, as has been stated, a portion of phosphate of lime. It is the constancy of its presence that proves, beyond reasonable doubt, that it answers some important purpose in the economy of the seed. It is never found in the straw of the plant: it does not exist in barley, or oats or peas, although grown upon the same land and upon the same circumstances, but as has just been observed, always in wheat. Now to regard this unvarying discrimination as accidental or to consider it as useless is to set to defiance the soundest principles of reasoning that philosophy ever bruited ... As little attention has hitherto been paid to these saline bodies, at least as they regard the subject of vegetation and much more as they respect the operations of husbandry, I have, for the sake of distinction, called them specific manures.'

Mr Grisenthwaite continues with the hope that the new knowledge will '... raise the operations of the agriculturist to a level with those of the manufacturer; and instead of committing the cultivation of the soil to accident, as if nothing were understood respecting it more than the mechanical preparations of it for the seed, it will serve to explain upon what causes growth and production, and consequently their opposites, abortion and non-production, fundamentally depend; and of course will enable him to provide against both ... The sun of chemistry has at length risen above our horizon, and dispersed much of the darkness of ignorance which covered former ages, and shed an illuminating ray over the various phenomena of nature . . .'

By the mid-nineteenth century the message was clear and Stephens, who thirty years before, had been '. . . disparaging of the power of chemistry to benefit agriculture . . .' had been partially won over to the cause. Yet the good, cautious farmer in him gave him a glimpse of future dangers.

'In reality, the regular system of breeding, and the regular system of husbandry, would both be destroyed by the reckless innovation. The mixed husbandry must therefore be maintained by a regular rotation of cropping. If extraneous food is purchased in lieu of raising a crop, the profit would be rendered dependent on the state of the markets, but the profit from the mixed husbandry is not immediately dependent on the markets, since the farmer breeds rears and feeds the same animals, and if any profit is obtainable at any period of the animal's life, he receives it. Extraneous food may assist the crop in producing a greater profit, but it may not necessarily produce a profit in lieu of a crop.'

Stephens' faith in technology was perhaps too little and he did not foresee the consequences of the Haber process for manufacturing nitrogenous fertilizers from atmospheric nitrogen which was to be invented some fifty years later. He was, therefore doubtful whether industry could ever supply sufficient specific fertilizers for all farmers.

'Such a plan cannot be generally followed,' he stated, 'for if all farmers purchased most of their manures extraneously where would the manure be found to supply them all? And if all purchased stock to consume the increased crop raised by the extraneous manures, there would be no breeders of stock, except in the pastoral districts, and these could not supply a sufficient number of animals. So that this significant fact ought not to be lost sight of by the farmer, that whenever he depends upon the resources of his own farm, he must adopt a regular course of cropping.'[1]

Stephens' *Book of the Farm* came out at a time when British farming was at a peak of productivity, brought about in no small measure by use of crop rotations, good soil drainage, and the application of an increasing quantity of South American guano and bone phosphate. Yields had risen accordingly and Stephens gives us a good account of harvests in the 1840s. Thus, we find wheat yields varying from as little as 1380 kilos per hectare (11 hundredweight per acre) to as high as 4266 kilos (34 hundredweight), barley from a low of 2000 to 4000 kilos per hectare (16 to 32 hundredweight per acre); oats from 1250 to 4770 kilos per hectare (10 to 38 hundredweight per acre);

meanwhile yields of up to 30 tonnes to the hectare could be expected for potatoes.

'It is as easy now, 1850,' said Stephens, 'to raise 32 bushels of wheat on an acre as it was 30 years ago to raise 24 bushels; to raise 54 bushels of barley as it was to raise 42 bushels, and to raise 60 bushels of oats as it was to raise 48 bushels. In like manner it is as easy to raise now wheat of the weight of 65 lb the bushel as it was then to raise it at 63 lb; barley now of 56 lb the bushel as it was then of 53 lb; and oats now of 43 lb the bushel as it was then of 40 lb.'

On that reckoning the average yields of wheat per hectare would have been 2320 kilos, of barley 3390 kilos, and of oats 2885 kilos. What is interesting is Stephens' remark that '. . . these results have been realized in the course of years, not so much from the superior as from the inferior classes of soil. The latter have increased more in fertility in that time than the former, and they became so entirely from ordinary good farming, and before the introduction of special manures.'

To put those figures in some sort of perspective: in 1960 average yields of wheat in Britain were 3700 kilos per hectare (29·5 hundred-weight per acre); of barley 3137 kilos; and of oats 2635 kilos. By 1977 they had been increased to 4890 kilos, 4617 kilos, and 4078 kilos respectively, mainly through the use of new short-stalked, high-yielding varieties and the application of large quantities of chemical fertilizer. Moreover, it must be appreciated that if the straw is taken into account, the older varieties are then as productive.

The fortunes of British farming depended very much on the political situation applying at the time in question. During wars farmers were exhorted to greater efforts to produce food and overcome the effects of blockades; when the war was over there was excess production and a slump. Such a slump followed the Napoleonic wars, but the new improvements in farming were beginning to make themselves felt and, despite both the Corn Laws and rapid population growth, British farmers kept pace with demand and even produced a surplus. Thus, Britain was producing an excess of wheat until the mid-1830s and prices were accordingly low.

After 1850 the situation improved; home-grown wheat could no longer meet demand and yet imports were still small enough not to bring prices down. Meanwhile, in 1848, Caird published his pamphlet *High Farming . . . the Best Substitute for Protection* in which he advocated the use of fertilizer to boost output. By then more than 100 000 tonnes of guano were being imported into the country, while superphosphates were being generated from the coprolite deposits in Cambridgeshire and from bones treated with sulphuric acid.

Between 1870 and 1901 the population in Britain rose by ten million and Britain's dependency on imports of cereals, especially wheat, grew commensurately. No longer could British wheat prices by sustained and they began to fall drastically until they received another boost in World War I. Then they began to fall tumultuously, reaching an abysmal low in the mid-1930s. What happened to the price of wheat compared to the price of bread is remarkable. In 1800 wheat was priced at 84·85 shillings the quarter; in 1810 the figure was 102·45 shillings; in 1850, it had dropped to 49·03 shillings; in 1900 it was 27·37 shillings, in 1915, during the war, it was up to 66·55 shillings and in 1930 right down to 5·97 shillings. Bread meanwhile was costing 11·7 pence per 4 lb loaf in 1850, and only 7·3 pence in 1930. Thus, overall wheat prices fluctuated over a fifteen-fold range while bread prices only halved.

Given such poor returns for their labour and investment in the late 1890s and in the 1930s it was hardly surprising that farmers should have turned their backs on the high-farming methods of their immediate predecessors. In Essex, for example, where wheat grew superbly on the heavy clay soil and which traditionally was the granary of the home counties, the cost of cereal growing proved too great for the farmers and they sold out, their place being taken by Scots who ranched their cattle over land which soon reverted to scrub.

It is against the backcloth of that terrible era of British farming in the 1930s that today's successes in boosting yields are primarily measured. In fact, the high-farming techniques of the mid-nineteenth century have now come absolutely into their own, and only a few aberrant farmers do not use chemicals on their land. Expenditure tell its own story. In 1949 farmers spent just over £36 million on fertilizers, four years later the figure had increased to £61 million, by 1970 it had almost trebled again, and in 1977 it was £436 million – a twelve-fold increase overall. Furthermore, farmers paid £354 million for feeding stuffs in 1960 and five times that in 1977.

What about their returns? Between 1960 and 1977 the farming net income increased three-and-a-half times to £1360 million and, for the immediate future, there are no signs of any recession. Clearly modern agriculture has become a successful economic venture; indeed, the value of land would not be able to escalate at its present rate if that were not so. Furthermore, it would seem that any alteration of the present farming strategy would be counterproductive and likely to lead to an unacceptable decline in the quantities of food produced in Britain. As for the farmers and farm workers, they now expect a similarly high standard of living to their brethren in the city, and it surely will not be many more years before the basic weekly wage for a farm worker is over £100.

Since self-sufficient farmers draw the line at using chemicals and at bringing in feedstuffs how ever will they be able to maintain any kind of productivity? Would not the result of any such attempt give rise to the contradictory effect of Britain becoming even shorter of food than ever before and having to import even greater quantities?

The answer lies in part, in a change in diet, or at least a shift. Indeed, one of the cries from the developing countries, especially India, at the 1974 World Food Conference in Rome, was that far more food would be available in the world if the millions of tonnes of fishmeal, oil seeds, and cereals currently being stuffed into livestock to fatten them for western consumption, could instead be directed straight to man. When animal or vegetable protein is fed to livestock at least 80 per cent is lost in the conversion. When man follows on, and consumes his own share of animal protein the loss is again 80 per cent and out of the original protein the overall loss is therefore 96 per cent. Professor Georg Borgstrom evaluates a country's ability to feed itself not by the food coming off the farms but by the total number of acres required to produce that food. Since feedstuffs are imported, then the area required is greater than that used in the country in question. Borgstrom calls those foreign acres 'ghost acres' since they never appear in official data on farm production. In his book *World Food Resources*, Borgstrom tells us '. . . most urban Americans rarely give thought to the fact that each one of them is dependent for food on 1·8 acres of tilled land and 3·2 acres of pastures and grazing lands. The British and Dutch boast about their higher yields and pride themselves that they need far less, merely 0·34 and 0·18 acre of tilled soil and 0·55 and 0·26 acre of pastures respectively. But these ratios as misleading half-truths. Both Britain and Holland depend on huge acreages in the North American prairies, in Argentina, in tropical Africa, and in Oceania. In the United Kingdom these non-visible acreages represent, in terms of domestic yields, 0·75 acre per person, or more than twice the tilled land of England; in Holland about 50 per cent more or 0·29 acre per person.'

Whether Britain or Holland can continue to rely on vast imports of feedstuff for their livestock is somewhat doubtful given increasing pressure on food resources all over the world; nor can Britain shrug off famine in India when its own food affluence depends in part on that continent. Furthermore, the EEC farming community is not in favour of the British farmer's bent for stocking his farms well above their carrying capacity and is threatening to penalize milk production in Britain on that account.

One argument for the continuance of food imports, apart from their 'beneficial' effect on the exporting country's balance of payments, is that the introduction of chemical farming in the exporting country will increase substantially its own food production. But Stephens' strictures about fertilizer shortage might then really begin to manifest themselves. Indeed, there is evidence that as a consequence of the 1973 hike in oil prices, ensuing oil embargoes and present-day petroleum supply problems, such shortages have already hit countries such as India which have been implementing the Green Revolution. The Green Revolution is based on the use of high yielding varieties of crops such as rice and wheat and large applications of fertilizer. Thus it is no more than the high farming of Europe or America translated into Asian terms. But the social consequences of the Green Revolution are disastrous. Only wealthy landowners can afford for the most part to make the transition from traditional farming; moreover, the new crops demand modern techniques which are in essence labour-saving. The result is that millions are displaced from the land and throng to the overcrowded cities. Professor Fred Cottrell of the University of Miami estimated in the mid-1950s that an increase in the average holding size in the more fertile parts of India and south-east Asia from the traditional 0·6 hectare (1·5 acres) per family to 10 hectares (25 acres) per family, would cause thirty million people to be displaced.

Another drawback is that seeds for the high-yielding hybrids have to be acquired from plant-breeding stations for each new crop, since their yields drop below those of traditional varieties if used in a second generation. The hybrids are also susceptible to disease, the control of which requires costly chemical spraying. Finally, the farmer is dependent on imported fertilizer since indigenous fertilizer production is usually far below that required for the country as a whole.

Calculations of the amount of nitrogen fixation which occurs naturally in the terrestial world indicate that it amounts to some 140 million tonnes each year. Already man is pouring on to the ground an additional fifty to sixty million tonnes a year, yet for all that, his nutritional requirements for nitrogen in the form of palatable protein amount to no more than nine million tonnes a year. Moreover, if agronomists have their way and industry can respond, by 2010 the plan is to increase the yearly application of nitrogen by a factor of four.

Scientists are now discovering the environmental consequences of applying nitrogenous fertilizers. Professor Barry Commoner and his colleagues at the Centre for the Biology of Natural Systems have studied fertilizer run-off from farms in Illinois, and they find a large proportion getting into waterways where it causes eutrophication. As Commoner points out, corn yields have risen significantly since 1945 when fertilizers first came into use on a large scale. Production has thereby increased from an average of 42 hectolitres per hectare (47 bushels per acre) in 1945 to about 77 hectolitres (86 bushels) in 1966 when approximately 78 kilograms of nitrogen per hectare (69 lb/acre) were being added. Since 1966 the average nitrogen application has doubled, yet the yields have risen only 5 hectolitres per hectare to 82 (91 bushels).

What has happened to the excess nitrogen? 'The relationship is strikingly non-linear,' says Commoner in *Ambio*. 'Up to an application rate of about 22–28 kg of nitrogen per hectare of watershed, river nitrate concentrations remain at about the level typical of natural rivers in those parts of the state not affected by agriculture – i.e. about one ppm of nitrate nitrogen. Where the rates of application exceed this level, the river nitrate concentration rises sharply, tending to exceed the acceptable concentration of 10 ppm (in the spring months) when the local rate of application is about 56 kg per hectare of watershed, no more.'

Commoner's study has its conclusions supported by the United States Environmental Protection Agency, which carried out a survey of 473 watersheds in the eastern half of the US and found that streams draining agricultural regions had concentrations of nitrogen which were more than ten times higher than streams draining forested areas.

There is a number of hazards associated with the excess nitrogren draining off agricultural land. Water with high nitrate levels can be toxic, causing methaemoglobinaemia or deoxygenation of the blood in babies – hence 'blue babies'; it can lead to nitrosamine formation in the gut, nitrosamines being carcinogenic; perhaps even more bizarre, excess nitrogen can lead to a diminution of the ozone layer through complex stratospheric reactions involving nitrogen oxides. Given the large quantities of nitrogen fertilizer likely to be used in the next century, it is conceivable that the ozone layer could shrink by as much as 8 per cent which itself would result in a 15 per cent increase in ultraviolet radiation at ground level. How life would be affected by such dramatic change is not clearly known, but it would hardly be advantageous. Other effects of nitrogen application are a depression of the activity of natural nitrogen fixers, increased soil erosion because of changes in the style of farming and consequent losses of soil humus, quality loss in the food being produced, (cereals, for example, tend to have a lower protein content than older varieties), and the socio-economic effects of agroindustrial farming in areas with a history of traditional farms based on the recycling of organic waste.

Because of the immediate good results obtained with chemicals, the farming world and its advisers have lost sight of the inexplicable rejuvenation of the soil brought about by allowing it to 'rest'. Those of the organic farm movement have often been accused of resorting to muck and magic, but there are sound empirical results to support their sticking fast to non-chemical farming. Indeed, a simple experiment carried out in the 1950s by the Soil Association on its farm at Haughley, Suffolk, indicated that the levels of nitrogen, phosophorus, and potassium in the soil could vary as much as ten-fold depending on the time of year. Furthermore, the researchers found the most variation – and the highest levels – on the plot dressed with organic manure, and the least on the plot kept free of animals and treated with NPK fertilizer.

Newman Turner, who had developed his own brand of organic farming at that time, based primarily on what he termed the deep-rooting herbal ley system, was scathing of the practice of farmers having their soil tested and then adjusting their fertilizer application accordingly. 'With fields of my size,' he said in *Fertility Pastures*, if a test were taken in January, I should have to spend perhaps another £100 more if I believed the salesman than if he had done his analysis in June or July when the phosphates and potash were up. It is much cheaper for me to wait till I have farmed the minerals into an available condition in my soil, than to buy them in synthetic form because the genuine organic potash and phosphates happen to be "out" the day the analyst calls.'

Like other organic farmers, Newman Turner is incredulous of the notion that soil fertility can be maintained by simple additions of chemicals based on some laboratory reckoning of a crop's requirements.

A crop of wheat of two tonnes, 250 kilograms to the hectare (2 hundredweight/acre) (which Turner obtained by organic methods) takes from the land 23 kilos (50 pounds) of nitrogen, 13 kilos (28·75 pounds) of potash, 9·5 kilos (21 pounds) of phosphoric acid, and 4·2 kilos (9·2 pounds) of calcium, even though the straw is returned to the land. 'In theory,' said Turner in *Fertility Farming*, 'by not using artificial fertilizers and not importing feedstuffs to my farm, I am exhausting its fertility.' But, as he explains, land in good heart contains many times more than the quantity of minerals required for a single growing season, and quotes the famous Broadbalk Field at Rothamstead. 'After bearing wheat for one hundred years with no manure of any kind and an average yield of 12½ bushels per acre ... still contains in its topsoil 2500 lb of nitrogen, 2750 lb of phosphoric acid and 6750 lb of potash. The next nine inches probably has nearly as much and a deep-rooting herb or a tree root going down as far as six feet can tap untold reserves.'

The basis of fertility farming is to create the conditions in the soil whereby the minerals locked away in it are made available in sufficient quantities to produce large healthy crops without the addition of artificial chemical top dressings. In the middle 1940s and into the '50s, men such as Newman Turner, Friend Sykes, and Arthur Hollins were deeply concerned at the consequences upon farming of the pressures exerted on farmers by the Agricultural War Committee and, by writing their own experiences, they tried to stem the swing towards chemical farming. All three were advocates of using deep-rooting herbal leys as the basis of their farm's fertility, rotating the ley after a period of four or more years with other crops. In general they found dramatic improvements in the soil and in the health and yields of their livestock.

Since grass, herbs, and clover are the basis of fertility in such organic farming, herbivores are a necessary step in bringing about the conversion of what for humans would otherwise be an inedible crop. Indeed Turner, Sykes, and Hollins all ran dairy herds. The vegetarians, who comprise no mean proportion of those seeking self-sufficiency, may find the idea of creating fertility out of herbal leys and livestock distasteful to them and would prefer a purely vegetarian system, or one which if it does use animal manure, gets it from humans. At first sight the vegetarians have some justification in their attitude. Thus, in Britain today, no more than 8·3 per cent of all farm land provides vegetable food for direct human consumption, the remaining 92 per cent being used for cereal growing and for livestock. Gerald Leach has calculated that the small amount under vegetable cultivation provides as much food for human beings in straight energy terms as the whole of the area given over to feeding livestock. 'In other words,' he says, 'farm animals in the UK use land resources which could, theoretically feed around 250 million people on an all cereal and vegetable diet.'

Leach himself is not advocating vegetarianism, he is simply illustrating a point, that Britain could be far more self-sufficient in food than it is. Yet he is assuming that vegetable growing will also be based on the application of chemical fertilizers, pesticides, and herbicides, and omits to mention that vegetarians are more likely to want organically grown foodstuffs. Leach advocates a move towards more dairying since '... the protein output would be 2·5 million tonnes, exceeding present consumption by nearly 50 per cent. The UK would therefore be more than 100 per cent self-sufficient for temperate zone foods. The energy output for supplying all food unprocessed would then be in the area of 309 MGJ rather than the 670 MGJ consumed by UK agriculture, fisheries, and food imports in 1968. All rough grazing would be left for the production of sheep and beef cattle.'

In order to produce Britain's self-sufficiency in temperate zone foods, Leach has postulated getting rid of factory farms and of systems like barley-beef, in which animals are fattened under intensive conditions. Presumably, too, by advocating greater dairying he is suggesting crop rotations and the use of grassland, yet Leach has by no means gone far down 'the small is beautiful' road. Rather, he proposes still larger farm units than are generally found today, because of their higher efficiencies in the use of energy inputs.

In fact Leach has overlooked the smallholding of 8 hectares (20 acres) or so, such as exist in abundance in counties such as Cornwall, where a family can still make a good living out of dairying – typically with Jersey cows. The productivity in terms of output of such farms is often extraordinarily high, much higher in fact than is usually found on large modern farms; moreover the costs of running the small farms are relatively low since there is less pressure to cover areas quickly with tractors and machinery. Those farming in such a way undoubtedly live more modestly than those owning large farms, and probably more so than the average farm worker, yet they claim they live well enough, and furthermore with a feeling of their own freedom and independence. Few perhaps are organic since they generally use chemical fertilizers, and undoubtedly buy in feedstuffs. Nevertheless, their example gives the lie to the notion that farmers must farm 80 hectares (200 acres) and more to make a living.

Thus, there are many different farming systems, and many different techniques from digging sticks, hoes, and sickles to ten-furrow ploughs, cultivators, and combine harvesters, and those seeking self-sufficiency must decide what system best suits their own purposes given the particular environment in which they find themselves. It is hardly possible in Britain, for example, to return to a swidden-type farming in which forested areas or scrub are cut and burnt, used for several years to be then abandoned, nor would one advocate leaving land fallow in the traditional sense, since crop rotations provide a productive alternative. Undoubtedly, too, the self-sufficient farmer will steer as clear as he can of an 'open-ended' system of farming in which he imports chemicals and feedstuffs on to the farm, for that kind of farming blatantly defies the principles of self-sufficiency. Moreover, it leads to a degradation of the soil, nitrogen run-off, and a balance of payments problem at the bank. The organic alternative on the other hand is increasingly a good one, even for those farmers who unhesitatingly use the latest machines. Thus, Barry Commoner's group at the Centre for the Biology of Natural Systems has investigated the economics of organic versus conventional farms in Illinois in the corn belt. The study compared the operation of a group of fourteen large-scale, commercial 'organic' farms averaging about 193 hectares (476 acres) that use no nitrogen fertilizer at all and no pesticides with matched control farms that use nitrogen fertilizer and pesticides. Both groups of farms were mixed crop and livestock and consequently were different from most farms in Illinois which commonly produce only grain. Both groups of farms also used equivalent amounts of machines and labour per hectare.

Two years were covered and the average yields on organic farms for soybeans, oats, wheat, and corn were 100 per cent, 95 per cent, 82 per cent, and 87 per cent respectively of the yields on the matched conventional farms. Overall the gross income of the organic farms per hectare of crop production was 90 per cent of the gross income of the conventional farms. But costs on the organic farm were lower since no nitrogen fertilizer was applied, and the net income was identical at 329 dollars per hectare (133 dollars/acre). As fertilizer and pesticide costs rise, the organic farm is bound to gain a relative net increase in income, especially if prices of crops at the gate are governed by the increased cost of conventional farming.

But farming need not be done with modern machines and technology to be productive. It can be just as effective or even better with simple tools. Oscar Lewis, an American anthropologist, stayed for long periods at the village of Tepozlan in Mexico and studied the different farming systems which were then in operation. Basically there were two types of farmer – the more wealthy who owned the best land, employed peones (peasants), and used oxen for ploughing and other field work, and the poor peasants who worked the more marginal land with hoes and other hand tools. Lewis reported that

. . . a comparison of the yields of the two types of agriculture reveals that hoe culture yields are equal to the best yields in plough culture and are generally about twice as high as the average yields of plough culture.'

In *Energy and Society*, Professor Fred Cottrell makes the point that hoe culture can produce more food from a given land area and more surplus energy than mechanized farming. 'As a matter of fact,' he says, 'hoe culture can more effectively make use of scientific practices as plant and seed selection, the selective application of fertiliser and insecticides than can machine cultivation. Thus once the techniques are developed more food and more energy can be produced from a unit of land without machines than with them . . . it appears that if the objective is to secure support of the largest possible population, hand methods of intensive cultivation provide the answer.'

Cottrell's statement is not far from the truth. Harris estimated that Chinese wet rice agriculture could produce 53·5 British thermal units (Btu) of energy for each Btu of human energy expended in farming it. In Switzerland a co-operative of some 700 small organic farmers, many of whom avoid the use of tractor-drawn machinery are not only able to produce as much food on their farms compared with their neighbours', they are able, through the co-operative, to market it at more or less the same prices in the supermarkets – thus exploding the myth that organically grown food must *ipso facto* be dearer than food produced through a system of high-energy inputs. One reason why organic farmers in Britain had to put higher prices to their products in the past was because they were competing with farmers who received a fertilizer subsidy. They have also had difficulties forming a viable marketing system. Swiss organic farmers have a number of advantages over their British counterparts. They live in a small country with an efficient rail and postal system, and their farms tend to be run by families.

The main trend in Britain is away from the small family farm; rather it is towards a highly commercial venture encompassing very large areas. Efficiency is measured by the units of food produced per man-hour of work, and here Britain is one of the most efficient countries in the world, yet no account is taken of 'ghost' areas abroad or of high fertilizer inputs the manufacture of which is based on non-renewable resources. Those who have small farms or gardens and who rigorously apply organic methods will know that they are highly productive; moreover relatively new techniques to Britain, such as the French intensive biodynamic method in which garden plots are deep dug, have shown that perhaps more than double the yield can be obtained from a given area than with conventional gardening methods. With knowledge, increased experience, the seeking of self-sufficiency should be able to make a very worthwhile contribution towards the problem of Britain being able to feed itself.

*

Soren Kierkegaard, who loved Christianity but hated priests, once asked whether all the priests would resign if it were proved beyond any doubt that Jesus never existed as an historical personage. Kierkegaard believed that in such circumstances the priests ought to resign, but that they were unlikely to do so because they would not willingly abdicate their wealth and power. The question has been asked many times and it is an interesting one. If Christianity depends entirely on the veracity of the life of Jesus as this is recounted in the New Testament, then clearly the exposure of that account as falsehood must invalidate the religion constructed upon it. On the other hand, if Christianity expounds an absolute truth regarding the relationship between man and the Universe, then such truth cannot be invalidated. An absolute truth is absolutely true, by definition, and it matters little how it was obtained. In this case the abandonment of the New Testament story might be traumatic, but it would not necessarily invalidate the religion founded not so much upon it as upon a deeper truth contained in it or derived from it. What is more, unless the religion expounds, or is believed by its adherents to expound, such absolute truth, it is essentially trivial. If we allow – and Kierkegaard probably would not – that a religion is entitled to employ priests, then the discovery that Jesus never lived would not be sufficient ground for requiring priests to resign. Either the religion would survive, even if modified, or it does not deserve to exist at all.

There are grave dangers in basing a movement upon purely technical arguments, especially where these arguments amount to a critique of some aspect of existing society. In the case of agriculture, for example, the criticisms advanced by Peter can be answered. If they are answered, does the case for alternatives fall? I think not, but to defend it I must shift the argument away from techniques and, indeed, away from agriculture altogether.

It is true that agriculture in the industrial countries has come to depend heavily on imported petroleum. This is a ground for criticism but only up to a point. In many cases the bargain is a good one and where it is not, it is possible to predict improvements.

Consider the tractor. It has displaced the horse and, before that, the teams of oxen that, surprisingly, remained in use in parts of Britain – such as Cornwall – well into this century. Of course, energy is used in its manufacture and use and it is fuelled by petroleum. However, its introduction has released land that formerly was used exclusively to feed draught animals. This is land that now feeds humans, so that in this case fossil fuels have been used directly to purchase food that otherwise would not have been obtainable.

Nitrogen fertilizers, too, are derived from petroleum or, more usually from natural gas. The problems that may attend their use have been overstated. True, fertilizers can and do leach into water as nitrates to raise nitrate levels above those that occur inevitably from the leaching of nitrates present naturally. It is difficult to say with any certainty the extent to which their introduction has raised agricultural yields. Comparisons with records from the past can be made only with great difficulty, for at best they are sparse and there is a tendency to compare the best of past yields with the average of present yields. Many nineteenth-century writers, including William Cobbett, have referred to yields of 2 tons of wheat to the acre but, apart from the fact that Cobbett was never the most reliable of reporters, such yields seem to have been exceptional. Furthermore, the 'acre' and the 'ton' were not defined absolutely until late in the nineteenth century and while this involved no great change for units of weight it did involve changes for the acre, whose size varied quite widely from one part of the country to another. Probably the best comparisons can be made where farmers grow crops alongside other farmers growing similar crops under similar conditions, one group using fertilizers and the other relying on 'organic' methods. Here it seems that the organic farmers achieve yields that are rather lower than those achieved with the use of fertilizers, but less dramatically so than many agricultural scientists might have expected. This implies not that nitrogen fertilizers contribute little that is useful, but that they are being used wastefully. Much of the fertilizer that is used fails to reach the crop and it is here that improvements can be made.

Even herbicides, most of which are products of the petrochemical industry, have been shown to be more efficient in their deployment of energy than alternatives to them based on mechanical or hand weeding.

We should not underrate the agricultural productivity of British farms, which yield annually more food than those of Australia and New Zealand combined. Nor should we assume that since the United Kingdom is a substantial net importer of food its imports derive from developing countries where they might be better used to feed the hungry. Such assumptions are doubly false. In the first place Britain does not import large amounts of food from developing countries and, if it were to become more self-sufficient in food, it does not follow that this would release food for those who need it most. In 1978, Britain imported 1 per cent of its beef and veal from Argentina, 82 per cent of its corned beef from South America and 2 per cent from Kenya, 4 per cent of its oilcake and meal from India and 1 per cent from Senegal, 9 per cent of its oils and fats from Malaysia, 9 per cent of its sugar from the West Indies, 6 per cent from Fiji and 17 per cent from Turkey. The only product for which we depend on developing countries for most of our imports is corned beef, and the amount involved is minute. The 1978 total amounts to about 54 million tonnes, which is around 4 per cent of our total annual supply of fresh beef and veal. Indeed, one of the criticisms that is sometimes advanced against the present world economic system is that there is too little trade between developed and developing countries, that if the rich were to buy more from the poor, the poor would become less poor. The best studies that have been made of the world food situation suggest that before the end of this century it will have been resolved by each country becoming completely self-reliant in food, either growing sufficient food for its own needs or paying for the import of food it cannot grow. This suggests that the total volume of world trade in food will decrease, and that there is not much we can do that will affect the trend. Where people are hungry it is invariably because they are poor and never because food cannot be supplied plentifully to those able to pay for it.

What, though, of the argument that an industry that depends so heavily on petroleum cannot be considered stable? The first answer is that dependent on petroleum though agriculture is, its total consumption is rather small as a proportion of total national consumption. The problem over resource shortages occurs not as a result of exhaustion but because competition for limited supplies bids up prices and produces economic disruptions. It is advisable, therefore, for such dependence to be reduced to avoid the disruptions. Agriculture is not able to contribute a great deal in this situation, and should there be genuine shortages in supply farmers could be given high priority. There is much they can and, in the next few years probably will, do though, to improve the efficiency with which they use energy of all kinds. We are likely to see a progressive reduction in the use of nitrogen fertilizer. Work on the fixation of nitrogen by biological means is well advanced, as one of the many biotechnologies that will become more prominent in the final years of this century. Biologically fixed nitrogen requires no fossil fuel of any kind, it is likely to supply nutrient more precisely to the crop so that losses are reduced, and the energy it uses comes almost wholly from the Sun. As this new technique is introduced in the developed countries, fertilizer manufacturers may look more closely to developing countries as potential markets, and eventually biologically fixed nitrogen may replace industrially fixed nitrogen almost completely in all countries. This would remove one resource objection to the expansion of agriculture in developing countries. Most of the problems of resistance and pollution caused by pesticides can be attributed to the methods by which the pesticides are sprayed. More sophisticated methods of integrated control, based on more detailed knowledge of the life cycle of the target organisms, coupled with more efficient spraying machines, are likely to reduce pesticide use substantially but without forfeiting the protection that pesticides have promised and sometimes given. Ultra-low-volume sprayers, for example, are sold for about one-tenth the price of conventional sprayers, they use between one-tenth and one-hundredth the amount of pesticide, and they are so much more efficient that fewer applications are needed. In years to come farmers will produce much more energy on the farm for use on the farm. Already some American farmers produce alcohol and add it to their tractor fuel, and the digester that can produce methane reliably from animal slurry on a farm scale has now been made to work in temperate climates. Its most sensible use is to generate electricity.

I find such developments attractive as well as optimistic, in the sense that they promise a degree of liberation from dependence on costly imported materials. I think, though, that their deeper significance lies in the fact that they are inherently democratic. The most telling criticism of modern agriculture is that for a generation or more it has grown increasingly elitist. Tractors are expensive, fertilizers are expensive, pesticides are expensive, and only prosperous farmers can afford them. The new technologies promise real economies that should make them available to farmers with less capital to invest. In this way they may overcome the single largest obstacle that lies in the way of improving yields from agriculture in the tropics and subtropics.

They are, then, technologies that may well appeal to the self-provider, They are designed to increase the level of self-sufficiency of those who use them. Yet they represent achievements of high technology and they are addressed to the future of farming, not to its past.

The environmental and self-sufficiency movements have been much influenced by a romanticized view of rural life set in some imagined golden age. There was no such golden age, and despite the criticisms of modern farming there are some ways in which it has improved greatly the quality of rural life. In the days when all farming depended on horses, farm workers were not paid for the hours they spent preparing the horses and their equipment for work, and removing and cleaning it, and grooming and feeding the horses at the end of the day. This was additional to the actual farming, and workers did it in their own time. The tractor freed them from that. We must remember that the drift of population from rural areas to nineteenth-century industrial cities, and the similar drift that occurs today in other countries, was and is due to the uncomfortable fact that conditions in the cities were and are better than conditions in the countryside. The romantic view of rural life is derived largely from such writers as Cobbett, who was nostalgic for a still earlier period, and who, in any case, at one time had views that were reactionary even by the standards of the early nineteenth century. Later he became a democrat. He did not believe that the children of the working classes should be educated, even to the stage of basic literacy, if this encourages the young worker to seek to change his place in society. 'I must hear a great deal more than I ever have yet heard, to convince me, that teaching children to *read* tends so much to their happiness, their independence of spirit, their manliness of character, as teaching them to reap.' And again, 'The *education* that I have in view is, therefore, of a very different kind (from formal education in schools). You should bear constantly in mind, that nine-tenths of us are, from the very nature and necessities of the world, born to gain our livelihood by the sweat of our brow. What reason have we, then, to presume, that our children are not to do the same? If they be, as now and then one will be, endued with extraordinary powers of mind, those powers may have an opportunity of developing themselves; and if they never have that opportunity, the harm is not very great to us or to them.' Such views fall strangely on the ears of those brought up to believe that each individual should be allowed freedom to develop and so make such contribution to society as he or she is able to make.

Perhaps, though, the nineteenth century was not typical and the centuries that preceded it saw better living conditions for the poor, and greater opportunities for personal development? It may be, as Peter suggests, that the fourteenth century provided such conditions. We must remember, though, that in 1348 Britain was invaded by bubonic plague, 'The Great Pestilence'. Now bubonic plague is associated, invariably, with poor living conditions. Today it is most likely to occur in the overcrowded cities of Asia in which sanitary conditions are poor. It is a disease of great poverty, and in the fourteenth century it struck first and hardest at the unhygienic and overcrowded quarters in medieval towns, the places that provided congenial conditions for *Rattus rattus*. It affected the wealthy much less, because they lived in more substantial houses built from stone and, in the countryside, it struck only here and there not because the housing of the poor was any better, but because the houses themselves were more scattered. I fear that the search for any golden age in the past is doomed to failure, unless we restrict its benefits to the rich.

But industrialization brought a fundamental change to manufacturing as well as agriculture. The change was a product of the development of capitalism and the expansion of trade. Goods came to be produced for trade rather than for use and labour became a commodity to be bought and sold in a market governed by impersonal economic forces. While the peasantry of former times were often oppressed and dealt with harshly, while there could be no question of their enjoying equality with the aristocracy in any aspect of their lives, while society did not pretend to any kind of democracy or fairness of treatment, at least oppression was possible because there was a human being to be oppressed. Perhaps the only right the individual enjoyed was the right to his or her human status. Inhumanity could be denounced as inhumanity. When the individual became the worker, and when the worker became identified as no more than a unit of labour, that humanity was forfeited. Slavery was denounced because it was inhuman but it was abandoned because it became economically inefficient. People became things, and employers were exhorted to improve working conditions not because this was their moral responsibility but because only by doing so could they maintain a high operating efficiency. This is the source of modern alienation.

The situation changed, of course, as material living standards rose. The fundamental injustice of the system was masked and later it became modified. World War II brought together men and women from different social backgrounds and so improved understanding. There was a widespread realization of the living conditions under which the majority of people were doomed to spend their days. Some sense returned of the responsibility of a society for the welfare of its members.

Almost by definition, 'self-sufficiency' or even 'do-it-yourself' implies a change to an economy that produces goods for use rather than for trading. The change is in emphasis only, of course. A trading economy also produces things to be used, and a 'use' economy does not abandon trade. The difference is that the purpose of production is the formation of things that people need rather than of things that can be traded. Since such a 'use' economy existed prior to the beginning of industrialization, perhaps it is natural that people should look to some period before the eighteenth century for their inspiration. To do so is dangerous, as I have tried to show, because oppression of the poor is not a satisfactory substitute for alienation of the worker, and because there is no point in the past that does not contain the tendency to develop towards the present. Even if we could return to a pre-industrial society there is no guarantee that we would not merely begin the process of industrialization all over again.

We must move forward, then, to a society in which all human activity is aimed towards the direct benefit of the individuals comprising that society, a society that restores human status to the human being but that does so without oppression. In this evolutionary process the ideas that lie at the centre of the self-sufficiency and environmental movements may provide the basis for the construction of a new political philosophy. It is on this ground that I would defend the movements and I think their manifestations extend far beyond agriculture. I would argue that 'self-sufficiency' is, more than anything, an attitude, a set of beliefs and values. Without this attitude the self-sufficient smallholder risks becoming just one more of the farmers Peter criticizes. With this attitude, I believe the 'self-provider' need make very little with his or her own hands.

Yet times have changed. Today our society claims to be democratic and we must consider whether dissidents exist only because of the tolerance of their fellow citizens. Is it possible to place too great a strain on that tolerance? To what extent is it permissible to change society from within?

5 What kind of world?

In an earlier chapter Peter suggested that the behaviour of large corporations and state monopolies is undemocratic. He meant by this that large organizations controlled by individuals appointed from within those organizations, and so not elected by the public, have no constituency. Their activities must be designed to benefit the organization and, if public benefit also follows from them, this is in some way a by-product, and incidental. In some spheres of life this may be of mere academic interest since it involves matters that barely impinge on the daily lives of ordinary people. In most cases, though, lives are affected directly or indirectly. The allocation of capital for investment, the kind of goods produced, the terms on which they are offered for sale, are outside the control of the ordinary citizen and to this extent individual freedom is curtailed. What is more important, the distribution of power within society, and so the political structure of society, is modified.

Peter has chosen to use agriculture as the most obvious example of an area in which those who seek to become self-sufficient may begin and, if we continue with this example, to compare food that a group of smallholders or a small community may grow for itself with the alternative that is offered commercially, some interesting and disturbing facts emerge.

Let us consider first the small community that has the use of an adequate area of land. Let us suppose that not all the members of the community are farmers or gardeners, but the community is small enough for everyone to know everyone else. Although there are, in respect of food, producers and consumers, the two sections of the community are close to one another. Within the physical limitations of the local environment it would seem to present no great problem for the producers to supply the consumers with an adequate amount of food and with the range of individual food items that people wish to eat. This range can be both wide and subtle. It may include, for example, not merely potatoes and onions, but many different varieties of potatoes and onions to cater for different tastes. People would be able to choose 'floury' or 'waxy' potatoes. Different potatoes might be grown for boiling, baking, roasting, frying, or for making into crisps. Onions would be large or small, mild or strong in flavour, and a similar range of choices might be extended to all other produce. To achieve this desirable situation we need do nothing more than devise a means for the consumers to make their preferences known far enough in advance for the producers to be able to respond, and for the producers to explain to the consumers such physical constraints as may make certain choices impractical. If we go a little further and allow the community to produce a surplus of some marketable commodity, we can extend their diet to include items they cannot grow for themselves, but which they can obtain by trading. Within this model we do not need to suppose an economy that uses no money, or one in which workers are not paid for their labour. People may choose to restrict the use of money, and on such a small scale it may be convenient for them to do so, but it does not imply a necessary departure from the conventional economic arrangements or media of exchange. Just because consumers are in close contact with producers it does not follow that they do not pay for their food in cash. The change that would bring about such a close relationship is mainly political, not economic.

If we consider now the situation that actually obtains in Britain, and probably in most advanced industrial societies, we find it is very different. The food industry is highly integrated and while the shopper may gain the impression that the goods in the supermarket are competing, the impression is largely illusory. Seventy per cent of the margarine on sale in British shops, 74 per cent of the frozen vegetables, 41 per cent of the ice cream, 63 per cent of the frozen fish, and 24 per cent of the sausages are produced by Unilever. Eighty-seven per cent of all breakfast cereals are produced by three companies, Kelloggs, Weetabix, and the National Biscuit Company. Ninety-one per cent of our bread is produced by three companies, Rank Hovis McDougall, Associated British Foods, and Spillers-French. Seventy-seven per cent of our canned soup is produced by either Heinz or Crosse and Blackwell. Eighty-five per cent of our sugar is provided either by Tate and Lyle or by the British Sugar Corporation. The list can be extended much further, but it is enough to show that the contents of the supermarket shelves are under the firm control of a very few corporations that are not answerable to the public or to any representative of the public.

The industry defends itself by insisting that the word of the consumer is its law. After all, no one is compelled to buy a particular food item and lines that prove unpopular must be withdrawn. Thus, the public gets the food it wants. Or does it? The Politics of Health Group, which comprises more than a hundred doctors, dentists, nurses, nutritionists, and other health and social workers operating in association with the British Society for Social Responsibility in Science has attacked what it calls 'the myth of consumer sovereignty'. It points out that to allow the consumer a genuinely free choice certain assumptions must be made. The food people prefer must be easily available to them, they must have the time, equipment and facilities to prepare it, they must be able to afford it, and their choices must be based on adequate information. 'For most of us, all this is far from the truth. For example, the time and effort required for shopping are often a problem, particularly if transport is inadequate. Small neighbourhood shops are rarely able to buy the bulk quantities for which manufacturers give discounts. The quantities in which foods are packaged are increasingly geared to family consumption and those who can afford a cash outlay, private transport and a freezer ... Then, of course, choice of food is strongly influenced by cost. White bread is cheaper than wholemeal – a fact determined by the milling industry – and more people buy it. It is claimed by the manufacturers that most people "prefer" white bread to wholemeal, and so that is what they make ...' The Group is no less critical of the information supplied to the consumer and points out that modern food processing separates the flavour and texture of food from its nutritional qualities so that the uneducated human palate, designed evolutionarily to identify nutritious foods, is no longer reliable. While the criticisms of the industry may be rather simplistic in some respects, there is much evidence that this separation of quality from the sensations by which we recognize quality leads to nutritional problems. The widespread use of sugar and fats in processed foods, for example, encourages their overconsumption by people who do not know they are consuming them. These problems are not spread evenly among the population. Contrary to another popular myth, the likelihood of a person contracting one of the degenerative 'diseases of civilization' changes in inverse proportion to his or her income and social status. An unskilled manual worker is much more likely to die prematurely from one of the so called 'stress' diseases than is a company executive. The poorer members of the community eat 55 per cent less fruit than the affluent, 20 per cent less fresh green vegetables, 30 per cent less cheese, 20 per cent less milk and 30 per cent less carcass meat, but they eat 32 per cent more sugar, and the cheaper meat products, such as pies and sausages, are more likely to contain large amounts of saturated fats.

Here, then, we have a situation in which an industry operating in a more or less free market produces adverse effects on the health of the community it serves and imposes these effects most severely on the poor. The industry is not answerable to the public either directly or by means of legislation that would restrict its activities and so, theoretically, distort the operation of the market economy. It is, as Peter suggests, undemocratic.

The matter is not trivial. Large though they are, the companies engaged in the food industry are very small when compared with some of the really big multinational corporations. General Motors, Ford, Exxon, BP, Standard Oil of California, are organizations each one of which is larger, economically, than many countries. It is a sobering thought that one of those private organizations could, at least in theory, buy a country the economic size of Saudi Arabia lock, stock, and barrel.

Now industry is not staffed by evil men and women. That is not the problem. If it were it might be dealt with more easily. The employees of large corporations are also citizens of their countries and con-sumers. As individuals, no doubt they are inspired by sentiments of the warmest affection for their fellow beings. They wish to improve the world, not to injure it. The problem is that when, collectively, they decide on a course of action, this action cannot avoid affecting directly the lives of large numbers of people who were not consulted because no mechanism exists by which they can be consulted. One of the reasons we may be certain that microprocessors will be manu-factured and used on a very large scale is that several of the big multinational corporations have invested heavily in the industries associated with them. Having decided that microprocessors will be used and that this is an appropriate area for investment, the scale on which the multinationals operate ensure that goods are produced and disseminated so that they make self-fulfilling prophecies. Governments can influence events only in minor ways. They may encourage or discourage and so alter by a matter of months the date by which a particular event occurs, but that is all. We may know, too, that the rate at which the nuclear power industry expands is influenced by the very large investment certain of the multinationals have made in the mining of uranium. It matters little whether you or I regard microprocessors or nuclear power as good or bad. That de-cision has been made for us and its results will be imposed upon us, if necessary by force.

If we would influence such decisions we must seek to do so within the multinational corporations as well as by taking action through

more conventional political channels. If we try to do so we will en-
counter the next in what promises to be an entire hierarchy of
difficulties. Being commercial organizations, corporations do not
reach their decisions in public. We have no way of knowing the
future investments they are considering and we have even less chance
of discovering just how decisions are reached and implemented. A
modern large corporation is so complex that power does not reside
at any particular place within it. There is no 'boss', 'leader', 'chairman' or 'managing director' whose word is final in the way it might
be in a smaller organization. If we were to liken the corporation to a
living organism we might say that the decision making process is
largely unconscious. The creature 'sleeps on it'. An idea may originate anywhere. It passes from office to office, receiving comments,
modifications, support, opposition, and as it does so it grows and
acquires a kind of impetus derived increasingly from the emotional
commitment of its supporters and the corporation time that has
been invested in it. Provided it is not killed outrght by some 'anti-
body' within the system, a point is reached beyond which it is almost
impossible to stop it. No one has made an overall conscious decision
on the principle of the new idea. To continue the analogy, the corporation may become conscious of it when funds are made available
for its further development and, at some later stage, the corporation
may announce it to the outside world. By that time the corporation is
committed to it, but by the time it became 'conscious' of it the idea
had already acquired great impetus. It needed such impetus to carry
it to the 'consciousness' of the organism. Although the idea could
have been killed in its early stages, these stages were not, and could
not be, accessible to anyone not directly involved.

We are led to the rather alarming conclusion that corporations
larger than many countries may be subject to only a limited form of
control, and that their behaviour may be governed by an internal and
purely economic logic. This may be mediated by the ethical code to
which their employees subscribe, but only to a limited extent. If the
multinationals do not engage in prostitution, say, or drug trafficking,
is this because their employees find such activities repulsive or is it
because the legal and administrative difficulties that would be encountered render these activities commercially unattractive? The
example may sound extreme, but it would not sound extreme to
suggest that their commitment to western democracy, to the 'free
world', and their hatred of totalitarianism would be sufficiently
strong to inhibit employees from involving their corporations in investment in certain countries. They might object to doing business

inside the USSR, for example, or the People's Republic of China, or Zimbabwe Rhodesia, or South Africa. They are active in all these countries and it is fair to say that the only countries in which they are not active are those from which they have been excluded or in which they see no resource to be exploited or market to be developed.

So we are brought back to our group of people living in a community that is more or less self-sufficient, and we must look more closely at the way in which they govern themselves compared with the system of government that obtains in the wider world outside. Is their system politically preferable? What relationship does our community have to the outside world and to what extent may it hope to influence it?

Many self-providers claim to be anarchists. That is to say, they espouse the principles of anarchism and believe they live within a system – in respect of the outside world a microsystem – in which government is unnecessary. I think this view is mistaken, and dangerously so, since the theory of anarchism contains a fatal flaw, at least if the term is interpreted in a literal fashion. This is simply that the moment a group of people act collectively they cease to act anarchically. A collective decision has been made and so a mechanism must exist for the making of that decision. This mechanism may take a variety of forms, but to deny its existence is to run the risk that what masquerades as anarchism is, in fact, dictatorship.

The fact that a philosophy contains a serious flaw is insufficient reason for dismissing it out of hand. There is no philosophy that cannot be criticized, usually for some quite naïve error. If there were, of course, philosophy would come to an end! In fact there is much in anarchist philosophy that is reasonable and attractive.

The anarchist believes that it is possible to conduct human affairs without establishing governments or institutions, without the promulgation of laws and so without need for police or courts of law to enforce those laws. Some people trace the idea back to Zeno (*circa* 334–262 or 261 BC) the philosopher from Citium in Cyprus who was one of the founders of Stoicism, whose principal exponent was Socrates. The Stoics believed in a God, or Lawgiver, who constructed the world as a single system, called Nature, to secure particular ends by natural means. Since all human beings are part of Nature they are bound to obey Natural laws, but not all of them do so willingly, and virtue consists in the willing obedience to Natural law, to the desiring of ends that are consistent with the ends to which Nature tends. Every individual contains a part of the essence of God, who is the soul of the world, and Natural law extends to the most minute detail of events. To live virtuously the individual must seek to discover Natural law and then further it. In this sense individuals are entirely free, since no outside force can take from them their awareness of Natural law or their desire to further it, provided only that the seeker after virtue has overcome all attachment to such worldly things as can be confiscated. The person who is truly virtuous can have no conception of property, for example. The result is a rather cold conception of virtue in which all passions must be subdued, including those of sympathy or love for others and, of course, the philosophy, like all philosophies, is flawed. If God is concerned only with the promotion of virtue through obedience to the laws of Nature how is it that the laws of Nature produce so many sinners? Further, cruelty, injustice, and the oppression of the weak by the strong cannot be opposed since these afford the best of all opportunities for the Stoic to practise virtue. It was the manner in which he faced his accusers and accepted his unjust conviction and death that made Socrates the foremost among Stoics.

In later centuries the philosophy became much modified because the people who adhered to it were often warm and humane in themselves and so were unable to live consistently according to its precepts. The philosophy became humanized and led eventually to most of our liberal beliefs. What was retained was the central core of Stoic belief: that man contains within himself and is guided at all times by a divine spirit tending towards good. Man is to be trusted, therefore, to behave well, provided conditions are such that his divine spirit is allowed to express itself. The idea arose again at the time of the Reformation, when the Anabaptists asserted that each individual is directly accountable to God and that daily life must be guided by personal faith. They rejected the baptism of infants and substituted a form of adult baptism in which the individual entered into a covenant with God voluntarily. They believed that the crucifixion of Jesus had atoned for the sin of Adam, so that original sin had ceased to exist and that every child was born into the world innocent and able to act virtuously or sinfully as soon as it was old enough to understand the meaning of such terms. This was a form of anarchism that emphasized personal responsibility, rejected violence as a means of imposing solutions to problems, and the Anabaptists refused to swear civil oaths or to support wars, just as many anarchists have done since. Today the descendants of the Anabaptists survive as the Mennonites and Hutterites, who live mainly in the western states and provinces of North America. They exerted great influence over the whole of Protestantism, although in the end they failed to shake the fundamentally pessimistic outlook of Christianity. The modern Quakers comprise one sect that continues to espouse their version of individualism.

The then eighteenth-century Stoic individualism assumed a secular, more political form, especially in France and England, with some subtle differences in emphases. While the post-Revolution French emphasized libertarianism and, in the writings of Rousseau, for example, the existence of natural rights, the more Protestant English emphasized natural duties. William Godwin, the most famous of the English anarchists (although he never used the term himself) urged a form of humanitarianism that anticipated in many ways the Utilitarianism of Mill and Bentham as well as the principles (though not the practice) of Marxism. He believed – and this is central – that man is infinitely perfectible and that virtue consists in the performance of natural duties and 'benevolence' based on a consideration of the general good.

'This end of the greatest general good was to be secured by the right-action-through-right-thinking of the individual, not by the intervention of the State. Godwin was against all forms of association on the ground that they obstruct progress and perpetuate evils. "Government gives substance and permanence to our errors." He hoped to see the State wither away – in this he is a Marxist . . .'

Although he modified his views later, Godwin originally proposed a society composed of small autonomous communities and a communistic distribution of property.

To this extent, historical anarchism would seem to accord well with the views of modern self-providers. Unfortunately, as I indicated earlier, there is a flaw in the concept.

Let us return to our small community and let us imagine there is some decision that must be reached that will affect everyone. We might imagine, for example, that a new communal building is to be constructed and a decision must be made regarding its location. According to strict anarchist principles, the person who first has the idea to construct the building is free to proceed. To do so, however, more than one person is needed and so the originator of the scheme must recruit others to help with the work. Each of these others is free to join or not. When it comes to selecting a site, however, different people have different opinions. A way must be found to resolve these differences.

At this point we may suppose two quite different views of 'natural' behaviour, views to which we will return later. According to the first view, each individual will seek to maximize his or her own advantage. People are inherently selfish and provided their perception of their own interest is accurate, benefit to the community will ensue. In our case such a person may wish the building to be placed either very close to or very far from his or her private dwelling. The other view holds that people tend to collaborate and maximize the communal advantage. They are inherently altruistic and derive individual benefit from the benefit enjoyed by the community as a whole. In our case such people might seek to locate the building where it will be most easily accessible to everyone, even though this may inconvenience a particular individual. These views describe motive and the ways in which people perceive their relationship with the community, but having reached an opinion by either route each individual must now make that opinion heard.

Let us suppose that each individual has an opinion regarding the location of the building. The interest of each individual will dictate that his or her opinion be the one that dominates. Each person seeks to become a dictator. Clearly this cannot be and some kind of compromise must be sought. It is at this point that the community ceases to be anarchistic.

It may be that when the community began, one person who was wealthy provided most of the capital to launch the project. Others may feel that this gives that person the right to make important decisions on behalf of everyone else. In a word, the community accepts this individual as its rightful monarch and the system is a monarchy. The monarch rules by the consent of the ruled, but is not bound to consult the subjects regarding each separate decision or, indeed, to inform them of the reasons for it. A wise monarch may listen to advisers, but there is nothing in the rules that requires it. Those who feel uncomfortable under this regime may leave.

Again, the community may feel that such a monarchy does not suit them but that nevertheless it is a good idea to allow one person to make decisions on behalf of everyone, provided the decision-maker can be held accountable. So they elect a leader and confer on him or her the powers of a monarch for life, for an agreed period, or until he or she is deposed by a popular vote in a referendum. This is an elective monarchy.

The leader may not be appointed at all. It may be – and in the real world often it is – that one person is able to dominate all the others by the force of his or her personality or physical strength. If this person becomes the leader he or she may be surrounded by supporters who form a kind of guard. The situation now is that the leader makes decisions and those who disagree may either confront the leader in an argument that the leader is almost bound to win, or may engage the leader or the guards in combat. Since both leader and guards occupy their positions by virtue of their strength, the outcome of the contest is a foregone conclusion. Dissenters may leave — with the permission of the leader. This is a tyranny and it differs from a monarchy in two ways. The tyrant does not rule by willing consent, and is not bound by a covenant to act in the interest of the subjects.

The final alternative is to institute a democracy. In a democracy each individual recognizes that everyone would prefer to be dictator and that the rule of one individual deprives all other individuals of any opportunity to make decisions. Therefore, the ruler is made the community as a whole, each individual exchanging the right to be overall dictator for one equal share in the government. Each person has an equal right to impose his or her will and this right is exercised in debate in which everyone may participate and try to persuade the others to agree with his or her point of view. At the end of the debate the matter is resolved finally by means of a majority vote for a simple 'yes' or 'no' resolution.

The important thing to recognize is that none of these alternatives corresponds to anarchism, but that one of them — or something rather like one of them — must be used if decisions are to be made at all and the community is ever to act as a community. Any of these systems will decide on a site for the new building, but anarchism alone will not. All the systems described have advantages and disadvantages, and history provides examples of the successful and unsuccessful application of all of them. The next thing to note is that one of the systems — democracy — requires the active collaboration of all members of the community in its planning, creation, and operation, and that another of the systems — tyranny — requires no planning, forethought, or participation on the part of anyone except the tyrant. This implies that in the absence of an agreed system of government the system most likely to emerge is tyranny. This is especially likely where members of the community espouse a belief that holds all government to be evil and unnecessary and so imagine they may live without government of any kind.

The dangers are very real. If, instead of following the anarchist argument along what some writers call the 'Protestant' path of William Godwin and his followers, we follow it along the less rational path of Rousseau and his followers, we find ourselves led, once again, to the cult of the hero. The view of government to which this leads is expressed clearly by one of the leading British writers of the romantic school, Thomas Carlyle:

Democracy, the chase of Liberty in that direction, shall go its full course; unrestrained by him of Pferdefuss-Quacksalber, or any of *his* household. The Toiling Millions of Mankind, in most vital need and passionate instinctive desire of Guidance, shall cast away False-Guidance; and hope, for an hour, that No-Guidance will suffice them: but it can be for an hour only. The smallest item of human Slavery is the oppression of man by his Mock-Superiors; the palpablest, but I say at bottom the smallest. Let him shake off such oppression, trample it indignantly under his feet; I blame him not, I pity and commend him. But oppression by your Mock-Superiors well shaken off, the grand problem yet remains to solve: That of finding government by your Real-Superiors! ...

... England will either learn to reverence its Heroes, and discriminate them from its Sham-Heroes and Valets and gaslighted Histrios; and to prize them as the audible God's-voice, amid all inane jargons and temporary market-cries, and say to them with heart-loyalty, 'Be ye King and Priest, and Gospel and Guidance for us': or else England will continue to worship now and ever-new forms of Quackhood, – and so, with what resiliences and reboundings matters little, go down to the Father of Quacks!

Carry Carlyle through to Nietzsche and it is but a short step to Hitler or Stalin:

The romantic movement, in art, in literature, and in politics, is bound up with this subjective way of judging men, not as members of a community, but as aesthetically delightful objects of contemplation. Tigers are more beautiful than sheep, but we prefer them behind bars: The typical romantic removes the bars and enjoys the magnficent leaps with which the tiger annihilates the sheep. He exhorts men to imagine themselves tigers, and when he succeeds the results are not wholly pleasant.

Anarchism has this tendency to degenerate into dictatorship and so to demolish those freedoms it was created to preserve.

We may avoid this trap by recognizing that while individuals have rights, they are none the less members of communities from which those rights are derived and by which they are protected, and from time to time they must collaborate in making decisions regarding their communities. At the same time, if their rights are to be preserved, they must make, promulgate, and observe laws that must be written in a language and style that makes them available to everyone. The alternative is either arbitrary law by the whim of the tyrant or monarch, or a law that is no less arbitrary by the whim of public opinion – mob law. As soon as our community has decided upon its preferred system of government and has agreed to make rules and observe them, it has ceased to be anarchistic, but it has the opportunity to preserve the best that the anarchist philosophy has to offer.

It is fairly easy to resolve the difficulties of our small community, of course, but what of those of a community the size of a modern nation and what is the relationship between the individual, or the small community, and the State of which it is part?

In a modern democratic state the democracy resides in an assembly or parliament whose procedures are democratic (more or less). The members of the assembly are elected by constituents whom they represent, and they are representatives, not delegates. This situation is now being challenged by some, especially within the British Labour Party, who hold that issues should be debated by the constituents themselves who would brief their delegate regarding his or her participation and vote in the Parliamentary debate. A representative, on the other hand, is apprised of the special interests and needs of constituents but participates and votes in debate according to conscience and to the political philosophy to which he or she subscribes.

Both views have advantages and disadvantages, but neither deals with the really difficult problem of minorities. In our imagined situation, members of our small community might well be considered a minority in respect of the larger society existing outside the group. They hold views that diverge from those of the majority on a wide range of issues. Geographically they cannot help being located within a constituency, but their representative does not agree with them, perhaps does not even understand or sympathize with them, and so, with the best will in the world, cannot really represent them. This may be unfair to them and if so they may be morally entitled to take certain action to draw attention to their condition or to make their views known.

In any society decisions must be more favourable to some members than to others, so that every general decision that is made must be unfair to some. What makes this unfairness discriminatory is the patterned distribution of it. The most fair system we can imagine is one in which each individual suffers from an equal amount of unfairness. The unfairness, then, is distributed randomly. If an individual or community suffers from more than average unfairness, this amounts to discrimination, and it alters their relationship to the political system. After all, the idea underlying the democratic system is that it distributes unfairness in a random fashion, so minimizing the amount of unfairness each individual must suffer. We may assume that it is on this understanding that individuals subscribe to it. If it fails and begins to act unfairly in a consistent fashion, then the victims of its unfairness are entitled to complain. The unfairness must be substantial, of course. It must restrict the freedom of individuals to behave in ways that are permitted more freely to others.

Apart from the victims of discrimination there is a second category of individuals who may take action to draw attention to their dissent. Where individuals or groups believe they have identified threats to the welfare of themselves or of society at large that arise from decisions made with the consent of the majority, they are entitled to draw attention to those threats in order to persuade the majority to reverse its decisions. This is a common form of dissent and in modern times groups have grown up to draw attention to threats arising from nuclear armaments, racial discrimination, American involvement in Vietnam, the loss of civil rights affecting certain groups in the United States and in Northern Ireland and, more recently, from the construction of motorways and nuclear power. Peter Singer, who has analysed such forms of dissent, concludes that it is legitimate to disobey certain laws to draw attention to the arguments of dissenters, provided the reason for such disobedience is made very clear and provided those who disobey submit to the judgement and punishment of the law.

This is important, for deliberate disobedience of this kind strikes deeply at the structure of democratic society, which is especially vulnerable to a withdrawal of consent from the governed. The laws of a tyrant may be disobeyed with fewer qualms since they were made without the consent of the governed and the system of government is not heavily dependent on their observance.

In an extreme case, though, does the individual who dissents have a right to withdraw politically from a society that discriminates against him or that is embarked on policies he believes must lead to catastrophe? In what sense does the citizen belong to society and, although we suppose that a democratic government governs by the consent of the governed, whose consent is, or ever has been, sought? The citizen may participate in the making of decisions, but who made the decision that created the decision-making system itself?

In our small community we can see that the system of government is created by the members themselves. Each of them makes a covenant, enters into a social contract, with the others, and so is bound, morally, to respect that covenant. A new member who joins later is informed of the nature of the system of government and is asked and expected to enter into a similar covenant. This is not to say dissent is impossible. It may be that on a particular issue some members find themselves unable to accept the decision of the majority. It is open to them to make their feelings clear and so they may be absolved from the covenant temporarily. For example, they may refuse to participate in the debate on a proposal, or they may participate but announce in advance that their feeling is so strong that although they will vote – according to their conscience – they cannot feel bound by a decision that goes against them. What they cannot do is to make no prior announcement, participate in the debate, vote, and then refuse to accept the outcome of that vote. Their participation without prior qualification implies their acceptance of the outcome whatever it may be, and to refuse to accept it after the event amounts to a violation of the convenant that strikes at the heart of the system and which other members of the community should not be expected to tolerate. Where a member is in frequent or perpetual disagreement, there remains the option of resignation or expulsion from the community.

In the world outside the community, life is not so simple. Individuals are born into societies whose procedures were fixed long ago and they are not asked whether they agree to accept them. If a covenant exists, it is implied. In *Leviathan* Thomas Hobbes overcomes this difficulty – or imagines he does – by quoting Biblical authority for his belief that children are bound by covenants entered into by their parents, all such covenants deriving ultimately from covenants made with God, whose representative on Earth is the sovereign power that rules the state. The glaringly unsatisfactory nature of his solution serves to illustrate the very real difficulties the problem raises. Modern writers tend to gloss over the matter by allowing participation in the system to imply acceptance of it. This seems to me to be a superficial view that holds only so long as no alternative system exists. We do not expect prisoners to accept the system that imprisons them simply because while imprisoned they obey prison rules and participate in prison life. Society is not imprisoning, of course, except in one important sense: we do not belong to it from choice and we cannot leave it. Since the smooth operation and, indeed, the survival of our democratic institutions depend on the willing participation and acceptance of the governed, and since all the known alternatives to democracy have disadvantages much greater than those of democracy, we have no choice but to assume the existence of an implied covenant by which each of us is bound, even though we cannot trace the origin of any such covenant. It is a necessary fiction.

Since the fiction is necessary, it follows that members of our imagined community are, and must remain, members of the larger society around them, whether they will or no. There is no way they can withdraw from it since secession is not so much illegal as impossible. They are bound by a contract into which they were born and which cannot be revoked. This being so, they may adopt a way of life that is different from that of the society around them only in so far as to do so does not contravene rules laid down by that society. They live by the consent of others and, although they may seek to withdraw from political participation in society, any idea they may have of isolation from it is entirely illusory. Indeed, however isolated they may be, they depend on society at large. It provides the guarantee that they can live unmolested, it protects them from military invasion – whether they wish to be protected or not – and it provides a large network of social and welfare services they are entitled to use by an entitlement they cannot resign. If a community member is injured while riding his bicycle along a public road (provided by the community at large) he will be taken to hospital by ambulance and given such medical treatment as he needs, and his right to such care will not be questioned.

This being so, it is more useful to consider what contribution the members of our community may make to society rather than the non-existent ways in which they may resign from it. I believe that their beliefs are founded on an idea that may be profoundly useful and that will appeal to many people who cannot adopt their way of life. To demonstrate what I believe to be the very radical nature of this idea we must look again at the political system we have inherited.

I have been assuming that within the existing political system all views are expressed and that citizens can choose freely those policies they prefer. In fact this is not the case. Electors do not choose the issues but are reduced to a choice between a limited number of bids. You may choose this set of policies or that, but there is no way in which the range can be widened in practice and even in theory there is no way in which individuals can advance their own policies for general consideration. The operation of an electoral system based on a simple majority vote, as in Britain, restricts the choice still further because the inevitable result is the emergence of a two-party system, with minority parties having no opportunity to influence the process. Where power tends to alternate between the two parties, there are long periods during which their policies are very similar.

The existence and operation of political parties have to this extent altered the basis of democracy into something other than that which was imagined when the system was conceived. A political party that is elected to office may consider itself mandated to carry out the legislative programme it announced prior to the election but, if it should depart from this programme without clear and unambiguous evidence of a change in circumstances that necessitates such a departure, its moral authority is undermined seriously. In practice, parties tend to avoid this difficulty by framing their proposals in very vague terms that are open to a range of interpretations. It has been proposed, for example, that to reduce government expenditure — which the ruling Conservative Party pledged itself to do in its election programme — measures to protect the environment should be relaxed and the obligation upon planning authorities to arrange public participation in planning should be ended. Since the most common criticism of methods for public participation in planning is that they are inadequate and discriminate, mainly financially, against groups of citizens objecting to proposals from large organizations, and since the most frequent criticism of environmental protection is that it is inadequate, it is fair to suppose that few electors consider that they voted for changes of this kind. These are proposals of special interest to environmentalists, but they form part of a package of proposals that affect a much broader section of the community through changes in education and welfare services, and there may well be many people who feel they did not vote for these reforms.

If the effect of political parties is to weaken democracy by converting it into a form of government by an elected aristocracy, an elite with almost limitless powers which must renew its popular support at intervals on the basis of its past record and its promises, the influence of large corporations, which we considered earlier, complicates the picture still more. When corporations act directly — say, by planning to undertake particular activities in particular places — they are subject to the existing political procedures which, for sake of argument, we may assume to be adequate for the protection of the public interest. Where their actions are indirect it is not so simple. Is the citizen bound to obey laws passed by a government where these laws have been framed under the influence of a particular sectional interest? This is not the same question as that created by lobbying on behalf of pressure groups within society because like all groups within society pressure groups are composed of citizens each of whom has indicated a willingness to accept the political framework by participating in it and seeking to exert influence through it. The multinational corporations are not composed in this way and, although their employees are citizens of particular countries, the corporations themselves are not, and are not bound by the political traditions of countries. Their influence works differently. Regardless of the views of governments, for example, oil will be produced and supplied only if the large oil corporations agree to produce and supply it. If they decided not to invest in the mining of uranium it is difficult to see how governments could proceed with plans for nuclear power programmes and, conversely, having decided to mine uranium the corporations can offer to supply it on terms that make nuclear power programmes appear irresistibly attractive. Having persuaded elected governments to take action that favours their interest, their subsequent behaviour is entirely within the law. This makes opposition very difficult for citizens who are bound to obey laws.

Yet political change is feasible. Within the next few years it will become technologically possible to convert the British political system to one based on simple, or direct democracy. It will be possible to use two-way television connected to private homes or at least to public buildings within every community to televise debates on important issues (and, presumably, on the selection of which are the important issues) and allow private citizens to participate directly. They will be able to see and hear politicians and specialists and they will be able to express their own views and contribute any specialist knowledge they may possess. At the end of the debate a motion may be put on which every citizen has the right to vote, the votes being registered electronically to produce a national result in a matter of minutes. It is possible, then, to extend the kind of democracy that can exist within a small community to national issues. I must emphasize that the technology required to do this exists now and that its installation and operation presents no difficulty that could not be surmounted. The capital cost would be fairly high, but not unacceptably so. Operating costs would be low, the system would require very little energy, the equipment would require very little maintenance and, provided it were not damaged physically, it would last for very many years. It would be simple to make the equipment secure from tampering, the administrative problems would be minimal and far less than those involved, for example, in changing the existing electoral system to one based on proportional representation.

Will it happen? It seems unlikely, at least in the near future, and the reason is political and not technical. It relates to the most important fundamental difference between the political philosophy that prevails in society as a whole and the philosophy by which our imagined 'anarchist' community is informed.

I mentioned earlier two opposing political views of 'natural' human behaviour and now I wish to explore these a little further. Our community (let us suppose) retains from its Stoic and Anabaptist forebears the view that individuals should be guided by their own consciences and that if they are allowed to be so guided, they will tend to act for the benefit of the community to which they belong. In other words, people prefer collaboration to competition. It seems unnecessary to refer to anthropological studies to find support for the view that by nature man is a collaborator rather than a competitor. Essentially it is moral and impossible to prove. It does seem, though, that in most human societies individual human behaviour is influenced more by collaboration than by competition. It is, of course, an intensely optimistic view of mankind, that embraces a belief in the moral perfectibility of the individual, and I imagine the anarchist would regard it as quite central to his or her belief.

In society at large this view is heretical. Western civilization is founded on a profoundly pessimistic view of man, but the heresy has persisted for many centuries. Whether or not Christianity supplied the pessimism, it expresses it lucidly. Because of the sin of Adam, all human beings are born in a state of sin that will lead them, inevitably, to eternal damnation. They can be rescued from this fate only by an absolute acceptance of the Christian faith. However, such acceptance amounts to much more than lip service or attending church on Sundays. It requires conversion, a radical change in moral outlook, a rejection of worldly values and, in effect, the cultivation of a hatred of the world and of men. The indulgence of human passions, including sexual passions and the reproduction of the species, is sinful and can be tolerated but not approved. Such conversion can be accomplished by few people. Thus, the number who will be saved is small. The vast majority of human beings, including, of course, all those who have never heard of Christian teaching, have been condemned. They are inherently sinful and so must be constrained. Without such constraint their efforts to maximize their individual advantage to indulge their passion for living will cause much injury to themselves and to the faithful. They must be governed, supervised, controlled by those best qualified for the task. In political terms this implies a form of government that at its kindest is paternalistic, with all power vested in a ruler or a ruling class. The people are not to be trusted to decide matters for themselves: they need leaders. The persistence of the heresy and the economic and social changes wrought by industrialization during the nineteenth and twentieth centuries necessitated some examination of this principle of government, but the only serious question that was raised related not to the principle itself but only to the method whereby the ruler, or ruling class, is appointed. The concession that was made amounted to the appointment of some rulers by a popular vote that is repeated at intervals. Even then, Britain retains a monarch whose position is inherited and an assembly whose members are not elected, but attend by virtue of their membership of a ruling class. The Christian church, meanwhile, has been criticized directly, for example by Kierkegaard, and by implication through the emergence of many fundamentalist sects, for trying to disguise its pessimism beneath a veneer of cheerful optimism.

This view and the view I have described as 'optimistic' lead to the kind of representative democracy that exists today since, without modern technological assistance, direct democracy is possible only on a small scale. It would be impractical to allow the entire population of a country to attend its parliament. The important question relates to the direction in which society is moving. Did it begin as a simple, direct democracy that grew larger and so evolved a representational system, or did it begin as an absolute monarchy or dictatorship that has been modified to its present form? This seems to me the more likely direction change has taken. However, it may be that it is close to the limit that can be achieved and if it is to proceed further along this path it must abandon its pessimistic view of humanity and substitute the optimistic view. It must learn to regard direct democracy as the normal and most desirable state of affairs and any lapse from that state as regrettable. We should be under no illusions regarding the depth of the change that this requires. It is indeed a profound conversion.

It seems to me that it is this concept of direct democracy based on an optimistic view of mankind that is enshrined in our notional community. Of course, I have no way of knowing whether such communities share this view in the real world, but I suspect that it lies at the heart of the self-sufficiency movement in general. The independence that suporters of this movement seek is, in truth, a political and moral independence. It is the right to think for themselves, to decide for themselves, to live their own lives according to the dictates of their own consciences. The actual performing of physical tasks is one way in which this idea may be expressed. The family whose power supply comes from its own windmill or water turbine derives no special benefit from this. The power would be the same – and probably more reliable – if it were supplied by the public utility. It might even be cheaper. The benefit is, if you like, moral and political. The family feels it has freed itself from a situation in which the amount, form and method of supply of power is decided by an organization that presumes to know better than they what it is they need and should have. It is an escape from paternalism, a maturing.

If an idea – any idea – is to be valid it must be available to everyone. If the idea is acceptable to many, but can be applied by only a few, then the many must accept, along with the idea, the formation of a moral elite. The kind of idea is typical of religious ideas, for example, where these allow the establishment of a priesthood and monastic orders. It is not acceptable, though, where the idea itself is that of democracy, which implies the direct involvement of all members of society. Either democracy applies equally to everyone or it is not democracy.

Clearly, then, the implications of self-sufficiency cannot be contained among those who seek to grow their own food or make their own furniture, because the great majority of people are excluded from such activities. Further, where self-providers seek to withdraw from society to which, thereafter, they make no economic, social, or political contribution, but to which they are bound by our notional and binding covenant, they are to that extent parasitic upon society. They enjoy a 'free ride'. It is this illusion of withdrawal and the unavoidable, if uncomfortable fact that in Britain today the average price of land is £3705 per hectare (£1500 an acre) that earns the self-providers their reputation as elitists. The idyllic smallholding is available only to the wealthy, and even those who may live on such smallholdings without owning them, must be free from financial commitments or in receipt of an income. It is not a choice that can be offered freely to, say, the family with children at school that has no capital and depends for its support on the earnings of, possibly, both parents. What is more, it is not everyone who would choose to live in this way. If we demand that subscribers to our political ideal must live in a way defined by us we impose a new form of dictatorship that is diametrically opposed to our most cherished libertarian beliefs. Can we resolve the contradiction whereby individuals can be 'self-sufficient' while continuing to live in a city and shop at a supermarket? I believe we can, provided we accept that the concept of self-sufficiency is moral rather than essentially practical. Any individual can develop an independence of thought and work within any community to establish a more directly democratic system. As the Stoics would have argued, anyone, under any circumstances, can practise virtue.

If such a philosophy is appropriate for would-be self-providers, is it equally appropriate for environmentalists? They might argue, for example, that environmental protection can be achieved only by legislation based on a firm concept of what is best for the environment to curb the activities of those who would cause environmental injury. This, quite clearly, is the traditional 'pessimistic' outlook that calls for a paternalistic form of government. However, there is an alternative even here. Our 'optimistic' view would encourage the emergence of new priorities, new social and economic goals, and there is good reason to suppose that these would concern the living standards and the quality of the environment most desired by the community as a whole. Industry might be reformed from within as each industrial organization resolved itself into a direct democracy whose members dedicated their skills to the production of goods to benefit society generally by techniques that were environmentally benign. This is no longer theoretical, for the idea has found expression in a number of British industries. The movement has been described by Dr Dave Elliott who was deeply involved in the development of the corporate plan drawn up by trades unionists at Lucas Aerospace. Although the corporate plan was largely ignored by the environmentalists from whom it should have drawn strong support, it would have altered radically the pattern of production in that organization to produce very real social and environmental benefits.

While some ecological theorists have been content to issue edicts as to 'what should be done' – presumably by them, once in power – trade unionists in a wide range of industries have been trying to put flesh on the ideal of 'socially useful technology'. This idea has spread well beyond its origin at Lucas Aerospace, to include campaigns by workers in the power engineering industry (C. A. Parsons, Clarke Chapman, etc.), Vickers, Chrysler and so on. These campaigns have their base in the need to fight for jobs in industries faced by recession or being subject to rationalization to increase profit. But the workers' response transcends this context: they are having to come to terms, in a practical way, with the question 'what should be produced – and how?'

As Elliott explains, this trend has close similarities with the changes advocated by the syndicalists and guild socialists of the late nineteenth and early twentieth centuries. For them, as for Godwin before them, socialism implied a society based on small, autonomous communities, linked in a federal structure, and governed entirely by their members. The central state would disappear under this system. Socialism as state centralism, derived from ideas developed by the Webbs and the Fabians for shared power in a social democracy, and influenced by the establishment of the centralized Soviet government in the USSR, represented a departure from the older socialist tradition. A return to that tradition may provide the means whereby self-providers and environmentalists find common cause with a broad spectrum of working people.

I have tried to show that modern industrial societies found their systems of democratic government on an essentially pessimistic view of mankind that leads to a form of paternalism. At the same time, as I suggested in the last chapter, the production of goods for trading to generate capital for further investment dehumanizes, and so alienates, the worker. The self-provider and, to some extent, the environmentalist oppose both these trends. The alternative that is proposed would substitute an optimistic view of mankind for the prevailing pessimistic view and it would found its political institutions on a principle of direct democracy. Industrially this suggests that instead of producing goods primarily for trading, goods would be produced for use. In other words, those who make the goods would aim to discover the needs and wishes of their customers and to supply them directly. This comes very close to an industrial version of the situation I imagined at the beginning of this chapter when I described the relationship between members of a small community that determined the pattern of production and supply of food. The aim in both cases is to supply goods or commodities for immediate use, rather than to supply them to a trading system.

The implications are profound, not to say revolutionary, but the idea is clear and simple. If, as I believe, this is the idea that informs the self-sufficiency movement, then we should be quite clear about what it is that our advocacy of self-sufficiency implies. The members of our imagined community are not, as they may suppose, anarchists; they are socialists in the original sense of that term, and far from practising no form of government, their government is direct democracy. If this definition is accepted it becomes possible to argue that far from being an elitist and somewhat parasitic movement confined to a tiny minority of eccentrics, the self-sufficiency movement forms part of the mainstream of European and American political history and it has allies within the society from which it appears to exclude itself.

*

In the Negev Desert, some 48 kilometres (30 miles) south of Beersheba, in a moonscape of sun-scorched hills, wadis and canyons, stands the ancient city of Avdat. Avdat was abandoned and lost for more than 1000 years until 1864 when an Englishman, Palmer, discovered it while tracing the caravan route from Arabia to Egypt. Palmer was amazed that Avdat could ever have existed in such a hostile environment and he could only assume that the Bedouin, with their flocks of sheep and goats, had denuded the desert of vegetation and left it incapable of supporting a large population.

There the matter rested until nearly a century later, when Professor Michael Evenari and his colleagues at the Hebrew University in Jerusalem also became enthralled by the mystery of how Avdat and other Nabatean cities in the Negev could ever have survived. To some extent Evenari exonerated the Bedouin, for he knew that the Negev had been a desert in Abraham's time, and he guessed that the invading Bedouin of the fifth century AD must have rather destroyed some special farming system.

What intrigued both Palmer and Evenari were the remains of terraces and a series of dams along the dry river beds, as well as gently sloping channels leading directly down from the surrounding hills. By repairing the channels, terraces, and dams, Evenari discovered that, after a heavy rainstorm, water would run off the hills and the wadis into the cleared areas which then became flooded. Through precise measurement he found that a rainfall of as little as 2·5 centimetres (1 inch) could be magnified through run-off into as much as 50 centimetres (20 inches) in the flooded areas, leaving the soil soaked to a depth of several metres and wet enough to sustain a crop through its growing season.

Beautiful in its simplicity, the system nevertheless showed a brilliant perception of the environment by those who first devised it some 3000 years before. The principles are a loess soil which forms an impenetrable crust when wet, hard rains, and then the water collecting system. Evenari and his colleagues have now established working experimental farms on the sites of two ancient desert farms – one at Avdat, the other at Shivta – and they are able to confirm that records of crops of wheat, grapes, almonds, and pistachios on a parchment from the city of Nizzana in the Negev are likely to have been accurate.

The collection of water within the city for drinking and washing was also a masterpiece of planning. Cisterns were dug under every dwelling and public building so that scarcely a drop would be lost.

Those Negev cities, surrounded by their run-off farms, are thus a classic instance of self-sufficiency. Without everyone's continual co-operation to maintain the intricate run-off system and to ensure the equitable distribution of water to each field in turn, life in the city would have been virtually impossible. Yet one would be absolutely wrong to imagine the city to be stark and gloomy, its inhabitants ever aware of their fate if they neglected their duties in the fields. Quite the contrary for, through the ruins, one can see the remains of what was once a prosperous life – of fabulous Byzantine churches, of spacious houses with courtyards, of wine-presses, and it is evident that the inhabitants carried on life to the full, embarking on all the various trades and occupations which make for a civilized society.

For all that, I like to think of each of them giving a hand with the making of the fields around and the run-off system, of being at hand at that exciting moment when the water pours off the hills and wadis, and of helping to gather in the harvest – the culmination of all the work for survival.

What a contrast modern Israel is. Not far from Avdat is the Kibbutz Sde Boker in which Ben Gurion made his home. It would seem that his dream of making the desert bloom has already come true; today Sde Boker is a lush oasis of green in a vegetation-sparse desert. Yet there is no miracle to that greening of the desert; water is piped in from the Galilee and the usual battery of chemical fertilizers and pesticides is employed to maximize yields. And, like most modern settlements in Israel, the buildings embody sheer functionalism; there is none of the aesthetics which manifest themselves at Avdat.

The kibbutz is a collective in which decision-making, essential tasks, and any accumulation of wealth are shared out among the members; in that respect the kibbutz is social democracy in action. And when the State of Israel was established, many members of the government were from kibbutzim, with allegiance to the kibbutz ideal. Indeed, politically Israel was moulded by their beliefs and attitudes. It could be claimed that Israel, in its handling of its Jewish population, approached the ideal state of democracy in which the great majority felt they had a voice in their country's affairs. Moreover, with state security a necessity, Israel had to create a people's army, which gave everyone who participated in it and in its battles a sense of unity of purpose.

Mike asserts that the search for self-sufficiency is primarily each individual's desire for personal freedom and that given that pure freedom is impossible in the collective situation of myriads of other human beings, the compromise is in participatory democracy. He has, therefore, even broached the idea of the two-way television set – a feasible technology – by means of which every individual could actually observe a parliamentary debate in action and vote for his preferences at the end of the day. But, whereas Ben Gurion would have considered the Israel of which he was prime minister, an example of social democracy and, being from a kibbutz, was a staunch advocate of certain principles of self-sufficiency, particularly with regard to the use of labour, the seeds from the dissolution of that myth were already inherent in Israel's developing economic and social systems. Israel today is a consumer society with a fixation on economic growth and development. The kibbutz movement, meanwhile, has lost its political status and is no longer representative of the modern Israeli's way of life; in addition, all notions of self-sufficiency have been cast to the four winds. Thus, labour is brought in from outside to do the more menial tasks, the food eaten in the communal dining-rooms is bought from a centralized manufacturing body, and high yields of each crop, increasingly of flowers for the European market, are sought through the use of chemicals.

Undoubtedly the search for freedom and independence lies behind the self-sufficiency movement, and Mike is correct in his analysis that such a search need not be limited to just those who return to the land with hoes and spades; anyone of any occupation can be part of the movement. But if one continues to shop at the supermarket, buying the products of the big monopolies, and drives around in one's car, then one is clearly still connected securely to the umbilical cord of industrial society. Indeed, for all the talk of action at Lucas Aerospace, their survival as a working group will depend on their competitiveness in selling their products in the market, and the mass of the population is governed in its choice by forces operating in the market, especially those of the big monopolies. Here, then, is the reason why the majority of those seeking self-sufficiency are looking for land for, by working it, at least the basis of existence can be independent of the massive industrial system which surrounds them. And in that respect, technics are important, since the degree to which one uses modern machines and chemicals symbolizes one's dependency on the very system one hopes to destroy. That is why there is seeming virtue in using antiquated machinery; not because it is necessarily better or more sparing in use of resources, but because it is no longer part of the modern manufacturing process.

The search for independence has another aspect, too. It is questionable whether there will be sufficient material resources for industry to expand given both dwindling reserves and escalating costs. Furthermore, industry is seen to lead to widespread environmental degradation. By reducing his consumption of industrial products, the aspirant to self-sufficiency is thus playing his part in the demise of the industrial state and simultaneously is contributing to the well-being of the environment.

But there is the rub that land is in short supply in a heavily populated country such as Britain and that its soaring price puts it out of reach of most people. Mike's misgivings, and they have validity, are that those who do procure land are part of a privileged elite and, that if land and self-sufficiency have to be integral and interwoven, then the movement must be both limited in size and politically unacceptable. Yet neither the supply of land nor its price have been determined through the self-sufficiency movement, but rather through the workings of the agroindustrial system with its power to control investment and labour. In common with true conservatives like Tocqueville, or radicals like Cobbett, I see the working community based around the land as the foundation of any stability in society. Not that each person has to be primarily concerned with growing food; there are many other occupations which are equally satisfying, but the person's connection with those who do work the land should be intimate and direct.

Mike has stressed the role of the individual in society, seeing democracy as the aggregation and then averaging out of a mass of self-interests. His view is purely an extension of the existing system which came into being as a consequence of the Enlightenment with its notion of rational man and equality. The industrial revolution in Britain and the social revolution in France were together the death knell of the feudalistic values of the Middle Ages. Rational man welcomed the transformation in society that followed, including those of social mobility, general education, and mass culture, but as those great nineteenth-century sociologists, including Durkheim, Tocqueville, and even Marx, recognized, what people gained in social mobility and in enfranchisement, they did not necessarily gain in independence and freedom. Indeed, the so-called democracies which came about in the late eighteenth and nineteenth centuries were little other than totalitarian bureaucracies with far greater control over the individual than had been the case in most feudal systems. As Tocqueville notes, 'The attraction of administrative powers to the centre will always be less easy and less rapid under the reign of kings who are still connected with the old aristocratic order than under new princes, the children of their own achievements, whose birth, prejudices, propensities and habits appear to bind them indissolubly to the cause of equality . . . In democratic communities the rule is that centralization must increase in proportion as the sovereign is less aristocratic.'

Under feudalism, the family remained a strong, coherent, and cohesive unit within the community with allegiances to guilds, the parish, and religion. The new democracies destroyed all the old orders, including the family, the guilds and the power of the church, for all men were now equal, a child as much as his father, and authority instead was vested in the state and in its legal advisers. In modern industrial societies that power of the state has become more absolute, the means of control more penetrating and subtle.

The seeker of self-sufficiency is looking both for independence and a stable society, and intuitively he has set out to recreate community. Durkheim's analysis of the role played by community in moulding the values and customs of individuals in society has never been repudiated, and it was his notion that the destruction of community was in itself sufficient to bring about anomie and alienation. Clearly the modern subscriber to self-sufficiency is not out to re-establish feudalism and the Middle Ages, but he is searching for a framework in which to generate new values, new ideas and customs. That will not come about through isolated individuals, lacking community but each striving independently to change the direction of the existing system. Change, I believe, will have to come from the grass roots and through the common voice of healthy communities. The adherence to the principles of self-sufficiency must play a role in those communities, for it is through an appreciation of limits and the discipline that derives from such awareness, that something approaching freedom becomes possible; for if each community is resourceful and limited in its demands on the environment, then a greater potential for equality naturally follows, since greed and envy of another's resources are eliminated.

Not that isolation becomes the order of the day. The Nabateans of Avdat were primarily traders by profession, transporting spices and precious stones between the great Arabian and African continents. They were part of the outside world yet they knew the value of self-sufficiency.

6 Energy and equity

Even after James Watt's improved steam engine of 1763, wind and water power were used to a remarkable degree throughout Britain. In Cornwall one can see the remains of innumerable water mills which, by the nineteenth century, provided practically every holding with its own power supply for grinding corn. Some assessments put the number of water mills which were working at that time in Cornwall at 3000. Indeed, many farmers went to great lengths for water power, tapping rivers more than a kilometre away and sinking water wheels below the surface of the ground to maximize the effect of flow. Still today one can stumble across such relics of the past – giant 7·5-metre (25-foot) diameter wheels, intact on their bearings and almost fit for work. As well as using water power for milling and threshing corn, by the end of the last century some farmers had adapted their water wheels for generating electricity.

But water- and wind-power had their limitations and, in Cornwall, the invention of the steam engine gave a big boost to the tin- and copper-mining industry, in danger of collapse because flooding was exceeding the capacity of water-wheel-driven pumps to clear the mines. Some claim that the industrial revolution derived its initial impetus from the need to improve steam engines for pumping out water from the tin mines. Certainly, the new engines Trevithick's included, enabled shafts to be sunk lower and workings to be extended.

Cornwall has not been self-sufficient in energy since the sixteenth century because of its tin industry. Indeed, in Elizabethan times charcoal had to be imported into the county from the New Forest for smelting tin, Cornwall's forests having already been denuded. Once steam was used, coal was brought in from the collieries of South Wales. Today, nearly all Cornwall's energy is imported. Even its electricity is generated outside the county, and most of that is derived from the nuclear power stations along the Bristol Channel; a point on which the Central Electricity Generating Board and United Kingdom Atomic Energy Authority are happy to remind antinuclear protesters.

If they give it a thought, most people would accept the need for importing energy from energy-rich areas to those that are lacking, such as from Wales to Cornwall. When an entire country is short of indigenous energy, then few would dispute the need for acquiring it from elsewhere. Cornwall, in fact, provided the greater part of the world's tin in the nineteenth century, and most would reason that the swap of energy and other resources for tin, was a fair one.

Energy provides power for industrial society, enabling people to travel in their own cars, to fly abroad, to have electrical gadgets in the home, to maintain comfortable house temperatures, to have mass entertainment, to eat prepacked convenience foods and, in general, to have a high standard of living. At present the greater part of this industrial energy is derived from the fossil fuels − coal, oil, and natural gas − which are consumed in ever-greater quantities as demand increases in the developed countries and as Third World countries struggle to catch up. That worldwide drive to consume is now rationalized into a kind of political credo in which each man, woman, and child has the right to a reasonable standard of living exemplified by adequate food, housing, education, recourse to medical facilities, and to a dignified livelihood. As a corollary, once people have attained a reasonable standard of living, it is assumed that they will behave responsibly by restricting the size of their families, so alleviating pressure on world resources and enabling each person to have a better bite of the ever-expanding materialistic cake. Curiously, when expounding such arguments people forget that the ability of couples to restrict the numbers in their families has less to do with modern education and to the possesion of a high standard of living, than with inclination and tradition. Indeed, in Britain the birth rate fell substantially from its high level in the nineteenth century to an all-time low in the 1930s, that fall being due neither to modern contraceptives which were then unobtainable, nor to a high standard of living. Equally, it is not the countries with a high population growth rate and a poor average standard of living which are the main consumers of the world's resources, but the industrialized nations and, in particular, the United States.

Nevertheless, implicit in the political credo is the notion of the industrialized state of man being better than a pre-industrial one; that the traditional way of life, with its customs, superstitions, hierarchical social structure, and consequent poor social mobility is a poverty trap for the masses and a block to freedom. In contrast, the life of modern industrialized man is conceived to be one of choice and opportunity, with jobs accessible to any man given desire and ability, from head of state down. In socialist societies this notion of freedom and social mobility is combined with egalitarianism in which the bounties of the industrial state are to be shared out among the populace. Industrialism is thus assumed to be the sole means by which people in a world of growing population can be given the chance of a reasonable life. In simple terms, the natural world is deemed inadequate to sustain man in either his present or his likely future numbers, and it increasingly behoves him to create an artificial world of his own, accessory to that provided by nature.

That world of artifice needs considerably more energy than that flowing through the natural system, so that man is hence driven to mine coal, drill for oil and natural gas, to shovel away at semifrozen tar sands and to work out the most economical way to burn uranium. Indeed that wondrous device of scientific engineering, the nuclear reactor, is increasingly deemed inevitable and indispensable for the future development of industrial society.

In general, the use of man-derived energy and the construction of an artificial world are considered complementary to that of the natural system, or at most an extension of it, but, as Edward Goldsmith points out, the man-made system is far from complementary and, in reality, is competing increasingly with the natural whose place it is consequently usurping. Thus, Goldsmith argues that the loss of agricultural land to motorways, urban development, and industry, is a clear indication of the technosphere – that technological activity of man – ousting the biosphere which incorporates under its mantle all natural biological activity. Clearly, the natural flow of energy through the organic system is brought abruptly to an end once the ground is plastered with concrete and smeared with the toxic excretions of man's industrial processes.

Not that modern agriculture is in the clear, even though the greater part of the energy it uses is sun-derived. Indeed, there are differences of orders of magnitude between the sum of energy used on traditional farms where either human muscle power or beasts of burden are used and modern farms wtih their large tractors, electric equipment, heaters, and their use of energy-rich chemicals such as nitrogenous fertilizers and herbicides.

The industrial revolution did not simply bring about changes in the method of manufacturing goods for human consumption, it led to a fundamental altering of human values. Thus, man's concepts about family, community, religion, and about his place in society all went by the board as the manufacturing industries made their claim for mass labour and for the payment of that labour in cash rather than in security of tenure on some agricultural holding. Ironically industrial society with its promise of individualism, and of freedom to choose an occupation as well as a place to live, has led to greater boredom, frustration, and anomie than probably at any time in human history. In *Working for Ford*, the sociologist Hew Benyon interviews shop-floor workers from Ford car factories in Britain who describe the soul-destroying boredom of their work and the pressures put upon them by management and unions alike to speed up and improve productivity. And in her remarkable book, *Woman's Consciousness, Man's World*, Sheila Rowbotham, also talks about the consequences of modern factory life on the individual and his family: 'The world of work occupies the worker body and soul for eight hours a day. Leisure is time not at work. It is what is left over to him. Leisure is time in which he is allowed to recover himself. But in fact the sep-aration of work and leisure is a fragile one. A man can't switch off eight hours of his activity when he clocks out. The capitalist product-ion process does not only occupy its operators at work, it pursues them in their rest, in their family, in bed, in their dreams. Do dreams change on Saturday night? Do strikes change the pattern of dream-ing? Work is something to live your life around. Love is something to be squeezed in between.'

As Emile Durkheim made clear, a consequence of a breakdown of all the old traditions and allegiances to family and community, to religion and to guilds, has been an unprecedented increase in the rate of suicide. Suicide, Durkheim suggested, was a consequence of man being unable to cope with his new-found individuality and hence, paradoxically, was the ultimate negation of that individuality. Thus, alienation is the antithesis of progress, and that being so, the pursuit of progress in the world is likely to lead increasingly to an alienated society.

The industrial society has been ascribed with some particular lib-eratory force in its bringing about the fragmentation of traditional society and the opportunity for men to break the shackles imposed upon them as a relic of the feudal ages. But the reality is that any freedom gained in industrial society has been won not because of some self-evident virtue within the system but through labour having to fight bitterly from the beginning for justice and a fair deal.

In effect, those rights were obtained through the organization of labour into unions and through strike action. Today, as Herbert Mar-cuse foretold, the differences between the aims and aspirations of those who direct and manage industries and those who work on the shop floor have diminished to the point where traditional Marxism has lost much of its power and attraction. The reason is simple enough for, as workers become more affluent and increasingly embroiled in the activities of mass consumerism —indeed they are the ultimate target of mass production — and as in effect they come to control the factories in which they work, increasingly they become victims of their success, and cannot afford for the sake of their own standard of living to bring the industry in which they work to its knees; they become, in fact, slaves to their own industry. Furthermore, as the rest of the world industrializes and begins manufacturing similar goods at cheaper rates, either because of closer access to raw materials, because of cheap labour or, most likely, a combination of both, so any action on the workers' part to make their own industries less competitive is counter-productive. In the end bosses and the men who work for them are increasingly in agreement; moreover, they all represent at different levels aspects of the same consumer society. Jet-setting to the Bahamas becomes, in fact, a shade different from the package tour to the Costa Brava. The net result, as Marcuse points out, is one-dimensional man.

Because of industrialization, because of the man-made world, man increasingly feels he has power to control his environment and hence his destiny. Yet that freedom from nature is illusory. Thus, the farmer who orders a battery of sprays to be applied at critical times, and then reaps a crop of 10 tonnes to the hectare of wheat, or 80 tonnes of potatoes, may feel that nature must dance to his tune, rather than he to its, but he has relinquished one master for another; for now he depends on agro-industry, on aeroplanes, on the weather man, and even on computers; perhaps most important of all, his viability depends on his relationship with his creditors, and on the sort of price he can get for his crops, with or without subsidies. Man's forays into space, however much they smack of a conquest of the forces of nature, are equally Earth-bound in the end, because they depend on Earth's resources to sustain them. Indeed, man's capers on the Moon and his endless orbiting around the Earth are nothing more than faltering, child-like steps into the immensity of space.

Modern economists, and many technologists believe that modern man has a better awareness of his environment than was possible before – primarily through the manifestation of nature's laws through the rigour of scientific investigation. Given that awareness, man has, therefore, a better chance of coping with environmental problems. But the primitive, however irrational his behaviour may seem, however barbaric in our civilized terms, does not need an objective viewpoint of his surroundings to live successfully. Rather the reverse, his subjective view, welling up from aeons-old experience and tempered by traditions passed down from previous generations probably gives him a better understanding of what is required for survival than does any dispassionate scientific viewpoint, which anyway is circumscribed by the degree of available information.

Nevertheless, certain primitive peoples behave in a wholly unacceptable fashion according to our standards of morality. Thus the head-shrinking Jivaros of Ecuador practise legitimized murder on their neighbours, ostensibly for reasons of status and prestige together with initiation rites. Dr Betty Meggers of the Smithsonian Institute suggests that the Jivaros and other neighbouring tribes carry on their ghoulish activities out of strict necessity to curb population growth, and she explains why such killings are endemic to that area of the Amazon and not to others further down the river in Brazil. Apparently millions of years of flooding and erosion have brought about a leaching of the soil in the upper reaches of the Amazon leaving the soil poor and infertile, and incapable of sustaining the richness of life achieved further eastwards. According to Dr Meggers the tribes living further down the Amazon in Brazil have a less compelling need to curb their own population growth and that of their neighbours and, with the release from that indomitable pressure, they are consequently more peaceable.

Whether Meggers is correct in her analysis is a moot point; other anthropologists claim that the head-shrinking activities of the Jivaros cannot be equated so simply with a need to curb population growth. Indeed, they point to other aggressive tribes, though not head-shrinkers, living in the more fertile lower reaches of the Amazon.

Whatever the reasons for head-shrinking, the Jivaros have probably lost sight of when and why it started, but before we condemn out of hand such an extreme case of tribal behaviour we must be careful to ensure that our own civilized societies offer those who live within them necessarily a better existence. Given our education and background it would be extremely unlikely that we would want to exchange our lot for that of an Amazonian tribesman but we have exchanged stability, tradition, and a coherent though subjective view of the environment for nail-biting instability, a breakdown of authority and tradition, and an increasingly complicated and unsatisfactory view of our environment. Furthermore we, as modern man, have unleashed wars such as no primitive would or could contemplate and, if the suffering we have caused were not enough, we continue to build more and more devastating weapons. We have also come to accept a terrible toll of road accidents, in the United Kingdom, for example, of thousands killed and injured each year, a certain proportion at least brought about through aggressive driving. The Jivaros would probably be aghast at such a volume of deaths, in so far as their own killings are at least limited in number and curbed by tradition. And what happens when we teach them our western values and they find themselves caught up in the backwash of development, living in slums, in poverty, with just as many deaths being caused by motor vehicles as was once brought about through private killings?

By no means all surviving primitive peoples are as aggressive towards their neighbours as are the Jivaros although many have ritual warfare to establish claims on territory. Maintaining a stable population, well within the carrying capacity of the land at the disposal of the tribe, is undoubtedly an active process among all primitive peoples, whether or not head-shrinking or any kind of killings are part of that vocabulary. Lactation taboos, by which sexual intercourse is curtailed during an extended period of breast-feeding is one mechanism encountered among Amerindian tribes, as is the killing of infants with tangible evidence of deformities. According to Dr Conrad Gorinsky of St Bartholomew's Hospital, London, some Amerindians use a form of chemical contraceptive – derived from natural sources – to supplement other forms of population growth.

The fundamental difference between the Pill and contraceptive techniques applied by primitive peoples is that the former is a license to unlimited sexual freedom, whereas population control among primitive people devolves around taboos and restraint. Furthermore, it is engineered around a total tribal viewpoint of the nature of man and his surroundings. The Pill too has unwanted hormonal side effects, particularly if used over long periods and its actual contribution to the curbing of population growth in the world is extremely limited.

As it is, the scientific world, is just as prone to irrationalities to justify its own existence as is the primitive. Thus while the primitive must live within the limits of his immediate environment to survive, modern man, trapped in his ferroconcrete jungle, has lost sight of the limits of existence, and hence is all too often intent on expanding his sphere of activities. His alienation from nature is well expressed by the economist Professor Wilfred Beckerman, who ironically enough, became a member of the Royal Commission on the Environment. Nature to him appears a nasty intrusion as far as man's affairs are concerned, and the sooner it is relegated to a subordinate role in the humanization of the planet, the better for man. In his *In Defence of*

Economic Growth, Beckerman takes it upon himself to spell out the advantages of the motorcar as a locomotory device over the horse, as if the horse itself had to justify its existence. Beckerman neglects to reckon on the roads, the factories, the mines and all the requisite paraphernalia that must go with keeping a car on the road but he tells us '. . . a car emits only six grammes of pollutant a mile, whereas a horse, over the same distance, emits about 600 grammes of solid pollutant and 300 grammes of liquid pollutant.'

In his deriding of the horse, Beckerman overlooks conveniently the different regard discerning people have for the effluent of the horse compared with the car, and the haste with which garden-proud Londoners used to run out into the road to shovel up the windfall from a passing horse to manure their roses. Instead, today, we hear of the effects of lead fallout on the health of children caused by heavy traffic flows as at the Gravelly Hill, Spaghetti Junction near Birmingham. But the purpose of Beckerman's argument, however facetiously put, is to show that if everyone rushed around on horses as they do in cars then the streets of major cities in Britain would get piled high in manure; furthermore, such numbers of horses as would be necessary would require a considerable proportion of agricultural land to maintain them. Ironically enough, there are nearly as many horses in Britain today as there were fifty years ago but, instead of being work horses, they are for riding and leisure.

Yet the alternative, that man somehow makes do without rushing around the globe is not one he contemplates with equanimity, for Beckerman, in line with conventional democratic thinking, justifies his economic theories by envisaging a time when each and every person, both in present-day developed countries and in developing countries, will have access to equivalent materialistic benefits, including the right to travel. There is no room in his analysis for doubts about energy resources and minerals, since man in his ingenuity, and given economic incentives, will push back conceivable limits.

Beckerman's is the prevailing view, and even the present worldwide economic recession, fuel shortages, and rapidly rising prices are seen as no more than hiccups in the smooth, progressive running of the world's economic machine.

In Defence of Economic Growth (Jonathan Cape, London 1974) is one of many treatises advocating increased industrialization in return for widely diffused material wellbeing. But, whereas Beckerman is caught up in the conventional matching of energy consumption with economic output, more recent analyses emphasize that the simple, almost linear relationship between energy and gross national product can be radically altered by applying energy conservation strategies.

Herman Kahn's *The Next 200 Years* is a veritable tour de force for those wanting to believe in a materialistically affluent future. Kahn, probably well versed in the consequences to society of a total breakdown in community and tradition, foresees great potential bleakness facing mankind once it has achieved his vision of Utopia, that is, unless mankind can learn satisfactorily to entertain itself. For those who find the planet Earth too limited in size and scope, Kahn suggests space travel, which two centuries hence may be as accessible to the tourist as the beaches of Benidorm are today.

There have been two major revolutions so far, the agricultural and the industrial, and the third revolution is in sight, says Kahn, if man puts major wars and other follies aside and concentrates on attaining material affluence. Kahn's prescription of some of the important facets of life in a truly post-industrial society will hardly appeal to all men, and especially not to those with an eye to practising self-sufficiency. (Kahn would, however, surely argue that in a super-affluent world, there is always likely to be room for drop-outs.) Thus, all the economic activities of today, those primary ones concerned with agriculture and extracting minerals from the Earth, those secondary ones concerned with construction and manufacturing, and the tertiary ones that provide an essential service to both the first two economic activities, will involve an increasingly small proportion of the world population. Implicit in Kahn's presentation is the notion that labour-saving devices will increasingly predominate in all three modes of economic activity and, moreover, that saturation effects will make themselves increasingly felt as the world achieves the requisite affluence.

The masses – presumably classless – instead of working, will be able to enjoy the bounteous fruits gained through the successful undertaking of the first three modes of economic activity, and will consequently be able to indulge in quaternary activities. These are none other than self-indulgent holidays. Sport, whether as spectator or participant, travel both Earth-bound and in space, an epicurean lifestyle at home, dabbling in the creative arts are some of the carrots Kahn proffers us should we attain the goals he sets the world. Nevertheless, he realizes that society without its taboos, religious affiliations, traditions and rituals, will in all likelihood disintegrate, and he suggests that humanity of the future may care to indulge in meetings at which community-binding strategies are devised.

The transition to a society principally engaged in quaternary activities – a transition likely to be well under way in the next century – will mark the third great watershed of human history. Future ages will undoubtedly look back at what happened in these four centuries of economic development and technological advancement as mankind's most effective and pervasive transformation – from a world basically inhospitable to its few dwellers to one fully commanded by its expanded multitudes.

Of course there will be problems. Some of them are likely to be: wishful thinking, illusion, decadence, educated incapacity and a kind of violence-prone boredom. Furthermore, we suspect that, even if society were to work as we outline in this image of the future, many of our readers will be somewhat unhappy with the prospect and wonder whether mankind really wishes to 'stagnate' in such a total quaternary society. We believe that at least for a time most people would generally enjoy this post-industrial society, but there would be many who would not. For them it simply would not be exciting and challenging enough; indeed it might be rather boring for many ambitious, advancement and achievement orientated people (though there will be fewer such people). We rather suspect that space will be a major focus for many of these people – as a locus of dynamism, initiative and entrepreneurship – and that the existence of such a frontier will be very healthy for the quaternary society that is developing on earth.

Kahn is undoubtedly right. There are and will be many appalled at the prospect of an Earth that is man-regulated and dull, with escape into space as one of the few remaining kicks. But we must give Kahn credit for illuminating the sort of world we are setting out to create and for showing us what it is likely to offer in terms of mother-comforts and living experience. It is interesting to note, too, the ease with which he believes such a comfortable leisure-full world can be made to happen. Economic growth is, naturally enough, the key but he and his colleagues make it clear that it will be growth within certain limits, and of a diminishing kind once the major bulk of development has been overcome. The yardsticks of Kahn's future world are a population flattening out at fifteen billion, give or take a factor of two, per capita income in the range of 20 000 dollars, 1975 value, give or take a factor of three, and gross world product at 300 trillion dollars. With growth there must be energy consumption, but Kahn reckons it will increase some fifteen times compared with a sixty-fold increase in gross world product; thus, it will go from the present day 0.25 quintillions (1 quintillion equals 10^{18} British thermal units) and flatten out at 3·6 quintillions by the year 2176. Since present-day trends in energy consumption show it to lag a fraction or so behind gross national product Kahn is suggesting a significant improvement in energy utilization. Nevertheless a fifteen-fold increase in energy consumption and a sixty-fold increase in gross world product are both very substantial and will demand an enormous commitment to resources. Kahn and his colleagues are sanguine about the world's potential for providing enough energy. Their first point is that there need be recourse to no other technologies than are either in use already or are in the making, under which category they include thermonuclear fusion, the use of fuel cells, hydrogen fuel, and flywheels. Thus, energy of the future will come from shale oil, coal liquefaction, fission and fusion reactors, from solar cells, from geothermal sources, all of which will somehow be made to go much further than in present society through the effective use of conservation strategies. The proposals for improving energy efficiency include better insulation for houses, a 60-per-cent conversion of fuels into electricity instead of the present 30 to 40 per cent, combined heat and power schemes, the use of heat pumps and automobiles with flywheels.

'The basic message is this': says Kahn, 'Except for temporary fluctuations caused by bad luck or poor management, the world need not worry about energy shortages or costs in the future. And energy abundance is probably the world's best insurance that the entire population (even fifteen to twenty billion) can be well cared for at least physically during many centuries to come.'

Not only does Kahn subscribe to the prevailing view that abundant energy is the key to material well-being, he also expects that such resources can be made available at reasonable cost, absorbing no more than 10 per cent of gross national product.

With an eye less to the long-term future and more to the immediate, Gerald Leach and his colleagues at the International Institute for Environment and Development, have come up with their 'Low Energy Strategy for the United Kingdom'. Since they are dealing with a country already considered 'developed' both by its own citizens and the rest of the world, there is no reason to extrapolate enormous growth rates into the future. Leach and his colleagues have set out to show that if Britons enthusiastically, and more or less to a man, take up energy-conserving technologies, then they can attain an even higher standard of living than today – or more important can attain it more generally – but at an even lower energy consumption. They give Britain some fifty years of gradual, relatively painless change to arrive at the energy-efficient, and materially affluent society.

The report is remarkably compact, replete with numbers, graphs and tables and many would say, eminently sensible in its conclusions. The IIED researchers have looked at every sector of the economy – the domestic, commercial, manufacturing, public, and transport – and disaggregated energy use for some 400 different groups within those sectors. Not only can end-use energy consumption be made far more efficient, through insulating houses and fitting heat pumps, for example, but so can delivery systems and, by assessing technological development, some already being implemented, others in the process of commercialization, they find the overall energy saved can be considerable. According to Gerald Foley, 'It becomes more a matter of finding ways to consume energy in order to take up the slack, than to try and cut out consumption.'

How about the feasibility of the programme? The IIED group notes that United Kingdom fuel consumption in 1977 was lower than in 1970 despite an increase in gross domestic product of over 10 per cent. Thus, with everyone having better housing, still being able to drive their own cars but with considerably reduced fuel consumption, able to travel abroad – in short having a better version of what they have today – Leach and his colleagues reckon on total energy consumption either falling slowly to its 1960 level in their low case, or climbing back to its 1973 level in their high case. Meanwhile gross domestic product rises to three times its present level in the high case and twice in the low case against a total population growth of between 3·6 and 4·5 per cent over the entire period until 2025.

Clearly the IIED study is in line with Kahn's study concerning the vast improvement in energy delivery systems and in end-use consumption but, whereas Kahn has gone on to a time when all the world has caught up and overtaken present-day industrial societies, Leach has taken his study to a critical time for Britain – when North Sea oil and natural gas might be on the way out as major energy resources.

Should Britain be building nuclear power stations in the intervening years to gain experience and to slot in when required? Nuclear power is best translated into electricity which, through station and transmission losses, and then end-use losses, is basically an inefficient and expensive way of getting energy to people. Amory Lovins, of Friends of the Earth in London, claims in *Energy Strategy – the Road not taken*, that the cost of delivering nuclear-generated electricity is some hundred times higher for the consumer than the cost of the traditional forms of energy used at the end of the nineteenth century. The second point, again Amory Lovins', is that to replace the fossil fuels, particularly oil and natural gas, and take over their roles in all sectors of the economy, nuclear power would have to be expanded at a rate far beyond the capabilities, including capital, of the most resourceful industrial country.

In *Environment*, the argument is taken a stage further. There, the marginal capital cost of delivering to the consumer one barrel per day of oil equivalent in electric power from a nuclear power plant in the 1980s is reckoned at least to be 200 000 dollars – in line with Lovins' assessment. That figure assumes 1000 dollars per kilowatt capital costs for a plant running at 60 per cent capacity factor, 10 per cent transmission losses, and 38 per cent transmission capital costs. Since the capital formation rate in the United States is about 7 per cent of the yearly gross national product of some 140 billion dollars, Kurt Hohenemser, professor emeritus for aerospace engineering at Washington University, St Louis, points out, that if 30 per cent or forty-two billion dollars is used for investments in nuclear electric power generation: '. . . a fraction that would actually rob the remaining economy of needed capital – one would obtain a yearly increment in electric power to the consumer of 0·21 million barrels per day of oil equivalent. To compare this electric energy with the energy from oil or natural gas that it is to replace one usually applies a factor of three, resulting in 0·63 million barrels per day of oil equivalent or 1·6 per cent of the total present US energy consumption of 38 million barrels per day of oil equivalent.'

The conclusion is inescapable: despite the assumption of a wholly unrealistic capital investment of forty-two billion dollars, the rate of substitution of electric energy for oil and natural gas would be inadequate and '. . . certainly would allow no room for even a modest growth in energy supply'

Visions of an all-clean, efficient, all-electric economy begin to vanish in the face of hard figures such as those of Professor Hohenemser. Amory Lovins has also added his piece of disfigurement to the vision in his recent study *Is Nuclear Power Necessary?* in which he estimates that a 50 per cent replacement of oil by nuclear power between now and the end of the century would require ordering one large power station every 3·5 days. Moreover if every oil-powered station in the Organization for Economic Co-operation and Development (OECD) in 1975 had been replaced by nuclear stations, the fraction of OECD oil which is imported would have only been reduced from 65 to 60 per cent.

One hundred years ago and more, when world energy demands were a fraction of what they are today, it was relatively easy to substitute one source of power for another. Such flexibility has become a feature of the past; the enormous capital investment required for obtaining energy whether from Athabasca tar sands, from North Sea oil, from the Selby coalfields, or from light water reactors, the long lead times and the uncertainties over economics, make sudden substitution of one energy source for another, virtually impossible. The attempt, during President Nixon's period of office, to launch Project Independence by which the United States would regain its self-sufficiency in energy is particularly telling in its almost total failure. Nor are the present fumblings by the new administration under President Carter to procure self-sufficiency more likely to succeed. According to Dr Ken North of Carleton University, for Project Independence to make any dent on the energy needs of the United States there would have to be: over a million new oil and gas wells (more than doubling the present number) involving 2700 new land rigs, 278 drilling platforms, 230 offshore rigs, 73 000 rig personnel, and 39 million kilograms of drill pipes; more than sixty new oil refineries, requiring ten million tonnes of steel and 41 000 man-years of engineering and technology; an equal number of plants for oil-shale development and for coal gasification and liquefaction, more than thirty new nuclear plants each year; more than 140 new coal mines in the east and more than 100 new strip mines in the west: thousands of kilometres of new pipelines, both on land and offshore, and half a dozen superports.

In 1975 the US National Petroleum Council estimated that by 1985 the tar sands could be yielding from 250 000 to 500 000 barrels a day; shale oil from 100 000 to 400 000 barrels, and coal around 80 000 barrels a day. The combined total of some 1·5 million barrels per day would have to be balanced against the projected demand of some 29 million barrels per day.

On every front, Project Independence has been something of a disaster. The orderings of nuclear power stations have dwindled away to next to nothing as a consequence of long delays during construction leading to exorbitant interest charges, of greatly increased capital costs through the up-grading of core-cooling devices and safety in general and, acting on all these factors, of a vigorous environmental campaign. The incident at the Three Mile Island reactor has already had repercussions, and the New York State Power Authority has abandoned plans to build a 1200 megawatt reactor in Cemento. The meltdown at Harrisburg is not the only reason — greatly increased costs have also played their part, estimates indicating that the reactor would cost at least 3·1 billion dollars rather than the 1·3 billion dollars estimated in June 1977. At that rate electricity generation from a nuclear plant would cost 2500 dollars per kilowatt, and that excluding transmission costs.

There have been some classic cases of self-delusion about the speed at which new energy sources can be developed. Too often people are beguiled by the sheer quantities of energy available in a resource forgetting, in their zeal to see it all extracted, that the infrastructure required is staggering and beyond the capabilities of even a superpower. The Athabasca tar sands are a case in point. In 1975, the then minister of supply and services in the Canadian Government, Mr Goyer, had the following to say: 'There is as much as 20 billion dollars in profits to be reaped in exporting synthetic crude produced from the Alberta oil sands by the end of the decade ... the Federal and provincial governments and the oil industry must act quickly to capitalize on the oil sands before the United States achieves self-sufficiency by 1980 ... We have very good customers, eager customers ... especially the United States, Japan and West Germany ... the United States should be approached to help develop the oil sands'

Mr Goyer even contemplated taking Herman Kahn's advice to implement Canada's War Measures Act in getting 30 000 to 40 000 Korean labourers to help get the oil out. With 1980 upon us neither has the United States achieved anything like self-sufficiency in energy, nor has Canada imported boatloads of Koreans to help it get at its oil. The realities are that of the 300 billion barrels of oil incorporated into the tar sands, little more than 10 per cent can be extracted by presently used open-pit mining methods. In 1975, the director of the Great Canadian oil sands operation pointed out that with twelve plants, each costing several billion dollars to put into operation, it would take some 100 years to extract the oil from the sands. Moreover, that total amount would hardly last the United States four years at the present rate of oil consumption, let alone providing for Canada's ever-growing needs.

Undaunted, the Vice-president of Shell Canada advocated a more intense effort to get at the tar sands, and suggested building one new plant to come into operation every year over the next thirty years, the target being to produce 200 000 barrels a day by 1977, 800 000 by 1979 and, together with oil from the frontier area to the north, 1·5 million barrels of oil per day by 1983.

Wholly cynical of such aspirations, Ken North has had his own views vindicated less than five years later. 'None of these targets can possibly be met and everybody in the industry knows it. No commercially exploitable oil has been discovered in any of Canada's frontier areas ... Even if a Canadian Prudhoe Bay were discovered tomorrow, it would not enable the National Energy Board projections to be met.'

As for the tar sands operation which would require seventeen plants in full operation by 1985 at a minimum cost of 20 billion dollars, Dr North had this to say: 'Such a programme would over-saturate Canada's access to capital markets and its ability to fabricate or purchase steel, cement or electrical components. It would require the services of more engineers, construction crews and machinery than we could possibly manage. No other major engineering undertaking of any kind could be attempted during the duration of this construction which would bring in its wake terrifying, social, economic and environmental consequences.'

The Project Independence of Nixon, which has been pursued rather hopelessly by Carter, may be an attempt at self-sufficiency in energy, but its outlook is clearly short term since the energies sought are primarily those which will yield liquid and gaseous hydrocarbons. The hope, then, is that other energy resources will conveniently appear such as fusion and a host of technologies for tapping the vast output of solar energy. But in the last analysis the same rigorous constraints that have doomed Project Independence come into play; especially those Amory Lovins refers to as 'rate and magnitude' problems by which new technologies have somehow to be made to grow at an unsustainable rate to yield energies which cost far more than those in current use. To make a Project Independence succeed without savage cutbacks in energy consumption must necessarily mean governments will have to provide gigantic subsidies which, in the face of faltering economies and rampant inflation, may be exceedingly hard to justify.

Such a conclusion leads inevitably to another; if the major industrial powers, including the United States, Japan, West Germany, and much of Europe, are incapable of achieving self-sufficiency in energy even when they have vast indigenous energy resources of their own, then the chances of the developing nations being able to haul themselves up to the sort of energy dependence found in the countries of the OECD, are slim indeed. Yet that is the direction most developing countries have set their sights on.

Escalating costs, together with the sheer size of any programme to substitute one form of fuel for another, have become the bugbear of all countries trying to sustain industrial growth. Thus, the dreams of unlimited energy from the atom tend to evaporate in the cold dawn of reality. The breeder reactor is capable in theory of utilizing all the energy locked up in uranium whereas conventional thermal or burner reactors utilize only the energy of uranium-235 which comprises no more than 0.7 per cent of the uranium found in uranium ore. The breeding gain is brought about by the transformation of uranium-238, comprising some 99 per cent of all uranium, into plutonium and plutonium, being fissile, is then used as fuel. Thus, the breeder reactor is simply a device with a mixed core of plutonium and uranium oxides surrounded by a blanket of uranium-238 which, in mopping up fast neutrons emitted during the chain reaction in the core, converts into plutonium, the plutonium being extracted through reprocessing.

But it is to misunderstand the nature of the process to imagine that the conversion of uranium-238 into plutonium takes place at once, and that at the end of the day the operator of a breeder reactor finishes up with sixty times or more the fuel he or she started out with. As Dr Walter Marshall, deputy director of the United Kingdom Atomic Energy Authority, made clear at the conference on the fast reactor held at the Polytechnic of the South Bank in November 1978, breeder reactors are rather poor devices for converting uranium-238 into plutonium, their capacity for that conversion being far outpaced by reactors such as the Magnox and Candu which operate on natural uranium. What is important is the 'doubling time' by which enough fuel is generated to sustain not just the reactor in operation but another reactor as well, for if the doubling time is sufficiently short – say twenty years or less – then an expanding programme of breeder reactors can be established. In fact, liquid metal fast breeder reactors such as the prototype reactor at Dounreay or the Phoenix reactor in France take twenty years at least to produce a plutonium gain equivalent in quantity to their initial charge and, since the overall lifetime of a reactor is approximately twenty-five years, such reactors are capable of little more than keeping themselves running in fuel.

With rare exception plutonium is a man-made element, formed within the reactor from uranium-238. Since thermal reactors are both cheaper to build than fast reactors and are more efficient producers of plutonium, clearly any long-term nuclear programme must depend on the two kinds of reactors, the former generating plutonium and the latter consuming it. The question is whether there is sufficient reasonable grade uranium in the world to allow enough plutonium to be generated to sustain a large breeder reactor programme, for in the last analysis plutonium breeding must keep pace with consumption.

The quantities of plutonium that can be produced depend on the quantities of uranium that can be mined and extracted from the environment, and they also depend on the kind of reactor and on reprocessing. Recently the International Atomic Energy Agency assessed that uranium could be in short supply at the same time as oil and natural gas are dwindling; hardly an opportune moment for the increasingly hard-pressed energy-guzzlers of the world. Indeed the four million tonnes of recoverable reserves of uranium must be matched against a world demand of between 178 000 and 338 000 tonnes per year – the uranium consumption forecast for the year 2000. While the fast reactor gives at best a net gain in plutonium of 189 kilograms (420 pounds) per year per 1000 megawatts a thermal reactor such as a pressurized water reactor will yield 275 kilograms (611 pounds) per year per 1000 megawatts [advanced gas-cooled reactors yield only 180 kilograms (400 pounds) of plutonium]. Thus, it would take some twelve years of maximum production and reprocessing for a thermal reactor to produce enough plutonium to fuel a fast reactor of equivalent size, in as much as the initial plutonium charge to a fast reactor is close to three tonnes per 1000 megawatts (electric).

Now we come back to a rate and magnitude problem. Professor Alvin Weinberg assessed in 1970 that the world would require the simultaneous operation of 24 000 reactors each of 5000 megawatts (electric), to reach a 1970 US standard of living and, since the world would have long since run out of uranium-235, he assumed all those reactors would be fast reactors consuming the plutonium generated within them from uranium-238 left over from the previous thermal reactor programme. In the light of studies indicating that energy efficiencies could be improved several times for the same industrial output, Weinberg has now reduced his requirements, and talks instead of 8000 reactors of 5000 megawatts each. To generate sufficient plutonium to get that number of fast reactors off the ground would necessitate a thermal reactor programme of 4 million megawatts operating at maximum production both of electricity and plutonium for ten years. In effect the 4 million tonnes of uranium assessed as being recoverable reserves would last a mere six years in such a programme on the basis that a 1000 megawatt plant requires some 180 tonnes of uranium each year.

For the promoters of atomic energy it is becoming a *Catch-22* situation. They need thermal reactors to build up plutonium supplies for fast reactors, and they need fast reactors to make good use of plutonium; yet the rate at which plutonium can be generated is too slow to keep pace with future reactor demand and, in trying to make good that deficiency, uranium-235 – the source of all fissile material – is consumed too quickly.

It is perhaps fortunate that Weinberg's fantasy is in never-never land; for his programme of fast reactors would demand that some 250 000 tonnes of plutonium are in circulation each year, half in the reactor core, and half outside being reprocessed. Given, too, that his programme is several hundred times larger than the full extent of nuclear power in the world today, reprocessing will have to become increasingly efficient so that the environment is free from contamination. Thus, each reprocessing plant will have to release virtually no radionuclides into the environment to remain within today's acceptable limits, and that requirement takes no account of any future authorized reductions in total discharges to the environment. There is simply no guarantee that such an extraordinarily high reprocessing efficiency can ever be attained at a cost which makes the whole operation worthwhile. Nor can reprocessing be dispensed with because without it, the fast reactor has no future, and without the fast reactor, fission power has no future.

To date reprocessing has proved the achilles' heel of the industry; this is the point at which the spent fuel is broken open and its contents released. Not only are shorter-lived radionuclides such as caesium, strontium, tritium, and krypton released but also longer-lived actinides such as americium and various isotopes of plutonium which, because of their alpha radiation, are particularly dangerous to living organisms if ingested or inhaled. Thus, once a nuclear programme of any substance gets underway, those isotopes will together present a fearful and intractable environmental problem.

With regard to cost atomic energy enthusiasts have been extraordinarily naïve. Because of the far lower fuel costs of reactors compared to fossil fuel plants, they believed that nuclear power would remain relatively impervious to rises in the price of fossil fuels and hence their competitiveness could only increase with the price hikes of oil and coal following Libya's take-over of its oil reserves in 1972. What they neglected to see was the absolute dependence of nuclear power on the fossil fuels, every operation in the fuel cycle, including the construction of the reactor itself depending on the processes fuelled by oil in particular and by coal. Furthermore the public has always been shielded from the real cost of nuclear-generated electricity which, from the beginning, has been sustained by government-sponsored research and development, and in the United States by reactor constructors promoting their reactors by sale-enticing, loss-making prices with guaranteed cheap enriched uranium. Now the industry and the utilities have had to concede, that nuclear energy is no more immune to inflationary trends than any other industry. In fact, between 1973 and 1976 the labour costs in uranium mines rose by over 50 per cent in North America; fuel and electricity costs tripled; the cost of chemicals used in refining the uranium and in reprocessing doubled; and, while between 1966 and 1974, approximately 2 dollars were spent in the exploration of every pound (over 4 dollars per kilogram) of uranium produced in the US; the costs are now over six dollars (over 13 dollars). Perhaps the last straw for the nuclear industry has been the five-fold increase in construction costs. One ironic indication of the dependency of reactors in the United States on fossil fuels is that all the enrichment plants are powered with electricity generated by coal-burning, a 1000 megawatt reactor requiring the generation of 45 megawatts for enrichment alone.

For many opposed to nuclear power, renewable energy resources have acquired an aura of unblemishable virtue, and they lament bitterly the gigantic discrepancy in funds made available for the research and development of nuclear reactors, especially the breeder reactor, compared with those for windmills, wave machines, photoelectric cells, geothermal energy, and other seemingly non-polluting self-generating sources of energy.

But if these people want the renewables to accomplish what is now accomplished with the fossil fuels then they are in for a great disappointment. For the renewables to replace present energy systems the rate and magnitude problems would be just as bad as we have outlined for gaining fuel from tar sands, coal, shale oil, and from uranium. Furthermore, renewable energy is relatively diffused and has to be concentrated, necessitating the use of large areas of land and of mineral resources for its capture. Thus a 1000 megawatt nuclear plant requires some 2 square kilometres (0·8 square mile) of land; a solar plant – using mirrors or heliostats to gather the energy and reflect it on to a central tower – takes up forty times more land, assuming similiar output to the nuclear reactor, and a hydroelectric plant with its water reservoir some 100 times more land still. Nevertheless, the nuclear plant is hardly an isolated machine, requiring fuel fabrication plants, reprocessing units, enrichment facilities, and, finally, somewhere to dump its small but potent wastes. As for windmills – the largest proposed are in the range of 1000 kilowatts or one megawatt – ther would have to be at least 1000 such units to match up to one average-sized nuclear plant. Each windmill would have 40-metre (134-foot) diameter blades, and would need to be supported by structures equivalent in size to those used for carrying 400 kilovolts for the national grid. To site as many windmills as would be necessary to replace just one nuclear power plant would clearly present great problems from the planning point of view. The same arguments prevail for wave machines – some estimates indicating that several hundred kilometres of wave machines would be needed to provide a reasonable proportion of Britain's electricity. None of such systems are free of technological problems: windmills would have to take gale-force winds without blowing over or losing blades, and wave machines would have to survive heavy seas and somehow be linked to an on-shore electricity grid system. As for solar power plants, a 100 megawatt (electric) plant would need a tower 260-metres (870-feet) high faced by a field of some 20 000 heliostats each 6·4 metres squared (21 feet squared) spread out over an area of 3·5 square kilometres (1·35 square miles).

Nevertheless, two American physicists, Professors Alvin Hilderbrandt and Lorin Vant-Hull claim in *Science* that it should be possible to get as much as 40 000 megawatts (electric) from such plants in the United States by the year 2000 and at a cost – given mass production of the heliostats – of no more than that cited for light water reactors (LWRs). They also point out that the energy amplification factor – which is the useful energy produced during the lifetime of the power plant divided by the capital energy required to create the plant – is some five times better for a solar power plant than for a nuclear power plant. Moreover the criticism levelled at solar power plants – that they perforce shut down at night – would perhaps be more significant if nuclear power plants operated at their maximum capacity twenty-four hours a day throughout the year. In fact, nuclear power plants have a duty factor at best some 50 per cent higher than that projected for solar power plants. As for development costs, Michel Rodot, director of research for Centre National de la Recherche Scientifique (CNRS) in France, points out that the construction of a dozen prototype solar power plants would cost less than that of one prototype nuclear power plant.

Even if solar power plants were the answer to the energy needs of the United States and of France with its warm Mediterranean climate in the south, they can hardly provide much of Britain's needs. Indeed, their contribution might be limited to flat plate collectors for heating water – a marginal enterprise given Britain's climate – or for small-scale electricity generation through the manufacture of sufficiently cheap solar cells.

Biomass fuels, as they have come to be called, are increasingly mooted as possibilities, with the advantage that they are concentrated forms of solar energy, akin in their usefulness to the fossil fuels. Thus, in his study of the energy requirements of British agriculture, Gerald Leach calculates that straw (if collected after combining, instead of being burnt in the field), would yield sufficient energy when converted to liquid fuel to meet most if not all agriculture's energy requirements, which amount to some 5 per cent of total United Kingdom energy consumption. Biomass is a massive store of energy. A rough estimate indicates that terrestrial and marine plants trap in organic form some 27 to 35 $\times$ 10²⁰ joules of solar energy each year – an amount which is some ten times greater than the present industrial consumption of energy in the world. Obviously it would be an impossible and ludicrous task to gather energy from vegetation to meet all the world's growing industrial needs. Neither would it be sound ecological practice, in so far as the soil itself, and its microflora, need replenishment from the breakdown of organic matter on the soil surface. N K Boardman and H D W Saddler of the Commonwealth Scientific and Industrial Research Organization (CSIRO) in Australia, calculate on a worldwide basis that vegetation might provide as much as 20 per cent of present world energy consumption. In Brazil chemical plants are already converting bagasse (refuse from sugar making) into alcohol which is added to petrol and in Australia a scheme is also being considered to convert timber waste. In China and India a growing number of villages are also provided with biogas plants which generate methane from sewage and animal waste.

In practice, biomass fuels, however much they appeal to the enthusiast, are hardly likely to make a real dent in man's future energy requirements. Take the fuel needed for transport. R Morse, director of solar energy studies at the CSIRO in Australia, estimates that 13 million hectares (32 million acres) of timber would have to be cut down each year in Australia to meet no more than one half of its estimated energy needs for transport by the year 2000. On that count it would take 26 million hectares (64 million acres) – an area the size of Britain – to provide all of Australia's transport fuel. And what would Britain do with its larger population and greater density of traffic?

Much of the rational thinking about energy self-sufficiency at the national level is purely short term, the hope being that necessity will be the mother of invention in generating new energy sources. Too little thought has been given to long-term self-sufficiency in energy because governments, administrators, and industry find it far easier to think in terms of a blanket of energy for the whole of society rather than of individual communities embarking on their own energy-providing ventures. Clearly the potential of becoming self-sufficient in energy in one area, one community, may depend on wholly different resources compared with another area. Where one country may have wind and water power, another with a drier climate might better be able to use direct solar energy, and biomass fuels may make more sense in the tropics.

In fact, self-sufficiency in energy is more likely to be possible if it is attempted at the individual and community level rather than from above through government mandate and, although technology will necessarily play its part, as it has with development of all human culture, the stress should perhaps be on individual choice and the opportunity for best using the local environment.

Leach has shown that proper insulation of all of Britain's nineteen million dwellings could reduce household energy consumption to as little as 14 per cent of its present annual average. The energy savings would be respectable because households consume 30 per cent of primary energy in Britain. But, in addition, there are innumerable systems for warming houses without necessarily resorting to heat pumps and other high technology. A conservatory along the south-facing wall can be a useful adjunct to any heating system, while having the virtue of providing a good environment for growing hot-house plants. An interesting and effective passive solar heating system has been devised by Professor Felix Trombe of the CNRS solar laboratory at Montlouis in the Pyrenees together with the architect Jacques Michel. Its main feature is a south-facing concrete wall painted black on the outside. The wall is covered with a double layer of glass leaving a few centimetres clearance. During the winter, air circulates from inside the house to the space between the glass and the concrete where it is warmed up. In the summer, vents are opened in the north and south walls so that the heated concrete wall draws a refreshing current of air through the house.

Ancient cooling systems are also remarkably effective in providing a pleasant environment in which to live. In Egypt, houses were traditionally designed with openings into small, shaded courtyards on the north-facing side and into large sun-filled courtyards on the other side of the house. The difference in temperature between the two courtyards created a current of air which was drawn in from the north side over porous pitchers containing Nile water. The air passing over the pitchers became much colder because of the latent heat of evaporation of water; moreover, any water which oozed out of the pitchers was filtered and could safely be drunk. In India food is also traditionally preserved from rotting by placing it in a glazed jar inside a porous one containing water. In *The Ecologist* Allan Cain and his colleagues point out that the Maziara jar used in Egypt can produce as much as 400 kilojoules (1700 kilocalories) of cooling per day, some 192 watts at a maximum, while the temperature within the jar remains relatively constant at 20 °C (68 °F) even though the outside temperature may rise to above 35° C (95 °F). The cooling achieved is very effective, and requires no more effort than to fill the Maziara jar once every morning. An air conditioner, on the other hand, yielding some 3000 kilojoules (12 700 kilocalories) of cooling, consumes some 2400 watts of electrical energy. In fact more electricity is consumed in the United States through the use of air conditioners than more than 800 million Chinese use for everything.

According to Ivan Illich, inequities in energy consumption, such as that between the United States and China, or between an individual with a rich life-style and a poor peasant are unbridgeable in the sense that one excludes the other. In *Energy and Equity* Illich develops the thesis that energy consumption over a particular threshold leads inevitably to negative consequences which primarily have to be absorbed by those in the poorer strata of society. Thus, more people trying to travel more swiftly leads to congestion on the roads, to speed limits, to the need for new motorways, and to the deprivation of those who cannot afford such means of transport and find themselves contending with an increasingly inadequate public transport system. The need for the high-speed journeys themselves is also suspect. In the last analysis most of the journeys are brought about through the need to create a flow of capital, whether for the oil companies, the motor manufacturers, businessmen, those in the tourist industry, or for governments who reap their harvest of value-added taxes and the like.

'Only a ceiling on energy use can lead to social relations that are characterized by high levels of equity ... participatory democracy postulates low energy technology ... What is generally overlooked,' Illich continues, 'is that equity and energy can grow concurrently only to a point. Below a threshold of per capita wattage motors improve the conditions for social progress. Above this threshold, energy grows at the expense of equity. Further energy affluence then means decreased distribution of control over that energy.'

In his usual devastating, controversial way, Illich overturns conventional dogma. People accept blithely that society benefits from the increasing centralization of energy supply, the notion being that it requires vast resources of capital and technology to develop such ventures as North Sea oil, Selby coalfields, nuclear power plants, and the like. Furthermore, the large bank of energy made available through such multinational, international, and national efforts is then supposed through market forces and through socialist .enterprise to diffuse down through the populace – providing goodies on the way. Illich disagrees wholeheartedly because what he sees is a failure of the bounties of that energy use to find its real target; consequently, he claims, it leaves real deprivation in its wake.

At this point we come back full cycle to those who are seeking some kind of self-sufficiency. Without necessarily being able to bring such hard, critical thinking to the problem as Illich, they too feel the inequities engendered in modern industrial societies through the un-bridled consumption of energy. They see too that industrial nations are hooked junkie-like on to energy and that, like the drug addict, there is no solution but to kick the habit entirely.

If society continues on its high-energy path, then clearly it will find it increasingly hard to procure the energy it requires. It might be nice if the palliatives of Leach and his ilk would work, but they would have to be imposed rigorously from above by a centralized bureauc-racy on a society that is composed of individuals seeking their own selfish interests. The idea of community action is somewhat lacking in the International Institute for Environment and Development (IIED) analysis: it is rather how people can have more and pay less in real terms for it.

Illich is right; if the world could do without its jet-setting, its high-speed trains, gas-guzzling cars, its mighty office blocks, its throw-away goods, then not only would far less energy be required but, at the same time, the need for vast energy enterprises would become unnecessary; nor could one country dictate world policies from its vantage of holding major energy reserves. Given the right kind of democracy there would undoubtedly be far greater equity in a society less smitten with the goal of industrialization than is apparent today, nor would that necessarily mean greater deprivation. If food, clothes, adequate housing, and proper work are the basic criteria for a reasonable life, then they can be obtained in a low-energy society. To travel throughout the Mediterranean and Middle East and see the increasing number of abandoned terraces and ancient dwellings is a dismal sign of the persuasive power of the high-energy society to destroy a way of life that once gave its practitioners, who at the same time, preserved and enhanced their environment, a reasonable stan-dard of living. Modern agricultural machines do not work as well as mules and donkeys on narrow terraces suspended above steep slopes, nor does the productivity of the terraces justify modern capital in-vestment; as for the labour to work those terraces, traditionally it came from within the family, but now it is being lured away by the promise of money and work in the city. And farm workers, with their values increasingly set by those of their urbanized fellows, cost far too much for the simple peasant with his terraces and mules.

Whether an individual, community, region or even nation, achieves self-sufficiency in energy is perhaps less important in the immediate future than that people should regain an awareness of both the limits of their environment and what they can achieve out of it, given resourcefulness and help. Houses built of local materials, whether stone, cob, timber, slate, tiles or thatch, still make attractive dwellings, especially when combined with modern plumbing and hygienic practices. Add then the technologies and designs to make more efficient use of energy flows, and for a reasonable capital investment such dwellings can become extremely comfortable. Decentralize electricity generation, make people aware that there must be limits to the amount of gadgetry they can operate at any one time, and the savings will become manifold. One simple device, an electronic control system fitted within each house, can increase the useful work done by electricity in a house while reducing the requirements for generating capacity overall. The original control system was designed in a private house in Plymouth and tested out on a generating system operating off an old Cornish water wheel. Indeed, peak generation can effectively be reduced and nigh eliminated, so making unnecessary vast quantities of 'spinning reserve'. Such simple electronic systems already exist and are utilized in conjunction with fluctuating power sources such as small hydropower schemes and wind turbines.

As Amory Lovins points out, much of the energy used in industry is to supply heat at temperatures little more than boiling. At such temperatures renewable energy sources, whether direct solar or wind, can be extremely useful and cost-effective and, once fitted, reduce the need for centralized generating systems. Moreover, all such schemes provide work for local labour, in contrast to giant centralized schemes which require a sudden influx of labour during the phase of construction and then a bare minimum of labour for the operating phase which is becoming increasingly automated. Thus, we hear of each job costing some half-million pounds or more to create.

The politics of self-sufficiency in energy demand, therefore, a concerted effort at the individual, community, business, and industrial level rather than at the national level. Attempts at creating self-sufficiency at the national level are doomed to failure in the long term, just as they have been in the United States over the past five years. Herman Kahn's dream of the quaternary era may be good for science fiction with its flights of fantasy into space but the reality is that man must first regain his notions of self-sufficiency before he will be able to make real his dreams.

*

The dilemmas that we face are essentially moral. As Peter suggests, we are asking ourselves questions about the kind of society that our technologies may compel us to create. This consideration leads us to speculate about the use of resources, the way in which access to them is shared among and between societies and cultures, and about the very purpose that our industries and, most especially, our science-based and high-technology industries are meant to serve. Why do we manufacture motorcars, say, or computers? Do they contribute in any significant way to our individual or social well-being and, if not, could they be made to do so? I believe that the debate over possible material 'limits to growth' is secondary to these considerations and in the next chapter I shall suggest that the entire question of resources and their availability has been misunderstood by many people. Yet to argue, as I would, that the imminent collapse of western industrial societies as a result of material shortage or for want of energy sources is implausible is not to imply that no problem exists. Very clearly it does because so many people have seized upon the issue of resources to criticize the society in which they live and the obvious implication of their criticisms is that this society can not, and should not, be sustained. There is a wish for radical change and this wish remains even when the supposed and superficial reasons advanced to justify the need for such change have been dismissed.

The questions may well be entirely new in human history. It may be that never before have so many people challenged the basic precepts of their society. This is not a matter of demanding the redistribution of wealth and power within society, although that forms a part of it. It is more a challenge to the basis of that wealth and power. This is a moral issue from which political issues stem. It is potentially dangerous because it is all too easy to allow such a fundamental confrontation with the philosophy that underlies society to lead to a rejection of the totality of that society. This line of argument develops into an extreme form of nihilism and, along the way, it persistently undervalues the positive attributes of modern civilization. Can we have the Olympic Games, orchestral concerts, cinemas, and cathedrals while rejecting nuclear reactors? I think we can, but if I were forced to choose between a package that included the bads as well as the goods and one that denied me both I think I would have to accept the nuclear reactor. As Peter says, it is in these terms that the choice is presented. I think that by and large it is presented honestly, in that those who present it to us really see it in these terms. All the same I think the presentation is incorrect and that the true options are much wider. To the extent that it is mainly the environmental movement that has mounted the challenge to accepted wisdom, and the self-sufficiency movement that has begun to explore alternative options, I think it is for them to take the debate to its next stage and to offer the wider range of choices they and I believe exists. This, again, is a moral task that leads to a political task for it must define the kind of society that might result. At all times, though, it must beware of the nihilistic threat that lurks beneath the terms of reference under which the inquiry is conducted.

Although the questions and the mode in which they are asked are new, they cannot be answered until other, much older questions have been considered. For example, Peter compares the number of deaths on the roads of the industrialized nations with the number of deaths that are caused by head-hunting practices among certain tribes. He compares one form of violent death with another to draw moral conclusions. If we are to do this we should prepare the ground in two ways. We should define quite precisely what it is we are comparing and, more important in this context perhaps, we should state the moral ground on which the comparison is made. Let us begin with that.

If we are to make moral judgements of behaviour in two quite different cultures we must decide whether there exists some absolute moral code that has universal application. Is the behaviour of all human beings everywhere subject to similar moral constraints? If it is, if there is some universal law that all of us are bound to obey, then judgements can be made according to that law. If not, judgements made on a universal basis can have no validity and behaviour can be judged only within the context of the culture in which it occurs. Comparisons across cultures cannot be made. Of course, all human societies have moral codes and in many respects these codes coincide. Universal acceptance does not imply the existence of any deeper universal principle, however. The coincidences may well be due to nothing more important than social convenience, so that the establishment of any form of society is impossible unless members agree to refrain from certain kinds of behaviour. Social convenience may be reason enough, but it is impermanent. It may vary quite widely from one culture to another and within a single culture at different periods in history. We may think it morally right for society to punish certain types of criminal by putting them to death at one period but not at another, for example, and we may be correct in our judgement on both occasions. Society has changed in the intervening period and what was useful once is useful no longer. Even then, we may accept that what is right for us may not be right for people elsewhere living under different circumstances.

This suggests that there is no universal moral law, that it is impossible to define once and for all what is 'right' and what is 'wrong'. If this is so, the comparison between the head-hunters and the modern motorist has no validity, and although it may well be true that the head-hunter would be appalled at the loss of life on our roads this can have no relevance to us or, for that matter, to him. His emotional state is caused by his misapprehension of the truth of the matters he is considering. He is not comparing like with like.

In fact, though, we behave as though there were a universal moral law because we have been educated to believe that such a law exists. If it does, its only possible authority must stem from God, and all moral laws that claim universal validity must be derived from a God. The law is clear, unquestionable – though often far from unambiguous – and requires no logical support. If we believe in the existence of such a law, then we can make comparisons and judgements. Indeed, we may have a duty to do so and to prevent behaviour that we find morally repugnant. Believing this, emissaries of many civilizations have set out from their homelands to subdue the barbarians. European colonial powers have condemned and finally stopped the practices of cannibalism and, where they have been able to, infanticide and head-hunting. Informed by ideas brought from western civilization people of many other cultures now seek to prevent the physical mutilation of one person by another such as by the infliction of facial scars, and by the surgical removal of the clitoris and sealing of the vagina in girls before they reach puberty. Is it reprehensible to interfere in traditional practices in these ways? It is if we hold that there exists no universal law to sanction such interferences, but even this is a narrow view. If the one God dictates such practices to be evil, then there can be no debate about the matter and the law must be observed. If, on the other hand, our moral code is based on social usefulness, we may still argue that the practices we seek to stop are harmful. We can try to show that there are practices that degrade their participants, for example, by robbing human beings of their natural dignity so that they are made to appear inferior. We may suggest that the unnecessary infliction of pain by one human upon another is degrading, mainly to the perpetrator, and that it is impossible to derive social advantages from the deliberate, often ritualized, degradation of members of that society. In the end, though, we are most likely to be motivated by our repugnance and, as a human being, I must admit that I find such infliction of needless suffering repugnant and I feel no qualms of conscience in denouncing it as 'barbaric'.

What, though, does the head-hunter think of road accidents? Again, the comparison is not valid. On the one hand we have the deliberate killing of one person by another person. The actions performed by the killer are intended, by him, to cause the death of his victim. Death is inflicted deliberately by a person who intends to inflict death. The motorist does not kill deliberately but as the result of mechanical failure over which he has no control, accidental misjudgement, or the sudden development of circumstances that he is not skilful enough to bring to a happier conclusion. Even where the fatal accident results from the criminal negligence of a driver, the driver did not intend to cause death. In a moral sense, therefore, even if we assume a common code under which both categories may be compared, we still cannot compare a deliberate act with an inadvertent one. Our own law, and so far as I know the law of all countries, forbids the killing of one individual by another, but it distinguishes carefully between the advertent and the inadvertent, allowing only a dubious area between the two in which the perpetrator behaves negligently or recklessly while knowing the risks, so that his sin is one of omission.

Nor is it true to say that modern societies tolerate high rates of road accidents. Perhaps they endure the grim statistics but they do not tolerate them. They pass laws to make cars safer, they impose regulations to constrain the behaviour of drivers, they build better roads, they conduct educative campaigns to warn motorists of the more common hazards, they cajole, exhort, and try to enforce better and safer behaviour. The fact that the incidence of road deaths remains high may show that the problems are very intractible or that the steps taken have been inadequate or inappropriate, but they do not show that nothing has been tried nor that society is tolerant of the situation. Morally, therefore, and provided, again, that we accept a universal standard, the motorist is preferable to the head-hunter. He remains preferable even when the scale of deaths is taken into account. There can be very few motorists who cause more than one fatal accident in the whole of their lives, but a head-hunter may kill deliberately on many occasions. We must be careful not to condone a deliberate and persistent murderer, but to condemn the person whose one error of judgement caused accidental tragedy that no one regrets more deeply than he or she does. That would be to take the nihilistic view that any situation is preferable to our present one. It cannot be held even on some supposed ground of comparative 'naturalness'. If we prefer the head-hunter because in some sense he behaves more naturally, then surely we would balance the situation best if we were to encourage our motorists to kill deliberately when suitable opportunities occurred? The idea is preposterous.

I believe that far from tolerating road deaths modern society is more sensitive to such wastage of life than it has been at any time in its previous history, and that this concern about the value of life and about its quality forms part of the questioning of the moral bases of our civilization. The concern spreads into many other areas of life, not all of them within the obvious compass of the environmental or self-sufficiency movements. We hear much, for example, about the ways in which our society is becoming more violent. Is it, though, that the victims of that violence include members of social strata that once were immune and who are articulate, or is it that we are all more sensitive to violence so that the extent of violence only appears to increase as the product of our increasing awareness? My own view is that while all three possible explanations may obtain it is the third that dominates. I am led to this view by two routes. In the first place I observe that the methods used to quantify violence are crude and limited. In essence, they consist of crime statistics and, perhaps, anecdotal accounts by the media of disturbances and especially of industrial disputes. I find it difficult to believe that these measure anything at all and, especially in the case of reported industrial disturbances, and in most cases the reports of political disturbances, the reporting is biassed heavily in favour of 'the forces of law and order', the existing political system and structure, criticism of whose basic tenets is not permitted, and employers, who by some curious manipulation are held to express 'the public interest'. Even crime statistics are suspect. Is crime being reported more frequently than it used to be, which does not suppose any overall increase? Are reports of crime being recorded in more detail by the police? To what extent are the police seeking to increase their own power and prestige by emphasizing the magnitude of the problems with which they must deal? Yet it has become part of the accepted wisdom of our day that society is becoming more violent and the response that is most popular politically is based upon more severe repression: an escalation of violence.

These are my doubts and they are reinforced by my own memories. When I was a boy attempts were made on my life almost every night, after I had gone to bed. Men flew over me in aeroplanes and dropped bombs upon me. Fortunately their aim was inaccurate, but their failure to kill me was not for want of trying. They killed many people. It seems to me that the war was extremely violent Compared to that, modern society is very gentle indeed. Perhaps, though, the war — though it did occur and I lived through it — was not typical of circumstances through which most people have lived. If I study living conditions before the war, however, I find poor families starving, workers brutalized by unemployment and, when work was found, inhumane working conditions, and, always, violent crime and a violent response to it. If I search back further in time, into the nineteenth and then the eighteenth centuries I find the incidence of violent crime increasing rather than decreasing. Where, then, shall I find the gentle age from which our present descent into savagery may be measured? If, eventually, I travel all the way back to our head-hunting tribesmen, I must conclude that my journey was fruitless, for his world was no less violent than the one with which I am familiar. There never was a time when society was not violent and, so far as I can see, it is becoming less violent rather than more so. What changes is the attitude to violence. We are persuaded of the view that a non-violent society is desirable and possible, that human beings can learn to live together peacably, and it is against this idealized society that we measure our own performance.

If, as I believe, modern society is coming to care more about the violence perpetrated by and against individuals, about economic and political violence and repression as well as about direct physical brutality, about the violence against non-human species and aesthetic concepts caused by human activities, and about the violence that is inherent in the consumption by the rich few of resources that otherwise might benefit many who are deprived, then, I would maintain, our civilization is becoming healthier and its prognosis may not be gloomy. We must look not at the habits and attitudes we inherited from the early phases of the Industrial Revolution but at those new attitudes, not yet developed to form habits, that we are beginning to acquire. The answers we must try to find will tell us how to seize on these new attitudes and extend them.

If my diagnosis is correct, the new society we build can and must include all that is worthwhile from our past. We must not fall into the trap of preserving every culture except our own or of assuming that our culture is something that was destroyed in the past so that we are left with only worthless and irrelevant relics. That route leads directly to cultural suicide.

This implies that in many respects our modern way of life will continue and that if it is to be changed the change must result from deliberate choices made with great care. A satisfactory future is unlikely to emerge from catastrophe.

For various reasons, then, the availability to us and to our children of the physical resources we and they will need is of some importance and it is at this that we must look next.

7 Limits to growth?

In the last chapter Peter developed the argument that the continued survival of modern industrial societies, at least in a form familiar to us, depends upon a continuing and reliable supply of energy at prices we can afford. Since our energy used in industry is derived overwhelmingly from fossil fuels, and since fossil fuels are categorized as non-renewable, it must follow that sooner or later supplies will be so depleted that prices will rise sharply. Energy will become very expensive indeed and the fundamental condition for the smooth functioning of our kind of society will no longer be met. When that time arrives either society will be organized differently so that its dependence on fossil fuels is no longer critical, or it will suffer severe perturbations leading, very possibly, to its economic and then social and political collapse.

This scenario is perfectly orthodox. There are arguments about the date beyond which dependence on fossil fuels will be unwise and there is great controversy over the means by which that dependence will be ended, but the central thesis is accepted by most governments. Peter argues that the adoption of a self-sufficient way of life represents an appropriate response to the situation; that it is, in this sense, a survival stratagem.

I believe this line of argument is open to several objections. Let us assume, for a moment, that the central thesis is correct and that modern industrial societies do face a major crisis regarding energy supplies. In this book I have tried to show that, while it is legitimate to propose reforms of society and that demonstrations of alternatives may form part of such proposals, there is no way in which an individual or group can dissociate from society. We did not choose the kind of society in which we live, which is why we may seek to alter it, but while we live in it we derive benefit from it which imposes obligations upon us. The coherence of any society derives from a relationship between the individual and the group, or what Hobbes would call the sovereign, in which the existence of a social contract is assumed. Eventually, of course, the contract may be defined in the form of a constitution. As members of a society, then, we are bound to obey its laws and we enjoy the protection of those laws. Its emergency services protect our lives and property, its schools educate our children as they educated us, and its hospitals, at least in contemporary Britain, accept us as of right. The benefits are conferred on everyone and it is impossible to refuse them under most circumstances. Indeed, it may be illegal to do so, as it is illegal to refuse to educate a child or to conceal a crime of which one is the victim, and we are bound to obey the laws of society. Consequently, the individual has a moral obligation to reciprocate by contributing to the welfare of society. Should large numbers of individuals evade this obligation, to a greater or lesser degree it would become impossible to provide the benefits. If the revenue from taxation falls below a certain level, for example, services cannot be financed from public funds. If the majority of people refuse to educate their children the following generation will have few teachers and so education will be much reduced. Now it is possible that the adoption of an alternative, self-sufficient way of life does contribute to the welfare of society and, perhaps, in an important sense. If one believes that the benefits conferred by society can be improved it makes sense to establish communities in which such improvements can be demonstrated. If an individual believes that the necessities of life can be provided more conveniently, more reliably, or more cheaply, then that individual may attempt self-sufficiency as a form of demonstration. Whether such communities or individuals succeed or not, their attempts are legitimate and valuable. It is almost as useful to know what cannot be done as to know what can. Further, and less predictable benefits may accrue in the course of the experiments. The self-provider, for example, may discover some novel and highly practicable way to utilize space, materials, or energy. The most obvious example is the development of the 'solar roof', in which a large part of the roof of a building is constructed in such a way as to act as a large, flat-plate solar collector. This idea was demonstrated first by a voluntary community and it was shown not only that it worked but that it cost no more to install than a conventional roof.

Persons engaged in activities of these kinds have not dissociated themselves from society and, in most cases, they have no wish to pretend to do so. Their contribution to society may be unusual but that may increase its value rather than detract from it.

If we relate this view of self-sufficiency to the suggested energy crisis, we can see that those who believe they have perceived this crisis in advance of the majority of members of society are quite justified in taking steps to bring it to the attention of their fellows. In fact, they have a social duty to do so. If they can discover ways to avoid the crisis, or to recover from its effects, then their contribution to social welfare is more valuable still. If their pursuit of solutions requires them to live under experimental conditions, then the self-interest of other members of society dictates that their path be smoothed wherever possible. If they need land, give them land. If they need building materials, give them building materials. If they need information and advice, send the wisest and most skilful of people to visit them, for their work is of high national importance. Of course, the real world is rather different from any ideal world and, in practice, such people seldom receive much official support and their experiments and investigations must be conducted hand-in-hand with the struggle for physical survival, often in a self-inflicted state of hardship. The lack of outside support may demonstrate the degree of bureaucratic myopia but it does not alter the moral standing of the experimenters.

There can be no doubt that the experimenters are responding to the crisis they perceive and we may assume, at least for the more intelligent among them, that the response is appropriate. It may be inadequate in some respect, but nevertheless it tends in the right direction. What matters is the motive of the experimenters and another motive is possible that may lead to rather similar behaviour. It may be that perceiving what they take to be a major crisis, some people seek personal solutions that will protect them from its effects. On a small scale this amounts to no more than prudence. I may lay in a store of candles during the summer because I anticipate power cuts during the winter. The information on which I base my supposition of impending crisis is available to everyone. I claim no special powers of prescience and I have access to no restricted information. My invest-ment is small as is the amount of protection it provides. Anyway, I could be wrong. At the other extreme, I might have access to infor-mation that is not available to everyone and from this I might deduce, with a fair degree of certainty, that a crisis looms whose proportions are very large. If I were rich I might buy myself a remote island, build a house upon it and stock it with provisions sufficient for a prolonged period of isolation. To protect my refuge I might refuse to divulge the special knowledge I had acquired. Most people might regard my actions as selfish, and this is how rich people who left Britain for neutral havens at the outbreak of the 1939–45 war were regarded. It was many years before their defection was forgiven. I think that the creation of a self-sufficient haven for purposes of self-preservation falls into this moral category.

The pursuit of self-preservation is a form of attempted dissociation from society. This kind of self-provider regards himself or herself as superior to other members of society and the attempt at dissociation is possible only for those who enjoy special privileges. The possession of special information that one is not prepared to share assumes superiority: 'I am fit to possess this information but you are not'. The belief that one's own comfort is of more importance than that of anyone else also assumes superiority. The ability to move to a new location at will, to buy land, accommodation, and provisions, requires the individual to have access to resources, especially financial resources, that are not available to everyone. It is morally reprehensible because it is divisive. In a literal sense it is antisocial. It seeks to sever the bonds of the notional social contract when those bonds threaten to become onerous. True, the individual who seeks to sever them demands no further benefit from society, but this is only because he or she believes that society will cease to possess the ability to confer benefits. It is not some kind of moral renunciation. Other members of society may reason that because everyone was bound together formerly in a cohesive unit to which all contributed and from which all derived benefit, loyalty to one's fellows requires the individual not to desert when times are hard. If, as is likely, most citizens continue to collaborate as best they can, enduring the loss of benefit but contributing to efforts to find solutions and so improve the situation, the defector may expect to be penalized for his or her defection. The defector who made no contribution to the resolution of a crisis will obtain a free ride if he or she returns later to resume enjoyment of the benefits. A parallel situation obtains in the case of the pacifist who opposes all forms of armed conflict but whose very existence may depend on the willingness of others to fight on his behalf. The individual who opposes a particular war, as being unjust for whatever reason, may defend his position consistently, but the individual who opposes all wars in which his society may become embroiled has no legitimate defence. Interestingly, such an all-out pacifist is tolerated in most modern societies, but the more rational individual who disagrees with a particular war only, and so passes judgement on his fellows, is not.

It is always dangerous to allow individuals to obtain free rides because, as we saw earlier, the very existence of society depends upon the participation of its members, and it is invariably in the interest of the individual to obtain a free ride. If I can obtain the full range of social benefits while evading the payment of taxes, the advantage to me is obvious. If I can enjoy the improved wages and working

conditions achieved in the industry that employs me without supporting the trade union that negotiated them, again I secure an advantage.
While a small number of free riders can be carried by the majority, in
the end the provision of benefits depends on the payment of taxes,
and the negotiating of improved working conditions and wages depends on the existence of trades unions with strong support. If they
become too numerous, free riders can erode the entire fabric of the
social system. For this reason, people caught evading taxes are dealt
with severely, many trade unionists favour closed shop agreements in
which only union labour is employed, and countless numbers of
ordinary people resent strongly the behaviour of individuals whose
pretence of self-sufficiency is supported by society at large. Of all
people, environmentalists and seekers after self-sufficiency should be
the last to try to obtain free rides. The implications of such behaviour
are spelled out with great clarity in 'The Tragedy of the Commons',
the essay by Garrett Hardin that was reprinted and cited so often in
the early 1970s that it acquired the status of something close to
scripture. It is appalling to fall into the sin one's behaviour was
designed expressly to avoid!

We may dismiss selfishness, then, as a motive of any moral worth
and we may count those who seek personal survival amid surrounding catastrophe as selfish. Morally they are of no interest and
politically we might not seek their company.

When it comes to it, though, are those who seek to persuade
society of the need for change of any greater moral interest? Does
their motivation provide us with a basis for a political philosophy? I
do not believe it does. Certainly they are not behaving reprehensibly.
They do not seek a free ride from society and the changes they
advocate may well be beneficial to society should their diagnosis of
impending crisis prove correct. It is here, though, that their moral
position is undermined. Their behaviour and the changes they seek in
society amount to a response to earlier changes that are beyond their
control. In fact, they amount to nothing more than expediency. Their
efforts to preserve the society to which they belong cannot be regarded as antisocial, but nevertheless they are self-seeking. Their
purpose is the preservation of society. Their success implies the continued receipt of the benefits of membership of society; their failure
implies the cessation of those benefits. Politically they may play a
useful role but necessarily it is a temporary one. The passing of the
crisis must rob them of their relevance whether they succeed in their
objectives or not. They may be likened to a faction that advocates war
(or negotiation) in a time of international tension. Such advocacy

may or may not be wise, and it may exert considerable political influence, but the easing of the tension or the launching of the war resolve the issue around which the faction formed. It must find a new role or it will cease to exist. This new role may require it to develop into a political party but if this is to be achieved successfully the faction must define a political philosophy that deals with every aspect of the society to which it speaks.

The question of motivation is of the greatest importance. Most people would agree, I think, that actions performed under duress have no moral standing. If I sign a confession to a crime while a gun is held to my head that, for all I know, will be fired should I refuse, my confession is worthless as a tool in securing my conviction, provided the circumstances under which I signed it can be proved. The person who performs a spectacular leap from a blazing building does not become a hero thereby. On the other hand, the person who enters the blazing building voluntarily to save the lives of those who are trapped is regarded as a hero. It is not the act that is heroic but the voluntary nature of its performance. At its most basic level we may infer that no act can be morally good unless it is wholly voluntary and is not intended to confer an advantage on the person performing it. Evil acts, on the other hand, are often performed out of self-interest, but even they cannot be performed under compulsion. They, too, must be voluntary. Only if an act is voluntary can it have moral significance and only if the performer expects to derive no benefit from it has it the possibility of being good.

If it is to be consistent, the standard is absolute and there can be no exceptions to it. It raises some quite profound difficulties, however. Clearly our ideally motiveless act cannot be good unless some good results from it. How, then, are we to define such good? It might seem that the saving of a human life must be unquestionably good. What, though, if the person whose life was saved later becomes an incorrigible criminal? Had Adolf Hitler or Joseph Stalin been endangered before they became dictators, would the person who saved them have behaved well? We may defend our hero by saying that at the time no one could know that these men would become dictators, but had they been in danger after they became dictators would it have been morally correct to save them or to allow them to die? We may appear to resolve this dilemma by declaring that all human life is sacred and must be saved if at all possible. Such a declaration may sound attractive, but there is no argument we can advance that will show all human life to be sacred, and so it needs support. Of course, we can argue that indiscriminate killing is socially inconvenient, but this does not defend 'life' as such. The support comes, and must come, from authority. Arguments based on nothing but authority have no basis in logic, and any human authority can be challenged, so the authority must be superhuman. In fact, it must be possessed by God. Now that we allow God to declare all life to be sacred we are safe because by definition God cannot be challenged. What is more, we may allow that God outlines a moral system that extends beyond the preservation of life to provide us with the skeleton of a moral, and so legal, code. Unhappily, we have travelled in a circle. We have defined moral behavour according to the degree to which it conforms to the will of God – or 'natural law', as we saw in Chapter 1 – and have accepted that all humans are bound to obey the will of God. This is compulsion and in most religions it is reinforced by promises of extreme bliss for those who behave well and extreme torment for those who behave badly. If he was a religious person, then, we may suppose that the man who leapt into the fire to save the trapped person, who may have been Hitler, was motivated either by a hope of eternal bliss or by a fear of eternal torment. His act was not motiveless, it contained a strong element of self-interest, and morally it was worthless. We are left with our absolute standard but no way of applying it consciously. In the last chapter I suggested that we cannot assume there exists any overall definition of 'good' and 'evil' that can be applied to all humans in all cultures throughout the whole of history. Now I am saying that there is no way we can define these terms satisfactorily even within our own culture and our own time.

The difficulty is very real, but it is not quite so morally paralysing as it may seem. By our absolute standard we may know that no act performed under constraint has a moral value and that no act performed from a self-seeking motive can be morally good, regardless of its outcome. Equally regardless of their outcome we may know that conscious but motiveless acts may possibly be good. To a moralist, this is as it should be. We may know with a fair degree of certainty when what we do is not good, but there is no way in which we can behave well deliberately. Were we able to do so, of course, our 'good' acts would be motivated and so they would cease to be good.

When we apply this argument to those who would change society, we find that if their purpose is the avoidance of catastrophe or, in any sense, the survival of society or of themselves, then it has no moral consequence. It is an act performed under constraint. It becomes morally significant only when the constraint is removed. At that point it may become self-seeking, in which case it cannot be good. If the self-provider aims by his or her way of life to improve the condition or quality of that life then, although the effort may succeed, it is of no moral worth. We are left, then, with one possibility of good. An attempt to change society may be good if and only if its success benefits society as a whole but confers no special benefit or advantage on those who bring about the change. We cannot be certain that such an act is good because we have denied ourselves any possibility of defining that word.

The argument may seem to turn upon a fine moral point – though I would maintain that it is fundamental and of the greatest importance – but it so happens that only the kind of morally positive act that I have outlined has the kind of political significance that might allow it to provide the beginning of a political base. As we saw earlier, a change that is advocated as a response to a constraint derives its relevance only from that constraint. If the environmental and self-sufficiency movements have political significance, therefore, this must derive from their moral significance which, in turn, must be based on the advocacy of changes that benefit society for no reason except that the advocates wish to benefit society.

Now, if the constraints that many people perceive are real, the chance that environmental and self-sufficiency arguments have any moral and political standing is much reduced. It is difficult to behave with a fine altruism when all about us is about to crumble. Perhaps we should consider, then, whether the constraints are real and whether, real or not, they are perceived by environmentalists and self-providers and form any part of their motivation.

Are there material limits to growth? The idea that such limits may exist is not new but it was revived during the late 1960s as environmentally oriented economists began to consider the implications of perpetual economic growth. They calculated, as many economists had done before them, that should the consumption of non-renewable resources increase, a point must be reached beyond which further increase is inhibited by the scarcity of those resources. The new element in the argument was derived from the way in which growth is measured. Invariably it is expressed in terms of gross national product, a crude measure compiled by adding together the value of all the goods and services produced or supplied within a country over a period of time, usually one year. Growth and decline are measured as changes in GNP from year to year. In fact, they are measured against a scale that shifts as GNP itself is recalculated. This means that change is measured as compound interest, in which proportional increments are computed not on the original capital but on the original capital plus all the preceding increments. If it continues, such growth may proceed exponentially and can be represented on a graph by a curve that rises very slowly at first but that reaches a near vertical alignment rather abruptly. The discovery that such growth cannot be contained within a finite system can make little claim to originality but it can be made to produce dramatic predictions of imminent collapse. It depends, of course, on our acceptance of certain premisses. We must accept that some resources are non-renewable, that the system is finite, and that economic growth must be based on the consumption of resources some of which are both finite and non-renewable.

It seems obvious that certain resources are non-renewable. Fossil fuels and most minerals are extracted from the ground and when they have been used they are not returned to the ground. Fuels are used entirely, but minerals can be recycled. The efficiency with which they are recycled in practice is a function of their value. Gold, for example, and the platinoid metals, can be recovered entirely after use and remade into ingots. Even the minute particles that adhere to the cloths that are used to polish articles made from such precious metals can be recovered. The process is expensive, of course, but the value of the metals is high enough to justify it. Other metals are recycled much less efficiently. There is wastage and the recovered metals are usually impure so that they are inferior to new metals and in some cases can be used only as diluents. Even if we allow a perfectly efficient recycling, however, the difficulty has not been resolved, because of our third premiss, that we must use more of them each year than we used last year. The circulating stock must be increased in size constantly.

In a literal sense, according to the theory of plate tectonics, minerals are all recycled and so it is not accurate to regard them as non-renewable. Eventually the durable wastes we discard are subducted at destructive plate margins to return to the magma from whence they came, their place being taken by new magmatic material supplied elsewhere. Thus, new minerals are formed constantly and materials are lost only when they are fired into space with the intention that they shall not return. Even most orbiting satellites return to Earth at last. This is not true for all metals – iron ores may not be formed in this way, for example – but it is true of most. They may be regarded as essentially non-renewable, though, if the rate at which they are used exceeds the rate at which they are formed and of this there seems little doubt.

On a larger scale, the matter from which the Universe is composed is finite, so that all our terrestrial resources are finite and the premiss that the system of which we are part is finite is a truism. It does not follow, however, that our activities will exhaust the resources on which they depend. These may be finite, but so large as to be in-exhaustible. The idea that particular resources are finite turns upon estimates of their size.

The idea that resources may become seriously depleted rather soon was developed first in the study made at the Massachussetts Institute of Technology on behalf of the Club of Rome and published as a series of technical documents and as a popular summary, which appeared first, called *The Limits to Growth*. *The Limits to Growth* study listed nineteen non-renewable resources: aluminium, chromium, coal, cobalt, copper, gold, iron, lead, manganese, mercury, molybdenum, natural gas, nickel, petroleum, the platinoid metals, silver, tin, tungsten and zinc. For each of these it used the rate at which consumption had changed in recent years, the size of the known reserves, and it calculated the date by which those reserves will be exhausted. The result was impressive and dramatic, but it contained some very fundamental flaws. This becomes evident in the prediction that aluminium may be exhausted in thirty-one years and that if the reserves are five times larger than the figure allowed, it will be exhausted in fifty-five years. In fact, 15 per cent of the weight of the upper 16 kilometres (10 miles) of the Earth's continental crust is accounted for by alumina, the oxide of aluminium, and the metal itself accounts for 8 per cent of the weight of the crust. Clearly a resource of this size cannot be exhausted at all, far less within about half a century. If it were to be exhausted there might be serious risk of the crust collapsing! Iron, which the study suggests will be exhausted in 173 years, assuming five times the known reserves, accounts for 5·8 per cent of the weight of the crust. Manganese, exhaustible in ninety-four years, is the twelfth most abundant element in the crust, with reserves in every continent, and the metallic nodules that are found on the sea bed in several places and in large amounts are rich in manganese. Even in the case of petroleum, the most obviously limited resources, the known and proven reserves increase each year despite the rate at which we consume petroleum products. A large region of fields has been found in recent years in Mexico; China has large but undisclosed reserves; and it is believed Antarctica may possess large fields, although this remains unproven. Conservative estimates hold that the present known reserves of about 750 billion barrels may eventually increase to 2000 billion barrels, and Professor Peter Odel of the Erasmus University, Rotterdam, suggests that the final figure may be in the region of 11 000 billion barrels.

Admittedly, Professor Odell is seen as a somewhat maverick figure by the oil industry and his optimism is not shared by all fuel economists, but even so the present reserve figure of 750 billion barrels is sufficiently interesting, because *The Limits to Growth* figure was 455 billion barrels. If this figure be increased five-fold, said the study, petroleum will be exhausted within fifty years.

Clearly, something was very wrong. In the case of aluminium, as Herman Kahn pointed out, the figure chosen to represent the reserves by the MIT team was more than doubled between the 1965 figure they used and the 1973 figures that were used for all other metal estimates. The reason for this is not clear. Kahn also shows the way in which the size of reserves changed between 1950 and 1970 not, as the MIT study might suggest, by decreasing, but in most cases by increasing very substantially. The 1970 estimate for phosphate reserves, for example, is more than 4400 per cent higher than the 1950 estimate, and chromite reserves increased by 675 per cent in the same period. There is a grave danger that we may end by playing games with huge numbers that are almost meaningless.

The MIT error was fundamental and semantic. They mistook the word 'reserve' for the word 'resource'. Technically, 'resource' means the amount of a material that is present on Earth. 'Reserve' means that part of the resource that has been located and for which mining plans exist, however tentative. Even then, figures for reserves proceed through several approximations. Most commonly the process begins with the surveying of land or sea areas to obtain a broad picture of their geological composition. Where the geology appears similar to formations elsewhere that are known to contain particular minerals, an estimate is made of the likely amount of the useful mineral that is present, based on the size of the formation and on information obtained from mining at other apparently similar sites. This is an 'inferred' reserve. Should it be desirable at some later stage to contemplate mining, drillings are made, rocks are analysed, and a more precise estimate is made of the concentration of the mineral. This is an 'indicated' reserve. Later still, if preliminary studies seem promising, mining operations may commence and it is not until mines have been opened and are in production that a final estimate may be made of the amount of material present. This is a 'measured' reserve. In the case of petroleum the terminology is somewhat different, but the principle remains the same. Surveys of these kinds are made by the mining industry or by government bodies on behalf of the mining industry. Their purpose is simple and restricted. The mining companies need to plan one generation of mines ahead. When existing mines are worked out others must be ready to take their place. Surveying and test drilling are costly, and no one can predict the demand for any material for very far into the future, and so the industry has no interest in exploring further into the future than about the lifetime of an average mine. For many minerals this is about thirty years. It is no coincidence, then, that assuming a constantly rising demand, the MIT study concluded that all the minerals will be exhausted in nine (gold) to 111 (coal) years, with most falling in the twenty to sixty year range. It does not mean that the minerals will be exhausted in this time, but that this is as far ahead as the industry has planned, so it is a comment on forward planning in industry rather than on resources or reserves, to which it has no relevance whatever. The size of the resource itself cannot be calculated except, and very approximately, by relating its known average abundance in the composition of the Earth's crust to the known mass of the crust.

It may be argued that although a substance may be plentiful it is found at such high dilutions among other substances that its extraction poses insuperable technical problems. In particular, the amount of energy required to extract metals from ores of extremely low grade may make the operation uneconomic. There are two answers to this. The first is that technological improvements have made it economically feasible to extract very low concentrations of metals whenever a market for them has existed. I know of no exception to this. Where it has been necessary to do so, the ability to work ever lower ore grades has been developed. Today mercury can be extracted wherever its concentration is 100 000 times greater than in common rocks, uranium wherever it is more than 1000 times more abundant, copper wherever it is 100 times more abundant and iron wherever it is more than ten times more abundant than it is in common rocks. In the case of uranium, recent work in Japan has shown that within a year or two it will be possible to extract the metal from sea water by a chemical process. With a concentration of only 3·3 parts per billion, uranium cannot be said to be abundant in sea water, but the total amount is considerable. It has been calculated to be about 4 to 4·5 billion tonnes.

This is not to say that mining for terrestrial minerals may not be constrained, most probably by its environmental cost. Even this constraint may be surmountable, however. Already plans are being made, and an exploitation treaty has been signed, for the mining of lunar minerals. By the end of the next century, and perhaps much sooner, it is perfectly possible that the Moon and perhaps the larger asteroids will be providing minerals to feed Earth-based industries. Curiously, this may prove far less costly than it sounds. The main capital cost will be incurred in moving people and equipment into space. Once there, and the space shuttle will reduce the cost to far below its present level, great economies are possible, due mainly to the absence of gravity in space and its low value on the Moon. It is said that one man can move with ease equipment that would weigh 9 tonnes on Earth. Minerals would be mined and processed in space and sent to Earth as pure metals or alloys and, of course, no fuel would be required to power their unmanned carriers for the greater part of their journey. Even energy may not be scarce. In space solar energy would be used, but even on Earth the most serious problems arise not from absolute shortages but from competition among potential successors to the fossil fuels, and the gravest dangers derive from strong governmental support for the wrong solutions. The British commitment to nuclear power, which as Peter has shown so persuasively, is irresponsible to the point of wilful sabotage of rival choices, may make it more difficult to ensure an adequate energy supply in years to come, but the fault is political not physical. The rate and magnitude problems, to which Peter refers, can be overcome. Solar cell prices are falling almost daily as new technological developments reduce the difficulties of manufacturing the unusual forms of silicon on which they are based. Solar cells could be mass produced easily, to supply electricity on a small scale just as efficiently as they can supply it on a large scale. Wind and wave technologies exhibit more intractible engineering problems, and are essentially large scale, but they, too, may contribute electricity, perhaps for the production of hydrogen — known already by the nickname LH2 in the aviation industry which is preparing to convert to it — which may replace petroleum as the most common liquid fuel. Fuel cells, improved batteries, and flywheel motors are also being developed.

We should not underestimate the rate at which changes can be made provided the incentive to make them is large enough. In 1939, for example, every building in Britain was equipped with efficient black-out materials, every person was issued with a gas mask, identity card, and ration book, thousands of children were evacuated from cities into rural areas, and air-raid shelters were built or improvised to accommodate urban populations, all in a matter of weeks.

The fact that within the next generation we are likely to move away from petroleum as the most important of our primary fuels and that this will be the first step in a more general move away from fossil fuels almost entirely suggests that the threat of scarcity encourages the development of substitutes. People who predict widespread resource scarcities admit this, but maintain that the depletion will affect so many materials more or less simultaneously that it will prove impossible to accommodate scarcity by substitution. This sounds plausible, but it must be examined because it refers to the third of the MIT premises, that economic growth depends on a continually accelerating consumption of particular materials.

This seems unlikely. It is impossible to predict the future, of course, but it is possible to look at three apparently critical resources that are being replaced now. The fossil fuels, as we have seen, can be replaced quite easily. The process may be ordered or not according to the relevance of the preferences of politicians, but the physical problem is not serious. My second example is copper. In the early 1970s it was being predicted that of all the metals, copper was the one whose exhaustion would prove most crippling. Copper was used in the transmission of signals, such as in telegraph wires and submarine telegraph cables. It was used to transmit electricity, in power lines, and it was used for wiring in transformers and in all other electrical systems. Today it would be more pertinent to predict the date by which copper will be obsolete, except for ornamental use. Submarine cables are being replaced rapidly by communications satellites which are cheaper, more reliable, and carry much greater volumes of information. What is more, they are simpler to service and to replace when their useful life ends. In power lines and several other electrical uses, aluminium provides a satisfactory substitute for copper. Its conductivity is only about 65 per cent that of copper, but since it is lighter, a bulkier cable need weigh little more than the copper cable it replaces. Plastics are being developed to conduct electricity and these may replace aluminium almost before it has begun to erode the copper industry's security. For overland communications systems, optical fibres made from glass – silicon – are likely to replace wires. Thus, the uses for copper are declining rapidly not because the metal is scarce, but because it is costly and inconvenient compared to its rivals. The real danger today is that the replacement of copper will cripple the economies of those countries, such as Zambia, that depend on its export.

Mercury is another rare and expensive metal. Most of the mercury that is produced is used to make switchgear in electrical equipment. New electrical equipment contains no mercury switchgear. The task is performed by a microprocessor, and at a cost that has fallen from something like £100·00 to £0·001 for equipment to perform the same task.

We are led to several conclusions. The first is that any figure purporting to stand for the amount of any resource cannot be better than very approximate and on no account must figures for reserves be mistaken for figures for resources. The second is that historically all the evidence must lead us to suppose that economic demand for a substance provides sufficient incentive to encourage exploration and extraction so that economically – though not necessarily environmentally – we need have little fear of declining ore grades. The third is that the normal evolution of technology makes it impossible to assume that demand for particular substances will be sustained. There is no simple relationship between industrial expansion and pressure on particular resources.

This is not to say that shortages cannot occur. As our experience with petroleum shows, they can. They are shortages that do not bear on resource depletion so much as on political instabilities and, even more, on economic instabilities that lead to wide fluctuations in demand and prices. Market instability has an inhibiting effect on marginal producers especially. The Cornish tin industry, for example, has suffered badly from the price swings that encourage investment in one year only to bankrupt the investor the next.

My purpose is not to show that resource limits will not be encountered at some time, but only to raise a sufficiently large question mark over the entire concept for us to be able to say that for the immediate future it presents no serious problem. Thus, to the extent that self-providers and environmentalists have been influenced by notional limits to growth they have been misled. If we are to develop a coherent political philosophy that embraces the views of the self-sufficiency and environmental movements we must try to remove constraints that tend to force those views in particular directions. As I suggested earlier, if the political outlook is to carry conviction it must be based on a sound moral position and this requires that the world it proposes is proposed for no reason other than that it would be better than the existing world. If it is the only world available to us, or if it amounts to no more than the most rational response to present contingencies, it can have no moral validity.

It has been necessary to examine the 'limits to growth' concept because references to it are frequent in environmentalist literature and, to a lesser extent, in the literature of self-sufficiency. Clearly, it has appeared to provide powerful support for the views of those who belong to both movements, but does it supply the only basis for those views? We may note that although neither movement is new, both of them have acquired their contemporary form since about the mid-1960s, when concern about environmental pollution emerged to reinforce the existing organizations whose aim was the protection of landscapes, the wild flora and fauna they support, and towns and buildings of aesthetic merit. Fears about the effects of environmental pollution are allied, through the levels of industrial activity that give rise to them, to fears of resource depletion and *The Limits to Growth* study included them in its forecasts. The results were no less mistaken. They assumed quite arbitrary causal relationships between the extent of pollution and human mortality, none of which can be substantiated. At present we may say that although pollution is very severe locally, and though there is now no part of the surface of the Earth where the presence of industrial pollutants cannot be detected, the threat to human life and the technical difficulties in controlling pollution levels have both been exaggerated. The true situation may have been described most accurately, and certainly most succinctly, by Dennis Gabor, who wrote that '. . . pollution is a major scandal, but a minor problem'.

If it were true that the environmental and self-sufficiency movements were motivated by nothing more than concern over such issues as resource depletion and pollution, the emphatic dismissal of their concerns would leave them with nothing to say. In fact, though, it seems they have much to say and a part of their message is contained in Professor Gabor's apparent dismissal of environmental pollution as an issue of great importance. Because pollution does not threaten to kill us that is no reason to ignore it. It is, as he says, 'a major scandal', and we refuse to tolerate it. If we seek to reduce levels of pollution, to impose controls on those who cause it and, more generally, to advocate reforms that would reduce the environmental impact of human activities, we may be called, and call ourselves, environmentalists. The message of the environmental movement, then, may be that we believe it is possible to achieve a satisfactory and satisfying way of life within a society that does not cause needless damage to rural and urban landscapes that we find aesthetically pleasing, or to non-human species. Those who seek a self-sufficient way of life may be saying something similar, but may be demonstrating their belief in a more extreme manner.

In elucidating this small piece of rather banal information we have achieved more than may be immediately apparent. There is no implication in this statement that man lives 'unnaturally'. There is no suggestion that his present state is morally inferior to some former state. There is no implied rejection of technology as such or of any technologies or industries in particular, except those that may cause 'needless damage'. Nor is there the slightest suggestion that any alternative that may be proposed as a consequence of the statement is a response to any material constraint. The statement is made freely, it looks to the future rather than the past, and it suggests only that an alternative social and industrial arrangement is possible and preferable. Thus, it appears to satisfy the moral criterion I outlined earlier. It is a statement with moral significance on which a political philosophy may be based.

That philosophy is a deal more radical than it may seem, and than many of its adherents may suppose it to be. Most obviously, it introduces a new criterion that industry must satisfy. No longer is it enough for a factory to produce goods for use or for trading, or for its operations to satisfy its accountants. It must also avoid causing 'needless damage'. By whom is this 'needless damage' to be defined? Presumably it must be defined by the community as a whole, assisted by advisers competent to judge whether or not a particular activity will produce changes that the community finds undesirable. Thus, the community assumes the right to control one aspect of industrial activity. It is more than it may seem, however, for if we are to take the view at its face value, and certainly in the spirit in which it is held by environmentalists, the activities of an industry are not to be confined to the vicinity of its factories. They must extend to the raw materials they use and to the factories that supply them with components they do not manufacture for themselves, and to the uses that are made of the final products. Nor are their environmental effects to be confined to the physical environment and to non-human species, for if they harm humans or impose social costs, then the way of life they imply is neither satisfactory nor, to the victims, satisfying. In deciding whether or not a particular industry should be allowed to operate in a particular place, the whole of the operations of which that industry forms part must be taken into account, with all their implications. We are assuming, then, that the community should have the right to regulate, by implication, all industrial activity. To many environmentalists this would sound extreme, but there are others who would accept it, and it does seem to follow.

Ways must be found to define 'needless'. The community must devise some kind of yardstick by which the usefulness of an industry may be measured. Here environmentalists must choose between two alternatives. They may decide that the most important activity is trading, so that goods should be produced for which markets exist elsewhere, the proceeds from trading being used to buy the goods the community needs. If the dominant factor is the existence or not of a market, it matters little what is produced provided only that its production is profitable. This route leads in the direction of the liberal market economy and it is difficult to see how it can be checked anywhere short of the kind of economy that exists today in the western world. In fact, the route describes a circle and leads the environmentalist back to the point from which he began and presents him once more with his original choice. It may be that this is the preferred choice, nevertheless. Our experience suggests that the regulation of an economy of this type and the imposition of controls upon its industries is very difficult, but it may not be impossible. It is quite likely that the introduction of new technologies will reduce the environmental impact of many industries, which will become far more benign than we have known them to be in the past. It is likely, too, that many industrialists will sympathize with environmentalist ideas, at least in part, so that a dialogue may be sustained and behaviour modified.

The other alternative is more radical. It requires the community to determine what goods are produced in the light of the needs of the community itself and, probably, the needs of other communities. It would shift the emphasis of the economy from trade to use and from a 'free' to a 'managed' market. To see how it might work in practice, let us return to the imaginary small community I invented in an earlier chapter. In such a community it is not at all difficult for members to decide what goods are needed.

Let us suppose that a would-be manufacturer seeks to open a widget factory near our community. Before he can do so he must convince the community that his factory will be beneficial. He may seek to persuade people that it will provide jobs, that it will bring money into the community that can be used to improve services, and he will seek to provide assurances that his activities will cause no inconvenience. If we are proposing a 'use' economy, however, such arguments will carry no weight. The community must know, as its first priority, whether it will be better off when it has widgets than it was without them. The manufacturer must defend widgets as things society needs. If he tries to evade the issue by claiming that even if the present community needs no widgets other communities elsewhere do, the response is likely to be the suggestion that he open his factory close to the community that needs the widgets. If he says that although it needs widgets, there is a compelling reason why that community cannot make them for itself, he may be told that his application to open a widget factory can be considered only if representatives from the widget-deprived community come and ask for them. The need for the product must be established before any other matters are even considered.

It is not difficult to imagine such a situation and to many environmentalists it must seem attractive, while to self-providers it must fulfil many of their requirements for industrial reform. Before it can be achieved, though, certain prior conditions must be satisfied.

By what right does the community permit or forbid the activity of the widget maker? What is to stop him buying a plot of land and building his factory with community approval or without it? In practical terms the community must be empowered to authorize or forbid the sale of land and the provision of facilities and services. No lesser power will be adequate to make unwelcome intrusions physically impossible. However, our cunning widgeteer may be able to out-manoeuvre the community. What can be done to prevent him making a private deal with a landowner and presenting the community with a *fait accompli?* We considered earlier the sanctions a community may visit upon one who breaks the contract by which members are bound one to another, but in this case they seem ineffectual. The ultimate penalty is expulsion, but the sale of his land indicates the willingness of the landowner to depart and his bulging wallet would help him on his way. Some greater control is needed and it is difficult to see how this can be provided without giving the community as a whole the actual ownership of all its resources, including its land. If the resources are owned communally, our widget maker can obtain the land and services he needs only by making a contract with the community, and provided the community is organized in an appropriate way and is not very large, even corruption of community members may be avoided. It might be, for example, that no such contract would be valid unless it bore the mark of agreement of a meeting which all members attended.

We have a situation now in which the land and its resources are owned by the community. This gives the community, the corporate body, something close to absolute power over its members. The ownership of the land on which my home stands, and perhaps of my home itself, gives the owner the power to evict me at will or to favour me by reducing my rent, and to regulate my life in countless petty ways. If the community is ruled by an individual, or by a small caucus of individuals, we have a regime that is too dictatorial for comfort. Power must be distributed fairly among members of the community. This takes us back to considerations of the political systems that obtain within communities and demonstrates the vital importance of establishing a fair system from the start. It is no use embarking blindly in the hope that an equitable system will evolve by itself. As we saw, it is far more likely that a community with no prepared political base will degenerate into some form of dictatorship. The community must be egalitarian.

Egalitarianism is a word that is often used loosely and it arouses strong emotions, usually triggered by misconceptions of what it can be used to mean. I would define an egalitarian society as one in which the benefits, privileges and duties that derive from membership of the society are conferred on all individuals in equal amount and in virtue of their status as members of the society and for no other reason. I do not mean that all individuals are equal in any sense, but only that they enjoy equal citizenship. I would hold that each individual has a right to an equal share in the prosperity of the society in return for the greatest contribution he or she is able to make to that prosperity: the old anarchist slogan 'from each according to his ability, to each according to his need'. It requires that every individual be given an equal educational opportunity, for example, and that the acquisition of a superior or different education by simple purchase be made impossible. It requires that each individual be treated alike in respect of such rules as have been drawn up by the community. This means that legal services be made available to everyone on equal terms so it becomes impossible to gain an advantage by paying higher fees to more skilled lawyers. It requires that those in need of help be treated equally, priorities being determined only by need, not by ability to pay. Such an egalitarian society would provide conditions in which talent would be recognized and fostered, but it would prevent the talented individual from using the rewards for that talent to buy privileges for his or her offspring. If we are to be reduced to considering life as a race, it does not follow that because we require the runners to start level we also require them to finish level.

Rather obviously, I have described a socialist society, because it seems to me that it is only in such a society that environmentalist criteria can be satisfied. The views of all members of the society must be heard, if for no other reason than that our experience of dictators suggests that they are inclined to sell our interests to widget makers at the first opportunity, whatever their expressed convictions, and even if they prove honest, can we trust their successors?

Experience of socialist societies is also experience of societies in which actual control is held, and very firmly, at the centre. Most socialist states tend to create monolithic institutions that are far from being democratic or even efficient and, by favouring members of the political party that holds the power and restricting membership of the party, they create elites whose power and social status are superior to that of the majority. In the final chapter I will propose that such dangers can be avoided best by ensuring that the communities in which power resides are themselves small. I will also propose that, to a large degree, they will be self-sufficient.

*

Mike suggests that my view of the future regarding resource depletion and the consequences on society of that depletion is 'perfectly orthodox'. In part he is right, for as far as mineral resources go, an environmentalist who is not a geologist and who therefore lacks expertise on the subject, must depend for information on someone else who is, and often the environmentalist and government official will fall back on the opinion of the same expert, particularly if events bear out that person's analysis. Concerning oil and natural gas there is now general unanimity between industry, government, and environmentalists that a peaking of world production is not many years away. Yet that consensus is by no means a long-standing one and, in large measure, has come about through the acceptance of one man's hypothesis on the relationship between rates of discovery, of production, and of ultimate recoverable reserves.

King Hubbert, a veteran geologist who worked many years for Shell, and is now with the United States Geological Survey, became something of a maverick in the United States oil industry with his gloomy forecast in the mid-1950s that their oil production would peak by the early 1970s and then go into decline. Hubbert was not speculating idly; he had carefully compiled all the data he could find on oil discoveries and production from the early 1900s until 1956, and he demonstrated that when one looked beyond the inevitable irregularities engendered by the occasional big find, there had been no increase in the rate of discovery for ten years. Indeed, when he fitted a curve to the data on the rate of discoveries against the years he found it to rise with increasing slope until the early 1950s when it flattened off and showed signs of going into decline. A curve of the production rate was similar, but lagging some ten years or more behind the discovery rate curve.

In *The Last Chance Energy Book,* Owen Phillips, Decker Professor in Science and Engineering at the Johns Hopkins University, gives a simple analogy to explain the mechanism behind Hubbert's graphs and his conclusions. Phillips supposes a shipwreck, a Spanish galleon, whose cargo of gold coins gradually spills through the rotting timbers and washes ashore. One day a coin is found on the beach and immediately leads to a rush to find more. Initially the rate of discovery is slow, but as time goes on, and metal detectors and other instruments are brought along, an increasing number of coins is found for every square metre of beach that is searched. Indeed, the treasure hunters have begun to get a clear picture of where the main body of the gold is. Meanwhile, lagging behind those locating the coins, follow those who are actually digging them up. As the search continues the rate of discovery begins to dwindle, first a little and then with increasing rapidity, for the searchers are moving increasingly to the periphery of the lost cargo. The story is the same for those digging up the coins, and as time goes on their efforts to unearth the coins become harder and harder, until the work is no longer worth their while.

Owen Phillips claims that the analogy to oil or to any other mineral ore is a fair one. Moreover, the greater the breadth of the search and the more data that accrue, the more Hubbert's hypothesis appears to be vindicated. Nevertheless, when Hubbert published his conclusions that the United States was soon to run out of oil, the oil industry and the Government were frankly incredulous, for how could the United States be running out of oil when production at that time was soaring to new heights? To refute Hubbert's claim, other research was invoked, particularly that of the geologist Zapp who, in contradistinction to Hubbert, believed that oil reserves should be assessed on the basis of exploratory distance drilled compared to the total amount of oil actually discovered. Thus, given only that a certain proportion of exploratory drilling had taken place, and that there were vast areas still untried, oil remained to be found in similar proportions per exploratory drilling as before. In reply, Hubbert and his followers explained that exploration was never a haphazard, hit and miss affair, but highly selective and increasingly so as a field was located, so that any attempt to equate a given quantity of oil to a given amount of exploratory work would lead, in their opinion, to a gross over-estimate. Time has borne Hubbert out, and not only did American indigenous oil production peak when he said but, despite improved exploratory techniques and a greater intensity of searching, the United States has become a big importer of petroleum. Ironically, it is now the moguls of the oil industry who warn governments and the public of the impending end of the oil boom.

Yet, whereas different factions in society may agree on the extent of oil and natural gas resources there is a world of difference between the view of radical environmentalists and what I would call the orthodox view concerning the future of industrial society. For while those leaning towards the conventional, orthodox view would rather invoke man's ingenuity and inventiveness to overcome the bottlenecks in production and to maintain the smooth running of industrial society, the radical environmentalist would see such efforts as ultimately self-defeating; instead he would stick to his notion of there being limits to growth, the challenge being to guide society towards some non-growth-oriented goal.

In fact, the rate and magnitude problems to which I referred in the last chapter are by no means nebulous hypotheses but are valid problems. Thus the breeder reactor works both in principle and in practice; the Dounreay reactor and its successor, the 250 megawatt prototype, are evidence of that, but try to build up a large programme of full-size reactors and, within one generation, the limits of growth imposed by a shortfall of plutonium are likely to manifest themselves. What on paper may have appeared a remarkable device for gaining cheaply enormous quantities of energy, becomes in real life a terrible economic failure on a scale far beyond the Concorde.

A parallel surely exists between Hubbert's hypothesis of the inevitable peaking of the rate of discovery of petroleum and the rate of discovery of new technologies and materials to overcome resource shortages. True, there will be technological successes such as the use of silicon chip technology to take over from mercury in electrical switching gear, and those breakthroughs will delude the Kahns and Beckermans into thinking that rate and magnitude problems will be overcome, but in the end the pace of demands on new technologies will exceed man's ability to conjure them up and then supply them. Indeed, because of the inexorable demands imposed by industrial growth, the pressures upon technologists to keep pace becomes increasingly difficult. In that respect technological success stories are no more than irregularities, like the discovery of a Prudhoe Bay oil field, which mar the otherwise rising and then falling curve of innovatory technology.

But I see that Mike is in something of a quandary. If I have understood him correctly, he disliked the idea that man's moral behaviour should be governed simply by expediency in the face of some limits to growth, whether imagined or real. Given that those pursuing self-sufficiency have joined the 'limits to growth' bandwagon, Mike berates them for a fundamental selfishness of behaviour. Indeed, by fleeing from would-be disaster into a haven of their own choosing, by having no compunction in leaving the rest of a society behind, such people have behaved immorally. Nor would it be an act born of morality if society as a whole decided to curb its excesses because it or its government realized the validity of the limits to growth thesis, since that again would be expediency and an act of self-preservation.

Mike wants society to be faced with a moral choice, which can only come about if there are no immediate limits of growth. Consequently he opens up for us vistas of unlimited quantities of minerals from the Moon and other extraterrestrial sources, or of new technologies like the extraction of uranium from sea water, which push back into the distant future any conceivable checks on growth. Man can now choose: either to proceed with his industries and the good life, or to set about the creation of a different kind of society imbued with egalitarian socialist principles in which mankind's real needs are better taken care of.

In an evocation of the Adam and Eve dilemma, Mike thus wants us to be forbearing in a garden of plenty, or at least to distribute the goodies we find there in a socially responsible manner. The idea that someone should cry out that there is blight and a poor harvest on their way, while staking out his claim to his own patch, however small, does not appeal to him. Nor indeed to me. But the self-sufficiency movement is more than simply a reaction to a belief in impending limits to growth. Undoubtedly its aficionados have come to use the limits of growth argument to support their case and to shake the industrial world out of its delusion, but their main desire is to create a better world to live in and that means one without poverty, without starvation and, at the same time, without environmental degradation and the callous selfishness of modern life.

Mike fails to see a moral act in rejecting modern industrial society and its consumer ethos. Indeed, to be moral, he says, we should stay with society because of the social contract and hence our obligation to it. Yet history is peppered with examples of people who, in good faith, have walked out of the societies in which they were raised, to live on their own or in communities. The Essenes thus lived in the desert by the Dead Sea to escape the corruption in Jerusalem and what they considered to be the defiling of the temple by the priests. Their seeking of a pure, untainted life surely had moral aspects, even though to the outsider or Jerusalemite it may have seemed bigoted, constrained and extremely selfish. In the end the Essenes could not escape the fate of the rest of Israel and their community was destroyed by the Romans.

There is a parallel with the self-sufficiency movement today, for however much its followers reject modern society and live a life on their own, their fate is bound up with the fate of society as a whole. To Mike the inescapability of any of us from the main thrust of society negates the point of rejection. From a statistical point of view he may be right, but for the individual there is satisfaction in trying to stick to principles and in trying to act accordingly. Moreover, the door is always open to anyone who cares to enter.

Self-sufficiency is an extreme form of environmentalism and, as such it may remain limited in scope. But it does set an alternative to a way of life that has nothing particularly moral about it. Indeed, socialism and egalitarianism have emerged in modern industrial societies to combat inherent ills and inequalities and in many respects, they have failed. Meanwhile self-sufficiency has been spawned as a consequence of the failure of the socialist ethic to create a healthy, equitable society. Thus, it is a reaction to bureaucratic socialism in which responsibility has been taken out of the domain of the individual and into the hands of faceless clerics. The notion that the individual should take care of himself and his family in co-operation with other members of the community and that he should become less dependent on the state are some essential first steps towards self-sufficiency. At first sight, that approach to life may seem more self-centred than one in which the individual makes a contribution to the state so that each and all may benefit, but in the end it brings caring for others back into the domain of the home.

In his conclusion, Mike is firmly for the small community which should be as self-sufficient as possible, but he is concerned lest power in that community should come to reside either in one individual or in a caucus of individuals. Unfortunately, it is impossible to dictate the affairs of men, since each moment in history has its own dynamic, and dictators flourish despite democracy. Yet there is a chance that given the present-day background of socialist principles people will generally want to see Mike's kind of egalitarianism put into practice. I would be all for that. Something of that nature already happens in Israeli kibbutzim, where talented individuals are sent to university or to other educational establishments by means of collective funds. Nor are other individuals prevented from leaving the community if they should so wish.

Ultimately nothing is so essentially destructive of communities as the growth ethic, since it imbues a sense of dissatisfaction and inadequacy. Awareness that one should limit one's horizons and instead live within one's means may well be behind the acceptance of the limits to growth thesis by those who are seeking self-reliance.

8 The self-sufficient society

Environmental awareness has become the privilege of those who in modern terms are able to improve their lot. Many socialists, the late Anthony Crosland, for example, claimed that such awareness was primarily a middle-class phenomenon and, as such, must be given less weight in terms of political action than in raising the standard of living of those presumably still classified as working class and underprivileged. That argument is somewhat circular since a polluted, unpleasant environment can hardly be synonomous with a high standard of living; hence, if making a high standard of living creates more pollution and environmental degradation, the raising of the underprivileged to a more satisfactory standard will be unattainable. At that point the argument shifts ground, and allegiance to the industrial effluent or the tax-collector seeking out evaders. Hence the question of controlling pollution and environmental damage rather than of limiting the scope of industrial activities.

Perhaps the distinction between middle-class environmentalists and those who seek self-sufficiency is that the latter do not believe that mankind can have both industrialism and a healthy environment. In fact they repudiate the notion that legislation and bodies of surveillance to control pollution and other aspects of industrial growth will achieve both a high standard of living and an environment worth living in. Thus, theirs is a rejection of the industrial growth ethic, and self-sufficiency is a term encompassing their aim to do away with products that most exemplify modern industrialism. But we live, as Mike points out, in an all-pervading society which leaves no nook or cranny untouched by its activities, whether that be industrial effluent or the tax-collector seeking out evaders. Hence the would-be self-sufficient is, to a large extent, trapped and he cannot escape into a world entirely of his own choosing.

His life then, is a compromise, and we must not necessarily damn him because we find him inconsistent in his approach to life. In fact what we must look for is the positive attributes of such a way of life; for the sense of self-responsibility and continual evaluation of what is good or bad. Indeed, to live a discriminating life requires

self-discipline which, so long as it steers clear of puritanical preju-
dice, provides a useful point of reference for those who continue to
believe that a high standard of living can be equated only with a high
level of materialism.

In settling on his few hectares, and trying to make a living, the
self-provider is battling against the trend of large-scale industrialized
farming and the influx of people into the city. Most governments
claim that increased mechanization on the land together with growing urbanization are inevitable aspects of development and progress,
and that they must provide accordingly. That provision is not only
costly in terms of resources it becomes self-reinforcing as an increasing number of people expect to reap its benefits. In time the needs of
rural areas and of its population become secondary to those of the
masses that have flocked into the cities, and mass needs have to be
met by mass production. It is then but a step to the call for a highly
centralized energy supply and the building of nuclear reactors; nor is
it surprising that atomic energy authorities should see their role as
the great providers, pushing back the encroaching Malthusian limits.

But how will mankind manage to make its cities keep pace with
the swelling demands? In the Swedish journal *Ambio* (January 1978)
Ken Newcombe and his colleagues have studied the basic 'metabolic'
requirements of Hong Kong as a test case of a rapidly growing city
which nonetheless has still a relatively low standard of living.
Indeed, Hong Kong's energy consumption on a per capita basis is an
order of magnitude below that of most western cities. The authors
have then extrapolated to a time twenty-five years hence when approximately 38 per cent of the world population will have become
urbanized (a percentage which is considerably lower than that found
in countries such as Britain) and they foresee certain limits to
growth. Such a city-bound population will necessitate the construction of 5000 new cities each with some 500 000 people. If such
cities are maintained at the 1971 Hong Kong level, the energy costs
of manufacturing the component parts of those cities and the costs of
maintenance will amount to five times the 1973 world consumption
of energy, assuming the same kind of energy mix and hence energy
efficiency as today.

What purpose does it serve mankind to have such an aggregation
of people in cities, especially when the requirements of building such
environments will far exceed the world's capacity to provide them?
Progress is undoubtedly a double-edged sword, and what may lead to
advantages for one person may indeed become disadvantageous for
another.

Thus, city life may have become the only possible option for millions of people who have lost their role in the countryside through the mechanization of their jobs; an uprooting the industrialist will call progress. The August 1979 issue of the United Kingdom Energy Authority magazine, *Atom* has an article on third world energy strategies in which nuclear power is advocated as an important energy option. What intrigued me was the caption beneath a photograph of a man ploughing with a pair of oxen in an area which looked decidedly like a modern industrialized region such as France or Italy. The caption read 'the backbreaking alternative to mechanized agriculture', which presumably referred to the heaving oxen and the man who was leaning forward to scrape off a stone or mud caught in between the coulter and ploughshare. To me, with my value judgements, the photograph represented a dignified scene of a hearty middle-aged man proud of the work he was doing, and (having ploughed with horses myself) gaining a great deal of 'job satisfaction'. Ironically, a tractor driver is no more exempt by virtue of his superior mechanization from having to leap down from his cab to clear a recalcitrant clump of couch grass or stone from one of the skims or coulters on his multifurrow plough. But with what pride the editors of *Atom* exhibit a photograph of a man holding a piece of electronic equipment 'for determining the quantity of nuclear material in sealed storage cans', the purpose being to prevent the theft of nuclear material and its potential for proliferation. In his white lab coat, and ugly environment, the man in question lacked the vigour and health of the ploughman in a field with his oxen and olives, and I for one have no doubts which profession I would prefer.

Does increased mechanization necessarily lead to a better solution for the masses than a more steady plodding pace in which individual skills are displayed. As I pointed out earlier, none of the major discoveries whether in agriculture or in industry, came about because of an intense drive to save mankind from impending disaster. They came about through ingenuity and imagination, of that there can be no doubt, but their taking over and their transforming of a previous way of life, was more a consequence of their seeming to provide their exponents with an economic advantage. That economic advantage is then whittled away as others pick up the techniques, and it is time for another experiment to be pursued. But that kind of progress does not of itself lead to a better quality of life. Thus, while it may be true that the farm worker now gets a decent industrial wage, it is at the expense of displacing four or five other men who would have been employed thirty years ago on the same area. Moreover the wage demands of the modern worker are now such that many farmers question whether they can afford to employ anyone at all other than themselves and their families. As for the job itself, today's farm worker is bound to the cab of his tractor and has become a glorified driver. What he may have gained in seeming comfort and ease of work, he will certainly have lost in innumerable other ways. The same can be said of those who have found work in industry and offices. The commuting to work in crowded trains, the humdrum routine, the noise of machinery, the stale air, and the cost of living are all obvious disadvantages of modern industrial life and they are counterbalanced only to a degree by home comforts and access to mass media.

The next stage in the unfolding strip of progress may be the introduction of miniaturized computers to organize and control all work whether or not it is considered humdrum. The microchip revolution may soon be upon us and many will be glad of escaping from the heavy routine of factory or of office existence, to pursue instead their own particular hobbies. But the introduction of silicon chip technology, albeit inevitable, will mark one more step in man's abdication from the responsibility of looking after himself. Its seeming advantages will, therefore, have to be weighed against the inescapable centralization that it is likely to engender particularly with regard to the instantaneous recall of intimate information about every individual in society. Indeed, its widespread use will almost certainly threaten the individual who deviates at all from the considered norm of society while simultaneously providing those who have gained power with a means of control such as has never existed before.

As a piece of technology, the microchip is no more the bearer of evil than the nuclear reactor. One famous anarchist figure, Murray Bookchin, actually delights in the opportunities offered by silicon chip technology, since he believes that man will gain his freedom only when work is abolished, and that state, he points out in *Post Scarcity Anarchism*, can be only when a system of non-human control over machines is devised. Bookchin lives in New York City and his highly intelligent and, to many, captivating view, is undoubtedly fostered by his appreciation of the cultural advantages of living in that kind of environment.

There is no reason why the basic technological principles involved in cybernating the manufacture of automobile engines cannot be applied to virtually every area of mass manufacture – from the metallurgical industry to the food processing industry, from the electronics industry to the toymaking industry, from the manufacture of prefabricated bridges to the manufacture of prefabricated houses . . .

It is easy to foresee a time, by no means remote, when a rationally organized economy could automatically manufacture small 'packaged' factories without human labour: parts could be produced with so little effort that most maintenance tasks would be reduced to the simple act of removing a defective unit from a machine and replacing it by another – a job no more difficult than pulling out and putting in a tray. Such a technology, oriented entirely towards human needs and freed from all consideration of profit and loss, would eliminate the pain of want and toil – the penalty inflicted in the form of denial, suffering and inhumanity, exacted by a society based on scarcity and labour.

Bookchin the anarchist is hardly different from Herman Kahn in his vision of the future: both see the elimination of work as a prerequisite of freedom from the shackles which bind one man to another. According to Bookchin there are two alternatives. Man may choose to work, if he wants, but at his own 'thing' rather than for someone else. 'Or,' remarks Bookchin, 'these humans of the future may simply choose to step over the body of technology. They may submerge the cybernated machines in a technological underworld, divorcing it entirely from social life, the community and creativity. All but hidden from society, the machines would work for man. Free communities would stand at the end of a cybernated assembly line with baskets to cart the goods home. Industry, like the autonomous nervous system, would work on its own, subject to the repairs that our own bodies require in occasional bouts of illness. The fracture separating man from machine would not be healed. It would simply be ignored.'

Unfortunately for Bookchin with his anarchist dream of a world of plenty where work is unnecessary and if done for someone else essentially degrading, the decisions taken by some human beings as to what should or should not be produced by the cybernated assembly line can hardly be free of value judgement, and it may not be to the taste of someone else. Can everything that everyone wants be produced so that no one suffers discrimination at the materialistic level, or is Bookchin's hope of anarchy hopeless given that the making of his Utopian dream will entail organization, technocrats, political will, capital investment? It may also have crossed his mind that the machines themselves, given so much scope through their free-ranging cybernetic controls, may not take kindly to being the slaves of an uncaring humanity; such a rebellion has at least been suggested in one of Arthur Clarke's short stories.

But why is Bookchin, or Kahn for that matter, so much against work? I would agree that many jobs of modern existence are 'thankless, repetitive, and boring' but Bookchin applies such adjectives to the work of the medieval stonemasons who would cut out stone after stone of exactly the same shape for the cathedrals. His dislike of such work is surely a hangover of the Renaissance debate over the Platonic notion concerning labour in which the conception of the object, whether it be a table or cathedral, was purer and hence more ideal than the work required to create it. Thus da Vinci tried to ridicule Michelangelo for his chipping away at stone when the more delicate art of painting could achieve a more lofty and complete concept. Michelangelo, on the other hand, expressed his debt to the family of stonemasons at Carrara who had brought him up and showed him how to chisel and mould marble, and he revelled in the actual physical work of creating his masterpieces. As for the repetitive, boring work of chiselling stones for the great medieval cathedrals, after the first Chartres cathedral was burnt down and destroyed, its replacement was built with incredible enthusiasm, even pilgrims and visitors lending a hand in whatever way they could.

As Michelangelo knew, the actual work of creation has its own rewards, and as long as the individual can see his contribution playing its part in the manifestation of the whole, he too will reap satisfaction even though he may be only one of a team. The production line, by way of contrast, is dehumanizing work where job satisfaction is virtually nil. Chaplin immortalized the inhuman drudgery of such work in *Modern Times* and statistics of strikes and labour problems in that epitome of mass production, the car assembly line, are evidence in themselves; for lack of money, even though the symbol of dissatisfaction, has never been the basic cause of factory walkouts.

We have come again full circle to the seeker of self-sufficiency. He is not afraid of work, not even of repetitive work, as long as he can see its significance in relation to a concept he has of his environment. In fact, in complete contradistinction to Bookchin, the self-sufficient individual believes that freedom cannot come from dependence on an inanimate technological world that has largely replaced the natural but only from his own contribution. In reality the totally self-sufficient individual is a fiction, or non-person, since there must be interaction with others, and dependencies. But here, instead of envisaging a community of individuals awaiting their free handouts from the faceless world of technology under its feet, self-sufficiency implies work in co-operation, with each person contributing as he can rather than as he must. One essence of a community of self-sufficient seekers is that it offers scope for individuals to carry out a multiplicity of tasks from agriculture and gardening, engineering, and woodwork to all kinds of artistic activities.

Self-sufficiency implies individualism and an egotistic concern with self-survival, but paradoxically it is a drive back to community and to mutual help. Modern industrial society, on the other hand, is an alienating force, splitting communities and families and bringing about isolation. But as we have pointed out, those concerned with the re-establishment of communities will have to show that their approach is not just inward looking and insular. The challenge facing them is to demonstrate that they can make a worthwhile contribution to the well-being of the larger corporation of those communities under the umbrella of the region, province, or of the nation–state. In a world of growing population and competition for resources, the self-sufficient movement cannot expect to survive in isolation. Its existence will depend in part on it being able to show unequivocally that it can provide surpluses for those who would prefer to live outside the world of production or manufacture. Thus, the communities should form a patchwork of interlocking, mutually supporting systems, with each unit capable of achieving some form of self-sufficiency, and at the same time of providing surpluses which can then be marketed and interchanged.

The Israeli kibbutz system has shown that communities based on Mike's egalitarian principles can exist satisfactorily and be productive units. The modern kibbutz has been able to achieve a relatively high standard of living for its members by western standards. When averaged out the land for each member family in the kibbutz amounts to some 4 hectares (10 acres), a figure some ten times less than that accepted officially in Britain as a minimum holding on which a family can live.

The British farmer does not usually have industry on his land in conjunction with farm work and, one reason for the kibbutz's financial success, is its mixture of enterprises. In that regard we are approaching the ideal we spoke of in which each community supports a wide range of activities that in their sum create a semblance of self-sufficiency.

Yet the kibbutz movement in Israel has turned its back on many of the ideals of its pioneers. Outside labour is brought in to help in the factories and on the land, the less pleasant tasks in the main going to those who are earning wages. This hiring of labour is in contradiction to the libertarian-socialist principles which many of the pioneers brought with them out of east Europe before and after the Russian Revolution. On the other hand, it could be argued that the mixed economic system of pure socialism in which each member receives an equal share of materialistic goods and of bringing in outside labour exhibits flexibility and realism in the modern world; moreover it enables non-kibbutziks to gain some insight into practical socialism at the community level.

The success of the modern kibbutz has brought with it fundamental problems which reflect in large measure those pertaining to modern industrial society. The high mechanization of all agricultural and industrial activities in the kibbutz has led to an increasing release of the members from a communal type of labour and has undoubtedly contributed to diminishing job satisfaction. The high standard of living within the kibbutz has also brought with it a certain ennui and lack of direction which is leading to increasing disaffection among the younger members. Thus, they find a discrepancy between the stories of the pioneers and the challenge they faced in reclaiming land by dint of hard work and enthusiasm compared with their own easy life. Furthermore, the social structure of the kibbutz in which they live has been ordained by the previous generation, and they may find a lack of flexibility and of understanding of their own particular problems.

One way out of their predicament is to leave the kibbutz in which they were raised to found new communities or to join another that is closer to their own aspirations. As a consequence, hardly two kibbutzim are identical in their basic principles. While children in one kibbutz will spend their lives in the children's home, separated from their parents, others will allow children to grow up with their parents; while one kibbutz will have a communal room with a television, others provide each member with his own house fitted out with a television and a hi-fi set. In one kind of settlement – the moshav shitufi – all work is done collectively, but each family is given the right and responsibility to do what he wants with his share of the earnings. At the other end of the spectrum is the moshav pure and simple in which work is done co-operatively rather than collectively and the receipts of each man's labour goes to himself and his family. Such co-operatives have their own insurance schemes to help others in the community who are in difficulty or who need some loan to develop their enterprise.

With the rare exception of the moshav-shitufi at Yodfat in northern Galilee, none of the kibbutzim follow the organic approach to plant and animal husbandry. Instead they are wholeheartedly committed to the industrial approach to farming and their use of chemical fertilizers and pesticides is second to none in the world. As a consequence, the Israel environment has become increasingly contaminated with nitrogen run-off and with the products of pesticides. At Yodfat the commitment to organic farming has a strong religious ingredient in that the members are followers of a Jewish mystic, Schechter, who had reverence for the natural cycles of life. Undoubtedly the religious approach to life of the members of Yodfat governs their appreciation of work in the fields and provides a deeper satisfaction than is apparent on the average kibbutz.

The same kind of reverence prevails among those following self-sufficiency principles in Britain, and inevitably the commitment is to organic methods of gardening and agriculture. Yodfat is economically successful because of an expanding market in west Europe for organically grown products of the Middle East such as citrus fruits and various nuts, including pecan. There is now an expanding market for all organically grown food and, in this regard, the organic grower has an opportunity such as never before. The task now open to him is to show that he can be productive on a long-term basis, and with far lower costs in terms of capital, materials, and energy than conventional farms.

Sufficient organic farms now exist to provide some basis of comparison with orthodox farms. The act of mechanization as such does not lead to higher productivity; it primarily replaces labour and speeds up specific tasks. In the main, the seasons themselves govern the growth of crops and the animals dependent upon them. But as I have pointed out earlier, a major question is whether organic husbandry by which land replenishes its own fertility is capable of sufficiently high production to provide the necessary surplus to feed those outside the farming community.

My own experience as a farmer has been extremely limited in scope but at least it indicates to my satisfaction that raising dairy cattle on organic herbal ley pastures in the way of Newman Turner is a viable proposition. With no more than 4 hectares (10 acres) of useful land I have been able to do without expensive machinery; moreover, part of the purpose of my farming is to get out in the fields and do physical work which, far from being degrading, has proved enjoyable. Over five years the land has improved beyond recognition, and I can now keep three times the number of animals that I could initially. Indeed, I provide all grazing and winter feeding for eight animals including a working pony.

A research student with a grant from the Ministry of Agriculture is now studying the profitability of organic farms throughout Britain, and a preliminary look at the figures of the farm indicates that I am more profitable than most conventional dairy farms. Out of curiosity I have now measured energy inputs and outputs and, although I use both a tractor and a petrol engine for milking, the farm appears to be ten times more efficient in energy use than the average dairy farm in Britain. Not that the productivity is higher; in fact, because I do not buy in large quantities of feedstuffs I do not stock the farm beyond its carrying capacity (an improved capacity at that) and as a consequence milk and animal protein production is approximately one half that of the average dairy farm on a per hectare basis. Nevertheless, we send a large surplus of food off the farm, and the cash coming in is enough to support a small family in comfort, although by no means at the standard and pace of living expected in the industrial world.

The farm has not been exploited to its full potential, mainly because of lack of time, nor is it worked on a proper communal basis. We are not self-sufficient either, even though we have our own vegetable garden and sometimes rear pigs for slaughter. If my smallholding could be combined in a co-operative with other smallholdings in the area, sharing certain enterprises, labour and equipment, then I have no doubt that the overall productivity could be brought closer to that of the national average while still being close to self-sufficiency in food for the livestock. Most important of all, the working of a small area, especially when done co-operatively, leaves a considerable part of the working day free for other activities. As in the Israeli kibbutz, a community of small farms could attract people who want to enrich their existences by having one foot on the ground and the other in some vocational activity whether it be in the arts or in some profession such as medicine, law, or engineering.

At present it is extremely difficult to get land-based communities together in Britain. The trends are towards bigger aggregates of land under either private ownership or business enterprises. Land is treated as a commodity like any other resource, and the prime concern is with productivity and profit margins. As a way of life, the land hardly features, but rather becomes a means of speculation as does property in general. Thus, prices soar putting land increasingly out of reach for those who would most like to commit themselves to it. And if they do purchase land, it is usually through a mortgage with an increasingly high rate of interest. Nor are governments and local councils in general well disposed to those who want to bring more dwellings into the countryside, because these bodies feel that services in the rural areas cannot support more people, and that more dwellings would spoil the countryside and decrease still further Britain's agricultural base.

It would clearly be wrong to open up the countryside to anyone who wished to purchase a hectare or so for building a private dwelling, particularly if that individual had no intention of working the land. Yet historically neither Britain nor Europe, for that matter, has suffered from the building that has gone on in the countryside in distinction from the towns. The villages, hamlets, farm cottages, and mansions that have grown up in the countryside over the centuries have, in general, enhanced the environment, at least in the human dimension, and if we are attracted to the countryside it is in large measure because of the activities of our predecessors.

Today thousands of hectares are swallowed up in creeping urbanization and industrial activities and, rather than tackle the real cause of agricultural land loss, the authorities try to check the age-old desire of people to live on the land and reap some bounty from it. Thus, people are refused planning permission for building up a home on a few hectares and must either give up their plans or must find an existing dwelling, usually at elevated cost. Meanwhile the farmer who wishes to expand his farm receives all manner of hand-outs from the government to defray the cost of his purchase.

One reason for the success of the kibbutz movement in Israel, as of the moshavim, is the support they receive from the government in terms of cheap land rental, water subsidies and grants for building. It is clearly a matter of government policy that such village-sized communities should be given every opportunity to flourish. In Britain we have no such policy even under a socialist government and the fragmentation of rural life that has now continued for the past 150 years has been considered an inevitable consequence of progress, the commitment of resources being turned towards the town and industries instead. Yet the number of people seeking a life on the land is steadily increasing and many of these people wish to be part of a community. No political party should overlook their needs nor the contribution they can make to the well-being of society. The Labour government at various times has raised the possibility of nationalizing land to be true to its socialist principles of doing away with private ownership. Unquestionably such nationalization would be disastrous in that it would lead to centralization of control and to potential disaffection of the farming work force. Furthermore, the Labour party is committed to industrial farming and certainly not to the establishment of communities based on the land.

On the other hand, it would be a significant step forward if a political party set out to acquire land for creating village settlements, providing at the same time basic training in agriculture, administration, and in other needs of the potential community. In Israel young people are given the choice when they leave school of going into the army proper or of being prepared for life in a kibbutz. A group of young people – the garin or future nucleus – is placed for two years in an established kibbutz where they can follow through all the activities that hold the community together. During those two years each member of the garin will find his or her particular niche so that when the time comes to establish the new kibbutz or to join an established kibbutz that sphere of activity will be his or her contribution. In Britain there is no tradition of such communities, and it is hardly surprising that many self-created communities disintegrate after a few years. Therefore, it is vital that training for the new community ventures should be at some 'model' centre which, as far as possible, aims at financial self-sufficiency. Such centres should be dispersed throughout the country to provide those who want to join or create communities a number of different environments with their own particular set of conditions. Then, after leaving the centre, a group of individuals who have decided to proceed with their own community should be given the opportunity to acquire the necessary area of land for their venture with help given for the building of homes and of community workshops and recreational areas. In time, as these new communities establish themselves, they can provide the training for a new nucleus and so on until a whole network of interlacing communities will grow up in a particular area. Ideally, the areas themselves will then link up and such communities will become major contributors to rural life. Not that each community will be exactly alike; far from it, for as in Israel each will develop along its own dynamic, determined by its individual members.

One advantage of such communities is that they can together organize a co-operative in marketing, thus ensuring distribution of goods and a fair competitive price. Another advantage is that each community will make an ideal unit for self-sufficiency in energy from whatever means, whether wind-power, water-power, biogas, or straightforward solar, and a good engineering facility will be an important component of each community. Meanwhile any innovations in self-energy technologies will be able to diffuse rapidly through all the communities, and government sponsorship as well as its own research and development will make an important contribution. In that way the self-sufficient communities will be wholly integrated into the nation-state rather than being drop-outs as they tend to be at present as a consequence of general disinterest at government level.

Awareness of the environment and of resource limitations will develop naturally in each community as it comes to grips with the land around it. And because each community will be responsible for the early education and health of its members a tradition of respect for the environment and the community is bound to grow, creating an allegiance that has become increasingly rare in modern life. The kibbutz experience in Israel has gone on long enough to prove its long-term viability. In Britain we must create the opportunity for such communities to come into existence. But they will be exposed to a new challenge, that of striving for sound resource management in the face of growing limitations.

There is a tendency today to evaluate everything in terms of economics, and, as a consequence, brute functionalism tends to become the dominant factor when any project is being evaluated. How little can be spent in return for the most profit is thus the criterion governing most planning decisions. By way of contrast the person seeking self-sufficiency is motivated by an aesthetic appreciation of the natural environment and, if there is a tendency to conservatism in the movement, that is because our ancestors were somehow more naturally given to aesthetics than we are today. One has only to look at the layout of old villages throughout the world to find a happy blend of buildings and environment. Thus, in the self-sufficiency movement the roles of aesthetics and functionalism tend to be reversed compared with the conventional world of economics and business and, if more time and hence capital has to be spent to create an enhanced environment, that will be the preferred path. A great advantage of the communities I have described would be that they would largely be responsible for the environment under their care. Under such circumstances there is a good likelihood that the interests of all the members of the community would be taken into account before any planning decision is made. Given, too, that aesthetic appreciation will be a prime motivation in decision-making, the chances that the environment will benefit are certainly improved.

We are now reaching the point in our history when political action behind the self-sufficiency movement could gain wide-reaching support. The acquisition of land to set up pilot communities would hardly tax the government compared to present-day expenditure on such money-guzzling ventures as the development of the fast reactor nor, moreover, do they require any more land than a nuclear power plant. Incentives, too, could be created for farmers to pass on their land for community ventures, and it may be that with proper compensation some farmers would be happy to be part of an experimental community. As it happens a number of centres are being established, such as the National Centre for Alternative Technology, where certain aspects of alternative life-styles are being evaluated. What we need now is a fusion of such interests at all levels of society and involving the whole spectrum of professions. With political will there is every reason for Britain to be restored as a country of extraordinary beauty in which the people have a satisfying and complete part to play.

*

The first rule of ecology is that within a community individuals are bound together in a complex web of relationships. Changes made at one part of the web often produce effects elsewhere. If the environmental and self-sufficiency movements are to acquire political influence they must take account of this and expand their views to embrace the wider effects of the changes they propose. They must speak to the whole of society, not just to a part of it. There is much for them to say, but before they can be heard I believe they must review certain of their attitudes.

Peter is right to point out that when the late Anthony Crosland suggested that environmentalists were motivated by middle-class elitism his argument was self-defeating. Of course it is true that all of us share the same environment whose protection benefits us all. At least, it is partly true. It is not a coincidence that in most European cities the fashionable districts are located to the west of the industrial districts and that the poor live to the east. The prevailing winds are from the west, so that the western districts are cleaner than those to the east. If we are wealthy we can buy clean air just as we can buy access to pleasant landscapes. When we campaign for environmental improvements it does not follow invariably that the improvement we seek will contribute directly to the general good. At times, most commonly when environmentalism shades into preservationism, campaigns can become quite blatantly elitist. Two recent campaigns conducted close to where Peter and I live illustrate the point. In the first the designation of an estuary as an Area of Outstanding Natural Beauty was opposed and in the second the removal of some bends and the widening of a road that twisted its way through a rather pretty valley was opposed. In both cases the main purpose of the opposition was the prevention of public encroachment on private land. In the case of the estuary, farmers objected to the planning constraints implied by AONB designation and supported others who feared the area would become attractive to visitors. In the case of the road, the valley that was to be protected is owned privately and it was feared that by widening the road cars would be able to park while their owners walked in the adjacent countryside. Such campaigns as these, and there are many of them, do not present themselves honestly by stating that their aim is to exclude outsiders from private preserves but masquerade as environmental protection. On occasion they may even win the support of environmental groups or of individuals who regard themselves as environmentalists despite the fact that, in some instances, such as that of the estuary, the campaign is actually anti-environmentalist in its objective. I had no access to the private thoughts of Mr Crosland, of course, but I suspect it was protectionist adventures of this kind that he had in mind when he made his quite gentle criticism of the environmental movement. There is nothing to prevent any person or group from advancing any view at all, but it is difficult to see how popular support can be won for policies that favour a privileged elite and offer nothing to the majority but contempt.

Again, it is true that it would cost the government little to buy areas of farm land and let them to tenants seeking self-sufficiency, but how could a government defend such purchases if the aim of the self-providers were merely to escape from a society of which they disapproved and, by implication, to which they considered themselves superior? If governments are to provide holdings in this way they must be persuaded that the search for self-sufficiency is likely to produce some benefit to society. The idea that the self-sufficiency movement aims for a type of land use that is described by agricultural scientists as 'low input low output' for a technology and social order modelled on those of some previous period in history and, again, for a philosophy that holds the majority of people in contempt, is hardly persuasive. Better arguments are needed, and these should seek to justify the provision not of a few small holdings for an elite but of very large numbers of holdings to provide for the needs of a popular movement. If it is held that society should be organized in small, more or less autonomous communities, then it should be made clear whether this requires major reform of land tenure or whether the communities are to be few in number and reserved for particular categories of individuals. Until then the self-sufficiency movement must accept the fact that membership is restricted to those with the means to buy land and to live without an earned cash income.

Appeals to nostalgia and eulogies over the virtues of hard physical labour and poverty should be abandoned entirely for they, too, are based on an elitist view. Of course, there is much satisfacton to be derived from the performance of a useful task to its completion, but this is far removed from saying that all work is beneficial. No one has suggested that the skilled craftsman will be replaced by a machine, even a machine controlled by a silicon chip or two. Indeed it is more likely that increasing automation will provide more employment for craftsmen rather than less. Automation provides machines to perform work that is arduous, repetitive, and unpopular, work of the kind that has been criticized repeatedly for being dehumanizing. There is no virtue in working for its own sake if the work could be performed better by a machine for, almost by definition, such work is not fit for humans. The use of farm horses falls partly within this category, although there is nothing to prevent people using horses if they prefer to do so. In the days when all farms were worked by horses, workers spent about an hour each morning preparing the horses and their equipment and a further hour each evening dismantling and cleaning the equipment, and grooming and feeding the horses. This work fell to either side of the normal day's work and it was unpaid. When horses were replaced by tractors the first beneficiaries were the farm workers and, although workers old enough to remember working with horses may be nostalgic for their lost youth, I have met none who would welcome a return to horsepower.

Poverty is a relative concept and acquires a precise meaning only in relation to the society within which it occurs. To people who are poor in modern industrial societies poverty does not mean the foregoing of a holiday abroad or riding a bicycle rather than driving a motorcar, it means going hungry and sending the children to school in shabby clothes that they have grown out of and that were second hand when they were bought. It means direct physical and social deprivation.

The fact is that throughout history life for the rural poor was hard. There has been some improvement in modern times, but it is still hard. Ann Heeley and Martyn Brown have reconstructed the life of a nineteenth-century Somerset farm labourer, John Hodges. Hodges was typical of the farm workers of his day. He was born in 1828 to parents for whom starvation was a familiar hazard. Compulsory education was not introduced until he was grown up and so he did not attend school and never learned to read or write. He started work as

a small child and by the time he was eight he was earning the equivalent of about 5 pence a week. At twelve he left home to live with
the shepherd for whom he worked. At that time he was earning
about 15 pence a week, working for twelve hours a day and six days a
week. He married in 1851, when his wages were about 35 pence a
week out of which he paid 5 pence rent for his tied cottage. He and
his wife subsisted on a diet of bread, potatoes when they were cheap,
and little else. Butter was expensive and although they drank tea,
about 7 grams (¼ ounce) had to last them a week. John grew vegetables in his cottage garden in his 'spare' time. He was lucky because not all farm cottages had gardens. A pig was kept in a sty in the
garden and fed on scraps. When it was killed and salted down it
supplied the Hodges with meat for the winter and enough of the
meat was sold to provide the price of a replacement piglet he bought
in the spring. Neighbours who had contributed scraps to the feeding
of the pig received a joint of meat each. He may have kept bees. For
fuel he gathered wood from the country lanes when he could, but he
had to augment this by buying coal and peat. His employer gave him
a jug of skimmed milk each day and when times were good he might
be given other produce from the farm. His wife died in 1859 soon
after the birth of their second child and probably because the family
could not afford proper medical care. John married again later in the
same year. He died in 1891, aged sixty-three, and a few years later
his widow was taken away to the workhouse where she died in 1908.
For most of his working life Hodges was employed by the squire, who
owned most of the land in the village and farmed the 80-hectare
(200-acre) home farm himself, with the assistance of fourteen farm
workers, ten gardeners and as many as twenty domestic servants.

There is nothing to be admired or envied in the harsh, squalid life
that robbed John Hodges of the three-score-years-and-ten his Bible
had promised him, but the contrast in lifestyles between rich and
poor only continued the social arrangement that had prevailed at
least since the Black Death in the fourteenth century that had caused
a shortage of labour, raised wages from their starvation levels, and so
commenced the destruction of the feudal system. That system was
much simpler because many workers within it were slaves. Today a
farm worker still lives in poverty on wages that are barely adequate
to support his family. In most cases wages must be supplemented by
growing vegetables at home – not for pleasure but for survival. Since
1976, agricultural workers who have been employed in the industry
continuously for not less than two years, and who live in tied cottages, have some protection from eviction. If such a worker loses, or

leaves, his job, he is entitled to remain in the cottage, paying an economic rent, unless the farmer decides that the cottage is needed for a replacement worker. The farmer must then take his case to a committee and if it is agreed that the accommodation is needed by the replacement worker in the interest of farm efficiency, the committee will instruct the local authority to rehouse its present tenant. A worker who has been in the industry for less than two years has no such protection and can be evicted by the farmer on the order of a court. In either case the farm worker cannot own his own home and his occupancy of it is much less secure than that of the ordinary tenant. The tied cottage and the low wages of farm workers are part of a system we should not seek to defend, far less perpetuate, and they show clearly why appeals to rural nostalgia and poverty in fact are appeals by the wealthy for the return of their lost privileges. They have nothing to offer the poor except further poverty. Politically they are unlikely to attract much popular support.

Farm workers are not alone among the poor in modern industrial society and some sociologists hold that the proportion who are poor may have changed little during this century. There is no great mystery about why this is so – wealth is concentrated in too few hands and poverty has been defined according to crude and out-dated concepts – but the fact that it is so presents the environmental and self-sufficiency movements with an opportunity to advance proposals for reforms that may be sufficiently radical to achieve substantial improvements.

The environmental and self-sufficiency literature says much about needs, and this is appropriate, so far as it goes. Perhaps, though, it is too concerned with the levels of material consumption it criticizes among the rich, and which it castigates, wrongly, as materialism. Materialism, in its true sense, is an entirely respectable theory about natural phenomena that holds that the Universe is composed of materials and energy, and of nothing else. It develops this theory into many fields, but nowhere does it advocate that which environmentalists and self-providers attack, and which most of us know as, but prefer not to call, greed. The glutton has lived among us since the dawn of history, but he is no less of a problem for that, and today as never before most of us are gluttons. If poverty is to be the alternative to gluttony, then poverty needs to be redefined to remove its connotation of deprivation. It is possible to live modestly but in comfort, eschewing ostentatious consumption but avoiding the grinding poverty that degrades and finally destroys human beings. Such a definition has been made and this concept advocated by Albert

Tévoédjrè, who is the Director of the International Institute for Labour Studies, based in Geneva. As we have seen, need cannot be defined simply in biological terms as food, clothing, and shelter. That is the crude mistake that has allowed large numbers of people to dwell in unrecognized poverty. Human needs include the need to be needed, to participate fully in the life of the family and the community, and the need to develop, enjoy, and then contribute to the community such skills as each individual possesses. As Peter has said, self-providers and many environmentalists recognize the need to create strong, supportive communities and to reconsider the ways in which society as a whole earns its living. This is their strength, which can be developed and increased so long as they remember that it is to the whole of society that they speak, and not only to one another. It is no coincidence that a society which is able to satisfy all the needs of its members is, by definition, self-sufficient.

The implications of such a redefinition are radical. As I suggested in the last chapter, they require that the objectives of industry be changed so that manufacturing be examined in terms of the utility of its products. Before we can consider and compare the costs and benefits of any activity we must decide whether or not we need the products of that activity; we must evaluate the supposed benefits as well as the costs. Peter and I would agree, I think, that at present the fact of production is usually considered to be benefit enough. In a market economy the manufacture of almost anything can be justified provided a market exists for it and, unless such a market is believed to exist, the manufacture will not be attempted. This we would regard as unsatisfactory. We propose instead that industry be held to exist to benefit the community it serves not only by employing processes, but also by producing goods, that produce local benefits to outweigh their costs. Until we are persuaded that we need widgets to enhance the quality of our lives it is pointless to consider ways to limit any environmental damage that might be caused by the manufacture of widgets. What we propose amounts to the ultimate consumerist society in which the consumers declare their needs and industry satisfies them if it can. Advertising, if it continued in such an economy, would play a radically different role. It would no longer be possible for the manufacturer to announce that he had produced a new article and to exhort the public to buy it. Instead he would have to propose an idea for the new article. This would start a debate at the end of which the public would decide whether or not manufacture should proceed. It would be a consumer-dominated form of advertising. It would become much more difficult to market products that proved later to be harmful – such as toys that contain toxic substances. Since the consumer had been consulted in advance, production and product standards would be set to ensure that the approved article met a specification devised by consumers after due and careful consideration.

Clearly, the public would be exerting far more control over industry than is the case today. In fact, the economy itself would be changed from a market to a command type. The injunction to industrialists would no longer be the simple 'Be profitable!' but the much more complex 'Make this, but not that'. Conventionally such a change might be enacted by a political party elected to office with an adequate majority. The change might then be implemented by means of a collaboration among the ruling party, the industrial workers, and the industrialists, to create, technically, a fascist state. Alternatively, it might be implemented by the ruling party, now the government, assuming direct control and ownership of industry, to create a socialist-centralist state. The party could occupy the radical right or the radical left. It could not occupy what we regard as the political centre. Equally conventionally, the control would tend to be centralized, decisions being made by a small group of high party officials entrusted with the guardianship of the doctrines they served.

The task could be approached in a different, but still more radical, way. The party might reason that if the purpose of the industry is the satisfaction of the needs of the community, then it must be the members of the community who declare those needs. What we may call the 'ecological imperative' suggests that each community is likely to be somewhat different from all other communities, so that its needs will differ. If these are to be satisfied in full, each community must have complete autonomy and devise the way of life that suits its members best. We have returned to our notional small community.

If the community satisfies in full the needs of its members from its own resources, then it must be self-sufficient. On a large scale, however, the concept encounters one of the traditional difficulties of such proposals. Resources are not distributed evenly across the face of the Earth. Some communities may find themselves inhabiting deserts or mountains, while others enjoy rich farm lands or extensive deposits of minerals or fuels. While normal trading will distribute resources evenly among communities that are equally, but differently, endowed, communities whose resources are few will be deprived. Traditionally this difficulty has been resolved by migration. People move from areas of few resources to areas of more abundant resources. It is why today people from poor countries seek to migrate to richer countries. The process is hallowed by history, has been used by the inhabitants of what are now the rich countries in times of hardship — to colonize the New World and Australasia, for example — and the xenophobia it arouses reflects the ignorance and greed of the rich. If we cannot permit the free movement of people among our communities we must devise a system of taxation for them that will compel the resource-rich to subsidize the resource-poor. This must erode the principle of self-reliance to some extent but, as long as the subsidy is provided as of right and not privilege, the erosion is not serious.

If communities trade to distribute resources, clearly they become self-sufficient in different ways. It is unavoidable that the idea of basing self-sufficiency purely on the production of food be abandoned, because we must recognize that not all land is capable of sustaining adequate agricultural production and that some is almost bound to produce surpluses. Once we allow this idea it can be extended. Can we consider as self-sufficient, for example, the group of talented individuals who form themselves into an orchestra and spend their time touring communities, receiving food and goods in return for entertainment? If the orchestra is not self-sufficient, in what sense is it not? It satisfies the needs of its members by the exploitation of their own resources and it contributes positively to the welfare of the communities it visits. If we allow the orchestra we must allow the theatrical troupe, the circus, and those who supply the countless services and goods that a modern society needs but that it would be impractical to duplicate in each community. Some industries, for example, do not benefit from operating on a small scale. The steel industry is one. So perhaps we may allow the steel workers to form a community of their own.

Such a society differs from existing society in only one respect, but it is profoundly important. Within it the producers and consumers of goods and services assume full and direct control for the planning and management of the way they live. If my community decides it would like to have electrical power, then we may see whether we can generate it for ourselves. If not, we may see whether we can import it from elsewhere in exchange for the goods or services we produce in surplus. This is conventional enough. What is less conventional is that if my community decides it does not want electricity there is no power on Earth that can compel us to install it. Nor is there any power on Earth that can compel us to allow the construction of a nuclear reactor, an aluminium smelter or an armaments factory on our land, although, of course, we can do nothing to prevent those who wish to build these things from seeking to persuade us to allow them. In the end, their need will have to be demonstrated to our satisfaction and, I dare say, they will have to bribe us fairly heavily: perhaps by allowing us to visit their rural havens to camp or walk in their countryside whenever we feel a need to do so.

The immediate objection to this concept, as to the idea of imposing full control over industry, is that it must stifle innovation. In the case of industry there is no reason why this should be so. Invention is to be encouraged, not deplored. All we require is that such new products as are made be of genuine use, but we have not lost our love of toys and novelties and the private inventor may be able to present his ideas to us as easily as the large corporation. Indeed, his chances will be improved, for if we like his ideas we have the power to order his inventions to be made. If we believe that such absolute local control will inhibit, for example, the construction of large and possibly dirty factories and that this amounts to an inhibition on innovation, then we must return to our redefinition of the purpose of industry. Industry exists to serve the consumer. If the innovation is popular, why should it be opposed? If nuclear power stations, shall we say, were not permitted by any of the communities occupying suitable sites for them, this might be taken to indicate an unwillingness on the part of the most affected sections of the public to accept nuclear power stations. If local objections are to be overruled then we must suppose an authority that exists to serve its own ends rather than those of the public, or that defines the public need in ways that differ from those used by most of the people. Though radical, the concept is inherently democratic, and it is not at all difficult to grasp.

Do we allow that our communities are to be governed by the direct participation of all their members? It is only if they are that they need to be small, for a dictatorship, or representative form of government can function more easily on a large scale. Democracy is dangerous, as most political philosophers have agreed. Plato did not approve of it at all. Peter, too, is made nervous by it, and with some justification. If people are allowed to choose the way of life they prefer I cannot guarantee that they will choose a way of life that suits me. For all I know they may fill the world with blaring transistor radios and sweet packets, offend my ears with their music, drowned occasionally by the scream of the aircraft that carries them to their packaged strips of Mediterranean coast, devour trash foods, and hold public executions of those who displease them. A benevolent dictator who possesses all power but uses it wisely and gently to guide his people, Solomon-like, to the promised land sounds more comfortable. My difficulty is that I cannot be certain that I will agree with the dictator, either. At heart we are all anarchists and since we must live together each of us would really prefer to preserve his or her autonomy by becoming dictator. My Solomon-wise benevolent dictator is myself, of course. This being impossible our best compromise is to forfeit our right to the throne in exchange for a share in that throne that is equal to everyone else's share. This is democracy, and the route by which I reach my advocacy of it. When I advanced it earlier Peter criticized me for it. We must make up our minds, though, between what I have called right-wing pessimism and left-wing optimism. Either people must be governed or they are inherently sensible and may be allowed to govern themselves by the willing co-operation of equals. I would suggest that democracy is worth trying and that it might not prove catastrophic, but in any case the environmental and self-sufficiency movements must make up their own minds whether they opt for the modified-anarchist or the modified-fascist. We abandoned the centre ground because it was economically untenable.

In fact, the difficulty is less serious than it seems. As Peter has said, and I agree, if we are to allow communities to decide matters for themselves we cannot at the same time impose systems of government upon them. We may expect, therefore, that political systems will emerge of every conceivable complexion. 'Eco-politically', that is the beauty of the structure. It provides for the greatest possible diversity and, we would hope, through its diversity on the small scale, stability on the large scale. Individuals who dislike the form of government under which they find themselves living may move to more congenial surroundings and even though some regimes may prove as oppressive as those that govern certain nation states today, it must be easier to escape from small-scale oppression than from large-scale oppression.

Within such communities, how will the weak and disadvantaged be protected? Who will care for the sick, the disabled, who will teach the children, feed, clothe, and shelter the aged infirm? Of course, each community will decide such matters for itself, but in doing so they should abandon another myth of the self-sufficiency movement. It is convenient to believe that in a small, strong community such social problems will vanish, the disadvantaged members of the community being cared for locally, as they were in the past. This is another manifestation of nostalgia. The fact is that in the past the disadvantaged were not cared for, that in the small communities we imagine we admire individuals were allowed to die in squalor for want of attention and care that the community could not supply. Efforts to provide more comprehensive care began in 1531 when the first attempt at a poor law was enacted. The welfare state, much along the lines with which we are familiar today, was outlined first by Tom Paine in *Rights of Man*, first published in 1789, and when that state began to be constructed in Britain about 150 years later, its purpose was not to satisfy the egos of bureaucrats hungry for power, but to care for those who were not being cared for and who cannot be cared for except by the community as a whole in a regularized fashion. Nor is it true that before the introduction of the National Health Service doctors treated the sick regardless of their ability to pay. They did not, and not because the doctors were wicked but because they, too, had to earn a living. The idea that if we leave things to themselves the problem will vanish is derived from the older, but still prevalent, idea that poverty is a vice rather than a misfortune.

Nor will it be easy for small communities to provide for themselves all the services they need. British hospitals were taken into public ownership not to enhance the reputation of politicians, but because it had become impossible to finance them from the proceeds of flag days, coffee mornings, and jumble sales. The 'free-enterprise' system simply did not work. Other social services must also be provided from the public sector for, while voluntary organizations often provide useful assistance, they lack the administrative resources and expertise that is needed to provide a comprehensive service available to anyone who may need it at any time of day or night. Education, too, must be supplied from the public sector. This is not a matter of political ideology but of practical necessity. It has been said that a civilization may be judged by the way it cares for its weaker citizens.

Once again, the degree of autonomy enjoyed by each community is eroded, but not in any serious way. As individuals we co-operate with one another and believe that the possession of friends and colleagues enhances the quality of our lives rather than detracting from it. There is no reason, then, why communities may not co-operate in a similar way and, if there be any that prefer to make no provision for the young, the old, the sick, and the disabled, that is their right – although the omission may be pointed out to them by those left to bear the impossible burden.

The idea of a society composed of such mutually and internally supportive communities is far from new. What makes it interesting is the advent of technologies that, perhaps for the first time, make it practicable. It is why the blind rejection of modern technology is so inappropriate. For the first time in history a community can be remote but not isolated. Communications technology can give them direct and immediate access to other communities and their voice can be heard as loudly as that of any group in society on matters that concern them. The best of education, including university education, can be supplied to community centres or directly into private homes. No longer will young people be compelled to leave their own community to seek education, or probably, employment, elsewhere. They may choose to leave, but they need not be compelled to do so as they have been in the past. As Peter says, communication and information technologies may also be used for surveillance, although logistically this is more difficult than it may seem. Since the introduction of the technology is inevitable, however, it might be more practical to recognize the benefits it may bring, work to ensure it does bring them, and oppose its repressive uses than to retreat into some kind of primitivist isolationism and hope the nasty thing will go away. It will not go away, and it is not necessarily nasty.

Communities of the future may offer a wide range of employment to their members. Peter mentions the example of the Israeli kibbutzim. I might add the Chinese communes. Both exist to provide their members with a high level of self-sufficiency, to which end industry, agriculture, and services are highly integrated. That the concept can be translated to Britain was argued as long ago as the 1930s – before the kibbutzim became world famous and long before the Chinese Revolution – by Sir George Stapledon. He observed that with the replacement of steam by electrical power in industry the location of industry was no longer determined geographically by the availability of coal and water. It could be sited anywhere to bring a synthesis of urban and rural ways of life. He also advocated a revival of apprenticeships, reformed to avoid the traditional abuses of the apprenticeship system, to shift some of the burden of vocational training from the public educational to the industrial sector. I tried to develop some of his ideas and to apply them to small communities some years ago, and concluded that the concept was very attractive and apparently practicable.

We are presented, then, with the possibility of creating communities that conform to most of the criteria established by earlier writers, and on a national scale. If we are to do so successfully, though, we must build the future, not the past. We must not delude ourselves that the recreation of the conditions of any former time is either possible or desirable. We must abandon notions of 'natural' man and 'natural' living, recognizing that we and the way we live are neither more nor less natural than the people or lifestyles of any other historical period. We must remember that no adequate definition of self-sufficiency can afford to omit reference to human creativity. We need to encourage artists, scientists, and philosophers as surely as we need to encourage farmers and carpenters. We must forget our fear of technology and embrace it, having established that it exists to serve us, the consumers. It is neither necessary nor possible for everyone to understand precisely how everything works. There is nothing wrong with living in a building even though we do not understand how it was constructed and although I could not build a typewriter I feel quite comfortable as I use one. Of course we owe it to ourselves to understand as much of the world in which we live as we can, but no one can hope to understand everything.

We are poised, then, to leap into a future that could be a great deal more pleasant than any period in the past. Before we do so, though, there is one final question we must consider. Who owns property?

Two views are admissible. Land and the buildings upon them that are used to produce goods or services may be owned privately, their owners collaborating in the management of the community, so that the structure comes to resemble a co-operative. If we suppose the community itself to be the ultimate authority, however, difficulties will occur. I suggested earlier that in the absence of any higher authority to which members of the community may appeal, it becomes impossible for the community to guarantee that its wishes are observed if there is a member who is prepared to flout them and against whom the available sanctions have no effect. If a private landowner wishes to sell out and the result of the sale will be a form of development of his property that is unpopular, there is no way in which it can be prevented. What is more, regardless of the system of government devised by the community, in fact power will come to reside with the owners of property whose agreement must be obtained before any change at all can be made in the use to which their property is put. Historically, such a distribution of power has tended to lead to a system of government that takes little regard of the needs or wishes of those who own no property.

The most obvious way to overcome the difficulty and to impose an effective control over landowners is to require that the community as a whole be given first refusal whenever property is offered for sale, and that any sale made without the community having had a prior opportunity to buy it be invalid. This power should be accompanied by the power of compulsory purchase to enable the community to carry out such changes as it thinks desirable if the owner of the property that will be affected objects.

In a small community, these safeguards are likely to lead in time to the communal ownership of all land. The idea is far from new. It was proposed by Thomas Spence in a paper he read to the Newcastle Philosophical Society in 1775, and in the nineteenth century Henry George revived the idea. Like many people, Peter is distrustful of land nationalization. His doubts are probably well founded if by nationalization we mean the centralized ownership and management of land, which might well create an unwieldy and insensitive bureaucracy. The communal ownership of land, and indeed of all industrial and business premises, is a very different matter. It amounts to ownership by the people who live and work on the property, whose knowledge of local circumstances must be more intimate than that of any outsider, and it allows the flexibility that is necessary for the community to adapt to those circumstances. I do not know who owns the land and buildings on a kibbutz, but in a Chinese commune that ownership is vested in the community itself, not in the party or the central government.

The concept of communal ownership of property should be acceptable to the more radical members of the self-sufficiency movement and to some members at least of the environmental movement. Those who admire primitive peoples, not least because they have no concept of land ownership, and who espouse anarchist ideals knowing that the most famous of all anarchist slogans is 'Property is theft', are unlikely to defend private ownership.

However, these are issues that Peter and I cannot resolve. All we can do is raise them to show that they relate to or derive directly from the matters that concern environmentalists and self-providers. They must be considered if the movements are to develop a coherent political platform.

If we date the emergence of the modern environmental movement from about the time of the publication of Rachel Carson's *Silent Spring*, in 1964, and the emergence of the self-sufficiency movement in its present form from a year or two later, we can see just how far both movements have developed in a mere fifteen years. The United Nations has an environmental agency and most governments have departments or ministries of the environment. No development proposal, anywhere in the world, can now be considered without at least lip service being paid to its environmental effects and ways of minimizing those that may be adverse. This amounts to considerable political influence. It is only within the last year or two, though, that environmental groups have entered the political arena directly, to contest elections. The move to do so has been controversial within the environmental movement, but since it has been made it seems likely that it will continue and that environmentalists candidates will come to contest elections regularly.

In some countries, such as France and West Germany, various environmental groups have formed loose coalitions to fight elections on particular issues. In other countries, such as Britain, they have formed an official political party. Regardless of what they call themselves, in fact they are factions, campaigning on a limited range of issues whose wider implications are barely considered. Since voters must take account of the full range of policies that affect every aspect of their lives, and since the overall political complexion of the environmentalists remain ambiguous, it is not surprising that their success has been limited. In the British General Election of 1979, for example, of more than fifty environmentalist candidates not one obtained as much as 3 per cent of the votes cast in the contested constituency, and many obtained less than 2 per cent.

If they are to improve their political position they must cease to be factions and become full political parties. They must consider their attitudes to the whole of policy, they must show how they would implement their policies and how they would finance them and, most important of all for the ordinary elector, they must state very clearly to which side of the political centre they stand. The debate that must precede the formulation of a broad political philosophy is bound to be divisive and it may be that more than one environmentalist party will emerge as a result. Far from damaging the movement, this could help it. As the differences that have developed between Peter and I have shown, more than one view can be advanced, and it would be tragic if people were deterred from policies they approve by their dislike of the society that would result from those policies. It is good that we may choose between left-wing and right-wing environmentalism. What is dangerous and misleading is to suppose that a political party may exist outside the traditional argument, which is not about rivalries between classes, but about quite different views of the role of the state and of the relationship between the citizen and the government.

If the self-providers and the environmentalists are prepared to define clearly their political objectives, there seems no reason why they should not become a political force as important as those movements that grew from the very similar debate that took place in Britain a century and a half ago. We could face a future of political, social, economic and so environmental reform.

Further reading

1 What is man?

A. Bilsborough, 'The diet of early man' *Nutrition Bulletin* 20 (Brit. Nut. Foundn., London, 1977)

E. Goldsmith, 'Adam and Eve revisited' *Ecologist* Vol. 9 No. 3 (Wadebridge, 1973)

E. Goldsmith, *The Stable Society* (Wadebridge Press, Wadebridge, 1978)

G. Hardin, 'The tragedy of the commons' *Science* Vol. 162 (A.A.A.S., 1968)

T. Hobbes, *Leviathan*, Chapter XIII

W. F. Lloyd, *Two Lectures on the Checks to Population* (Oxford University Press, Oxford, 1883)

T. R. Malthus, *Essay on Population* (1798)

H. Marcuse, 'The struggle against liberalism in the totalitarian view of the state' *Negations* (Allen Lane The Penguin Press, London, 1968)

Plato, *The Republic* Book IV

D. Ricardo, *Principles of Political Economy and Taxation* (1817)

Bertrand Russell, *History of Western Philosophy* (Allen and Unwin, London, 1961)

A. Schmidt, *The Concept of Nature in Marx* (NLB, London, 1971)

2 The technological solution and the myth of progress

Sir Alistair Hardy, *The Living Stream* (Collins, London, 1965)

Lewis Mumford, *The Myth of the Machine* (Secker and Warburg, London, 1967)

David and Marcia Pimental, *Food, Energy and Society* (Edward Arnold, London, 1979)

P. J. Searby, *ATOM* (November 1969)

Stuart Struever (ed), *Prehistoric Agriculture* (Natural History Press, 1971)

Robert Waller, *Be Human or Die* (Charles Knight, 1973)

3 Human Creativity

D. Attenborough, *Life on Earth* (Collins/BBC, London, 1979)

E. Goldsmith, *Ecologist* Vol. 4 No. 6 (Wadebridge, 1974)

J. Hemming, *Red Gold, The Conquest of the Brazilian Indians* (Macmillan, London, 1978)

See J. Lyons, *Chomsky* (Fontana, London, 1970)

L. Williams, *Challenge to Survival* (Allison and Busby, 1978)

4 Living off the land

Georg Borgstrom, *World Food Resources* (ITC, 1973)

Barry Castleman *Ecologist* Vol. 9 No. 4 (Wadebridge, 1979).

W. Cobbett, *Cottage Economy* (1823)

S. Enzer, R. Drobnick, R. Alter, *Neither Feast Nor Famine* (Lexington Books, Lexington, Mass., 1979)

Jean Gimpel, *The Medieval Machine* (Gollancz, London, 1977)

M. B. Green, 'The energy balance of pesticide use' *Biologist* Vol. 26 No. 3 (June 1979)

G. M. Howe, *Man, Environment and Disease in Britain* (David and Charles, Newton Abbot, 1972)

S. Kierkegaard, *The Last Years – Journals 1853–55* edited and translated by Ronald Gregor Smith (Collins, London, 1965)

Gerald Leach, *The Man-Food Equation* (Academic Press, London, 1973)

MAFF, Food Facts No. 3 (1979)

Peter Mathias, *The First Industrial Nation, an Economical History of Britain 1700–1914* (Methuen, London, 1969)

Howard T. Odum, *Environment, Power and Society* (Wiley, Chichester, 1971)

Michael J. Perelman, *Environment* (October 1972)

Roy Rappaport, *Scientific American* (September 1971)

Henry Stephens, *Book of the Farm* (Blackwoods, 1851)

Newman Turner, *Fertility Pastures* (Faber, London, 1950)

5 What kind of world?

P. P. Bunyard, 'Making the desert bloom' *Ecologist* (Wadebridge, May 1975)

T. Carlyle, *Past and Present* Book III Chapter XIII (1858)

D. Elliott, 'Can there be green socialism?' *Resurgence* Vol. 10 No. 2 (1979)

W. Godwin, *Enquiry Concerning the Principles of Political Justice* Vol. 2 (1793)

R. G. Grylls, *William Godwin and his World* (Odhams Press, London, 1953) *Guardian* (10 July 1979)

R. A. Nisbet, *The Sociological Tradition* (Heinemann, London, 1966)

Politics of Health Group, *Food and Profit* (British Society for Social Responsibility in Science, London, 1979)

Bertrand Russell, *History of Western Philosophy*

P. Singer, *Democracy and Disobedience* (Oxford University Press, Oxford, 1973)

C. Wardle, *Changing Food Habits in the UK* (Earth Resources Research Ltd, London, 1977)

6 Energy and equity

Wilfred Beckerman, *In Defence of Economic Growth* (Jonathan Cape, London, 1974)

K. Hohenemser, *Environment* Vol. 20 No. 3 (April 1978)

Ivan Illich, *Energy and Equity* (Calder and Boyars, London, 1974)

Herman Kahn, William Brown, Leon Martel, *The Next 200 Years* (Associated Business Programmes, 1976)

Gerald Leach, Christopher Lewis, Ariane Van Buren, Frederick Romig, Gerald Foley, *Low Energy Strategy for the UK* (IIED Science Reviews, 1979)

Amory H. Lovins, *Soft Energy Paths* (Penguin Books, London, 1977)

7 Limits to growth?

D. Gabor, *The Mature Society* (Secker and Warburg, London, 1972)

G. Hardin, The Tragedy of the Commons' *Science* Vol. 162 (1968)

Herman Kahn *et al*, *The Next 200 Years*

D. H. Meadows, D. L. Meadows, J. Randers, W. W. Behrens, *The Limits to Growth* (Earth Island Ltd, London, 1972)

P. Odell, World energy in the eighties – the significance of non-OPEC oil' *Guardian* (21 August 1979)

I. Tabushi, Y. Kobuke, T. L. Nishiya, 'Extraction of uranium from seawater by polymer-bound macrocyclic hexaketone' *Nature* No. 280 (1979)

8 The self-sufficient society

M. Allaby, *Inventing Tomorrow* (Hodder and Stoughton, London, 1976)

R. Blythe, *Akenfield* (Allen Lane The Penguin Press, London, 1969)

A. Heeley and M. Brown, *Victorian Somerset – John Hodges, a farm labourer* (Friends of the Abbey Barn, Glastonbury, Somerset, 1978)

B. Inglis, *Poverty and the Industrial Revolution* (Hodder and Stoughton, London, 1971)

G. Stapledon, *Human Ecology* edited by Robert Waller (Faber, London, 1964)

A. Tévoédjrè, *Poverty: Wealth of Mankind* (Pergamon, Oxford, 1978)

Index

A Book of Honey

Eva Crane

Honey is a splendid, entirely natural food, which has been treasured by people the world over from earliest times. Its production does not impoverish the environment, but actually enriches it, as bees pollinate the flowers they visit. Today honey is a commodity with an annual production of 800,000 tons, but it is only recently that research has shown how bees locate flowers containing nectar, and produce honey.

The book opens with a clear exposition of the amazing instinctive behaviour of bees, and of the composition and properties of honey. The use of honey in the home is discussed: as a gastronomic delicacy (and the author provides mouth-watering recipes, some new, some several thousand years old); as a remedy (for such ailments as hay fever and hangovers); and as a constituent of cosmetics. Dr. Crane goes on to tell the fascinating story of honey, from times before prehistoric man to the present day, and to show how bees have figured in the minds of men as magical or sacred creatures. Numerous literary references show the value accorded to bees through the ages, as agents of industry and thrift, and as objects of superstitious belief. The hive is considered, too, as a political symbol.

Know & Grow Vegetables

P. J. Salter, J. K. A. Bleasdale, and others

Gardening is usually considered to be an art but in fact 'green fingers' are *not* required for producing good vegetable crops. The simple instructions and practical advice given in this book are based on modern scientific research and will work in your garden, because the essential feature of science is that it must be repeatable.

All the authors are members of staff at the National Vegetable Research Station, Warwickshire, and they have been involved for many years in research which has made a major impact on commercial vegetable production in the U.K. They are all enthusiastic gardeners well used to communicating their knowledge to the amateur vegetable grower.

The book deals with spacing, sowing (including the novel method of fluid sowing) and planting, feeding, and watering different vegetable crops, and also describes how the vegetables can be protected from pests and diseases. The reader will be able to interpret the advice in a way that will meet his own particular needs. Some old garden lore is shown to be soundly based while other myths are exploded. Packed with a wealth of practical advice, the book will be invaluable both to the beginner and to the experienced grower.

Cottage Economy

William Cobbett

With a preface by G. K. Chesterton

'I view the tea drinking as a destroyer of health, an enfeebler of the frame, an engenderer of effeminacy and laziness, a debaucher of youth and a maker of misery for old age.' First published in 1822, Cobbett's classic handbook for small-holders was many times revised and enlarged, and is now reissued in its latest edition (1850). Cobbett tells us, among much else, how to brew beer, make bread, keep cows, pigs, bees, ewes, goats, poultry, and rabbits. And the book is full of splendid passages of social and political invective, making it a manifesto for Cobbett's philosophy of self-sufficiency. 'A couple of flitches of bacon are worth fifty thousand Methodist sermons and religious tracts.'